The Story of the Blues

NORTHEASTERN UNIVERSITY 1898–1998

Music advisor to Northeastern University Press
GUNTHER SCHULLER

The Story of the Blues

PAUL OLIVER

Northeastern University Press

BOSTON

Northeastern University Press

Copyright 1969, 1997 by Paul Oliver

First published by The Cresset Press in 1969;
new edition first published in Great Britain in 1997 by
Pimlico, an imprint of Random House UK, London.
First published in the United States of America in 1998
by Northeastern University Press, by arrangement
with Random House UK.

Library of Congress Cataloging-in-Publication Data
Oliver, Paul, 1927–
The story of the blues / Paul Oliver. — New ed.
p.   cm.
Includes bibliographical references (p.   ).
ISBN 1-55553-355-8 (alk. paper). — ISBN 1-55553-354-X
(pbk. : alk. paper)
1. Blues (Music) — History and criticism. 2. Blues musicians —
United States. 3. Afro-American musicians. I. Title.
ML3521.O46   1998
781.643´09 — dc21   98-12192
MN

Printed and bound by Thomson-Shore, Inc., Dexter, Michigan.
The paper is Glatfelter Supple Opaque Recycled, an acid-free sheet.

MANUFACTURED IN THE UNITED STATES OF AMERICA
02 01 00   5 4 3

Contents

Acknowledgments

In 1964 I was invited by Francis Mason of the United States Information Service to prepare an exhibition entitled *The Story of the Blues,* which occupied the ground floor of the American Embassy in September that year. Well over 500 photographs and reproductions were displayed and these became the basis of the book of the same title, published by Barrie and Jenkins five years later. In the ensuing three decades literally thousands of photographs of blues artists have been published in books and magazines.

As the first comprehensive history of the subject, it seemed necessary to place blues in its cultural context; now, after the passing of so many years and with the original milieu of the blues forgotten, simplified or largely unknown to many enthusiasts of its later forms and influences, it seems desirable to do so again. The illustrations have been reduced and selected with a view to showing as far as possible the background of the blues as an African American music and how blues singers were seen in performance or presented by the record industry to a larger black audience. The period of 'discovery' (or redis-covery) of the blues, its singers and players is also represented, though the subsequent development of the blues as an international popular music is not.

While the majority of the pictures in the exhibition and the first edition of the book were taken by myself or were drawn from my collection, many pho-tographs were generously provided by blues enthusiasts, record companies, publishers and archives. This is the case with the present, revised edition. For a complete listing of illustration acknowledgments, see page xii.

Music transcriptions done by Donald Kincaid are printed in their original form, with my sincere thanks.

As for the text, a number of minor adjustments have been made. These are mainly biographical, reflecting the emphasis of research in the past quarter-century. For this edition I owe a special debt of gratitude to Alan Balfour, who has advised me on biographical data and has assisted with corrections to tran-scriptions. I have also taken his advise that the emphasis and thrust of the book should remain as it was originally conceived.

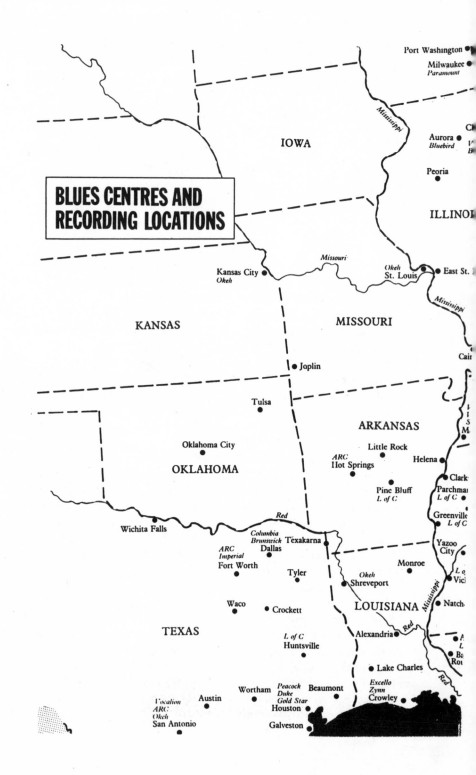

BLUES CENTRES AND RECORDING LOCATIONS

Port Washington
Milwaukee
Paramount

IOWA

Mississippi

Aurora
Bluebird

Peoria

ILLINOI

Missouri

Kansas City
Okeh

Okeh
St. Louis

East St.

Mississippi

KANSAS

MISSOURI

Cai

Joplin

Tulsa

ARKANSAS

Oklahoma City

OKLAHOMA

Little Rock

ARC
Hot Springs

Helena

Clark

Pine Bluff
L of C

Parchma
L of C

Greenville
L of C

Red

Wichita Falls

*Columbia
Brunswick* Texakarna

Yazoo
City

*ARC
Imperial*
Fort Worth

Dallas

Tyler

Okeh
Shreveport

Monroe

L o
Vic

Waco

Crockett

LOUISIANA

Natch

L of C
Huntsville

Alexandria

Red

A
L
B
Ro

Lake Charles

TEXAS

*Vocalion
ARC
Okeh*
San Antonio

Austin

Wortham

*Peacock
Duke
Gold Star*
Houston

Beaumont

Galveston

*Excello
Zynn*
Crowley

Red

Detroit
J & B
Fortune
Modern

Cleveland

PENNSYLVANIA   Philadelph
                     Gotham

Pittsburgh

Baltimore
MARY-
LAND

Washington

cago
Decca
alion
ebird
Chess

Gary

Wabash

Kokomo

OHIO

Columbus

Ohio

Vocalion
Indianapolis

King
De Luxe
Cincinnati

Richmond
Champion
Gennett

WEST
VIRGINIA

VIRGINIA

Lynchburg

Richmond
L of C

INDIANA

Ohio

ouis

Louisville
Okeh
Victor

KENTUCKY

Durham

Knoxville

Winston-Salem

Raleigh
L of C

NORTH CAROLINA

Charlotte
Bluebird

Nashville
Bullet
Excello

Spartanburg

Greenville

SOUTH CAROLINA

Jackson

TENNESSEE

Chattanooga

ocalion
ictor
un
emphis

Rome

Columbia
Okeh
ARC
Atlanta

Columbia
Vocalion

Charleston

sdale

Drew

Gennett
Birmingham

Macon

Statesboro

Savannah

MISS.

ALABAMA

GEORGIA

ARC
Trumpet
Jackson

C
ksburg

Selma

Columbus

Hattiesburg
ARC

Montgomery
Federal

Waycross

ez

ngola
of C
ton
ge

Columbia
Victor
De Luxe
New Orleans

Mobile

Biloxi

Pensacola

Tallahassee

FLORIDA

Tampa

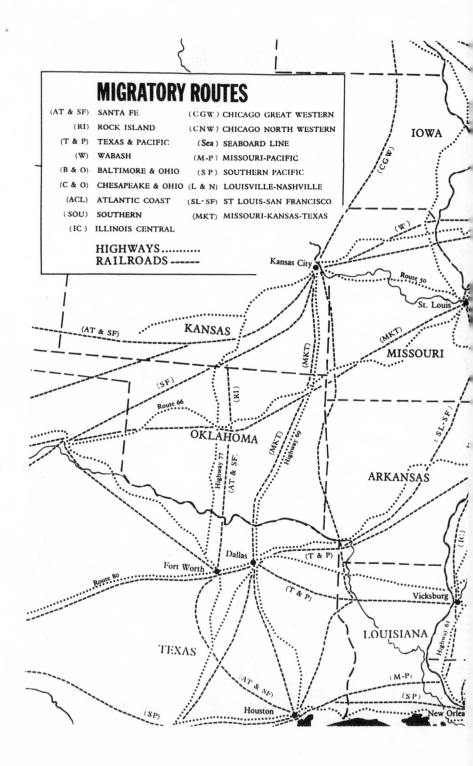

MIGRATORY ROUTES

(AT & SF)	SANTA FE	(CGW)	CHICAGO GREAT WESTERN
(RI)	ROCK ISLAND	(CNW)	CHICAGO NORTH WESTERN
(T & P)	TEXAS & PACIFIC	(Sea)	SEABOARD LINE
(W)	WABASH	(M-P)	MISSOURI-PACIFIC
(B & O)	BALTIMORE & OHIO	(S P)	SOUTHERN PACIFIC
(C & O)	CHESAPEAKE & OHIO	(L & N)	LOUISVILLE-NASHVILLE
(ACL)	ATLANTIC COAST	(SL-SF)	ST LOUIS-SAN FRANCISCO
(SOU)	SOUTHERN	(MKT)	MISSOURI-KANSAS-TEXAS
(IC)	ILLINOIS CENTRAL		

HIGHWAYS..........
RAILROADS ------

IOWA

Kansas City

Route 50

St. Louis

(AT & SF) KANSAS

(MKT)

MISSOURI

(SF)

Route 66

(RI)

OKLAHOMA

(MKT)

Highway 69

(SL-SF)

ARKANSAS

Highway 77

(AT & SF)

Fort Worth Dallas

(T & P)

Route 80

(T & P)

Vicksburg

(AT & SF)

LOUISIANA

Highway 61

TEXAS

(M-P)

(SP)

(SP) Houston

New Orleans

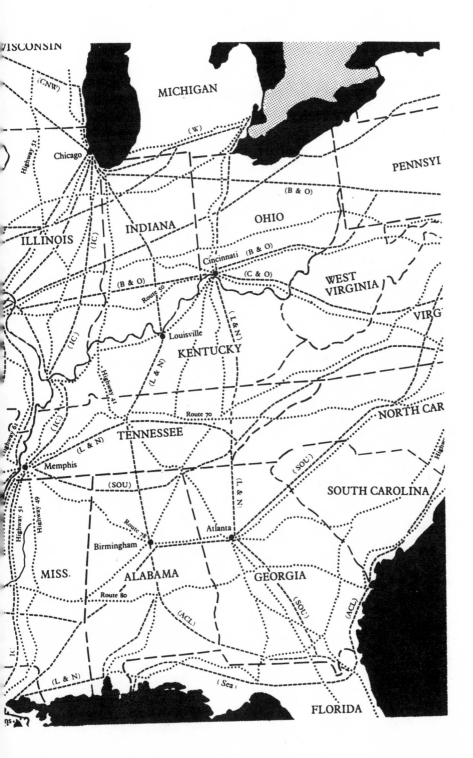

Illustration Acknowledgments

The following codes have been used to identify illustration credits:

Illustration sections

BB   Background to the Blues
DHB   Down Home Blues
BS   Blues on Stage
UC   Up from the Country
BR   Blues on Record
CB   Chicago Bound
PWB   Post-War Blues
DB   Discovering the Blues

Position on page

t = top   c = center   b = bottom
l = left   r = right

Thus, DHB.3tl indicates the photo section titled Down Home Blues, third page, photo at top left (Huddie Ledbetter [Leadbelly]).

Photograph credits are as follows:

Lawrence Cohn: DHB.3tl

Jacques Demetre: BR.8t; CB.6bl; PWB.2tr; PWB.3t; PWB.8t

David Evans: DHB.5tr

Farm Security Administration, Library of Congress: BB.3b; DHB.1t; DHB.1cr; DHB.1b; DHB.2b; BS.2b; BS.3t; BR.8b

The late Langston Hughes: CB.2tl; CB.2tr

Library of Congress collections: BB.5t; BB.6b; DHB.2t; UC.1b; CB.1b; CB.2c; CB.5t

George Mitchell: BB.8b; DHB.8t; DB.3br

New York Public Library: BB.1b; UC.1t

Paul Oliver: BB.4t; DHB.4tr; BS.2c; BS.3b; BS.6br; BS.7t; UC.2tl; UC.2b; UC.3tl; UC.3b; UC.5t; UC.5b; UC.6t; UC.6b UC.7br; UC.8t; UC.8b; CB.2br; PWB.4tl; PWB.4bl; PWB.4br; PWB.5b; PWB.7br; PWB.8bl; DB.2b; DB.3bl; DB.4b; DB.5tr; DB.5b; DB.6t; DB.7tr; DB.8tl; DB.8b

Valerie Oliver: DB.4t

Harold Oster: DHB.2c

The late Bill Russell: BS.2t; CB.3tr

Chris Strachwitz (Arhoolie Records): DB.3tl; DB.6b

University of North Carolina Press: pp. 19, 79; BB.3tl; BB.3tr

All other illustrations, including ephemera, publicity photographs, record labels, record catalogues, and historic photographs are from the Paul Oliver collection. The original maps compiled by Paul Oliver from data selected for this work are reproduced from the first editions.

Introduction

Roll over, Beethoven! When the Beatles recorded the iconoclastic title it wasn't only Beethoven who had to move aside but the composer of the song, the rhythm-and-blues singer, Chuck Berry, as well. When the Rolling Stones were *Confessing the Blues* they were confessing, too, to the influence of Walter Brown and B. B. King; when the Animals acclaimed the *Big Boss Man* the real boss man was Jimmy Reed. It was Lightnin' Hopkins who was preserved when The Lovin' Spoonful put the *Blues in the Bottle;* it was a Mississippi Black, Bukka White, on parole from Parchman Farm, who was Bob Dylan's muse for *Fixin' to Die Blues.* Using the words and music of a Memphis 'gum-ball raker', Gus Cannon, the Rooftop Singers offered the invitation to *Walk Right In.* Popular music has been walking right in on the blues ever since.

So pervasive has been the influence of the blues on pop music since the early 1960s that it is already difficult to recognise it. Once the twelve-bar, three-line structure was peculiar to the blues; now it is a commonplace. Sliding bottle-necks on guitar strings, back-beat drumming, crossed-harp harmonica – these have become the familiar sounds of the Top Twenties. Electric guitars and electric basses, amplified harmonicas and shouting singers play the music of Chicago blues bands on college campuses and in British teen-age clubs; the blues has been assimilated. This book is not about the current trends in pop music but about the blues, attempting to show the changing patterns in the evolution of a modern folk music until it moved from the circumscribed world of a segregated minority to become the inspiration of popular music throughout society.

When blues singers could be heard in any Southern courthouse square on a Saturday afternoon and the porches of country stores and plantation cabins were alive to the sounds of idly-picked guitars, there were few who stopped to consider the nature of the music. Blues singers were part of the total scene, no more to be remarked on than were the mules that drew the wagons to the cotton gin, or the watermelons ripening on the vines in the spreading patches. There's a certain appropriateness in this for 'it's in the nature of a folk music that it is the creation of the people and not separate from the whole fabric of living.' At the turn of the century, few collectors of folk music who were studying African American song attempted to note the blues as it appeared. They were far more concerned, when they listened and wrote, to preserve the musical forms which the blues threatened to displace. Occasional verses and fragments were noted but generally the collectors looked upon the blues with hostility, regarding it as a degeneration of the folk-lore they were anxious to save. Their endeavours were worthy but the lack of any accurate observation of the blues at its inception is irreparable. Neither were there any chroniclers of the blues as the music developed: no chroniclers except the blues singers themselves.

Today it's no longer possible to hear the history of the blues from the mouths of many of those who shaped it. The survivors of the first decades are few; memories are dimmed by age and scarred by experience. Time and pride have coloured some recollections, distrust and envy may have distorted others. Fingers are no longer nimble when old men are asked to play; blues that were sung in youth may have little meaning when the heat of the moment has been long forgotten. The problems of piecing together the story of the blues are many. It's a sociological axiom that the observer changes the nature of the subject observed by the very act of observation. Not only does his presence change the circumstances that exist when he is not present but the structure of his own research, and the kind of interpretation that he makes from the material he gains, may subtly distort the image of the subject. This is a principle which is evident in the differing ways in which the blues is seen today. For some people it is infinitely glamorous, for others it is a symbol of the oppression of a racial minority. For some African Americans today it is part of a proud tradition while for others it is the last brand of the plantation, and humiliating. There are some who view the blues as a music of protest and some who consider it a music of self-pity; there are those who consider it important primarily as an influence on jazz, and those who use it to inspire their own music making. For each and every other category the significance of the blues is different. And, of course, there are those for whom the blues has no significance at all.

Seen from any point of view, the blues is both a state of mind and a music which gives voice to it. Blues is the wail of the forsaken, the cry of independence, the passion of the lusty, the anger of the frustrated and the laughter of the fatalist. It's the agony of indecision, the despair of the jobless, the anguish of the bereaved and the dry wit of the cynic. As such the blues is the personal emotion of the individual finding through music a vehicle for self-expression. But it is also a social music; the blues can be entertainment, it can be the music for dancing and drinking by, the music of a class within a segregated group. So the blues can be the creation of artists within a folk community, whether it's in the deep, rural South or in the congested ghettoes of the industrial cities. Blues is the song of the casual guitarist on the back stoop, the music of the piano-player in the barrelhouse, the juke-box rhythm-and-blues hit. It's the ribald 'dozens' of the medicine show, the floor-show of the edge-of-town club, the show-biz of the travelling troupe and the latest number of a recording star. Blues is all these things and all these people, the creation of renowned, widely-recorded artists and the inspiration of a man known only to his community, perhaps only to himself.

So the story of the blues is the story of humble, obscure, unassuming men and women and it is the story of some whose names became household words – in black households, that is. Of many of them nothing remains as evidence of their skill except the few brief minutes of a phonograph record or two made sixty years ago. Even some of the most important of bluesmen are known only for their records; we may never know the features of Willie Brown or Pine Top Smith or Cleo Gibson. Many of the places where the bluesmen worked remain unlisted and undocumented; the shacks and juke joints have been reduced to splinters of dry wood and torn fragments of tarpaper, fallen to the bulldozer and the wrecking crew. Automobiles stand on the sites of old T.O.B.A. theatres and the medicine shows no longer set up on vacant lots of Southern townships. Yet there are jukes still; the cotton still blooms in July though it is cropped with a mechanical picker. There are the ghettoes still and the kitchenette apartments have not ceased to demand exorbitant rents.

Blues is music and blues is song; blues singers are people. Blues is not text and blues singers are not pictures. But they aren't discs of shellac or vinyl either. As the disembodied voices that struggle to be heard above the needle-scratch of old records may give some impression of the sounds of the blues, so this brief outline may place the blues singers in the contexts of the times and places where they lived and worked, and sang, and sometimes died; the mind's eye might clothe these instant images of the camera with flesh and blood and animate the figures frozen in southern cottonrows and Southside clubs. You won't find all the singers and all the settings here which make up the story of the blues, but perhaps there is sufficient to show the rich variety of forms of the blues, the many personalities who created the music, and the world of experience which inspired them.

Long Hot Summer Days

'I hadn't slept more than ten minutes when I was awakened by what seemed to me terrible screams coming from the Quarters' wrote Charlotte Forten in her diary entry for December 14th, 1862. She was a young black woman who had been born free in the North and having qualified as a teacher had come to Edisto Island in South Carolina to instruct the slaves. The screams disturbed her all the following day, Sunday, and she came sadly back from church. 'Nearly everybody was looking gay and happy; and yet I came home with the blues. Threw myself on the bed and for the first time since I have been here, felt very lonesome and pitied myself. But I have reasoned myself into a more sensible mood and am better now.'

Charlotte Forten's entry is one of the first recorded references to 'the blues' as a state of mind. She did not record how the slave suffering in the quarters worked off *his* misery when she 'reasoned' away her blues. If she, an educated African American, had been writing her entry shortly before she died, fifty years later, she would doubtless have rationalised her worried state in much the same way. But the slave's successor might well have sung away his unhappiness with a blues song.

A few days before she had noted in her diary that 'Lucy McKim has set to music some of the songs of the "contrabands" here. She has sent *Poor Rosy, poor gal* as the first of a series, to Dwight's Journal.' It was a song used to accompany work. 'On the water,' wrote Lucy McKim herself, 'oars dip "Poor Rosy" to an even *andante*; a stout boy and girl at the hominy mill will make the same "Poor Rosy" fly, to keep up with the whirling stone; and in the evening, after the day's work is done, "Heab'n shall-a be my home" peals up slowly from the distant quarters.

> Poor Rosy, poor gal, Poor Rosy, poor gal,
> Rosy break my poor heart,
>
> Heaven shall be my home.
> I cannot stay in hell one day,
> Heaven shall be my home . . .'

Said one old slave-woman 'I likes "Poor Rosy" better dan all de songs, but it can't be sung widout *a full heart and a troubled spirit.*'

A full heart and a troubled spirit has been the inspiration and the reason for countless blues. Charlotte Forten herself had been noting some songs, 'but of the manner and singing it is impossible to give any idea', she apologised.

> I wonder where my mudder gone
>   Sing, oh graveyard,
> Graveyard ought to know me,
>   Sing Jerusalem.
> Oh carry my mudder in de graveyard . . .

'It is a very strange wild thing,' she wrote. It was a religious song but in feeling and expression it had much in common with the blues; with, for instance, Red Nelson's *Crying Mother Blues*:

> Dear mother's dead and gone to glory, my old dad gone
>   straight away,
> Dear mother's dead and gone to glory, my old dad gone
>   straight away,
> Only way to meet my mother, I will have to change my
>   lowdown ways.
>
> Tomb-stones my pillow, graveyard gonna be my bed,
> Tomb-stones my pillow, graveyard gonna be my bed,
> Blue skies gonna be my blanket and the pale moon
>   gonna be my spread.

In its way Red Nelson's voice is strange and wild too; his unexpected falsetto on the syllable 'tomb', his marked vibrato on 'spread' equally defy transcription. To the unaccustomed ear the quality of the blues singer's voice may seem strange, the timbre harsh and the notes off-key, much as did the singing of the slaves in the fields who were heard by occasional observers. 'The odd turns made in the throat and the curious rhythmic effect produced by single voices chiming in at regular intervals seem almost impossible to place on the score',

wrote Miss McKim a few years before E⌐
the comments of earlier witnesses, like t⌐
actress Fannie Anne Kemble who married
kept between 1838 and 1839 her *Journal*
Plantation. Some of the songs she hear⌐
wild and unaccountable. The way in v
with the burden between each phrase ⌐
single voice is very curious and effectiv
that she was listening to a work song in w⌐⌐⌐
of the labour by singing and his fellow slaves answered in ⌐⌐⌐
was a pattern heard by many travellers in the South; William Cullen
Bryant for example, who was in South Carolina a few years later, in
1843, and who commented on the 'singularly wild and plaintive air'
used as a corn-husking song:

> *Leader:* De nigger-trader got me . . .
> *Chorus: Oh, hollow!* . . .

This leader-and-chorus form of singing was a direct link with a
widespread African tradition. In theory, the importation of slaves
from Africa was illegal after 1808 but in practice it continued until,
and perhaps clandestinely, even a little after, the Civil War. According
to Stephen A. Douglas, who was not an opponent of slavery, more
slaves were landed in the United States in 1859 than at any time during
the years of legal trade. There had been a sustained contact with Africa
over more than two centuries, and in spite of the barbarities of the
slave-ships, the inhumanity of the auction block and the brutalities
of the slave-drivers which were all designed to break the spirit, the
African displayed a remarkable capacity for survival under deplorable
conditions. In America he was classed as a chattel, he had no rights and
his sole function was to work. His culture was rigorously suppressed
– unless it happened to aid his labour. Though his tribal identity
had been destroyed, if his skills could be channelled into effort
that was to the advantage of the slave-owner, he had a chance to
survive. This applied to the traditional leader-and-chorus songs which
accompanied group work in Africa. Other traditions were expressly
forbidden, as in Mississippi where the Black Code laid down that
slaves should not play drums or horns – instruments which could be
used for codes and communication purposes as they had in Africa, and
which could be employed to incite insurrection. African survivals in
America are therefore conditioned by their appropriateness to life in
a strange country and by the degree to which they were permitted

In spite of a remarkable tradition in West Africa, wood soon declined and the sculptors, who were often also ths, were put to blacksmithing. Only a decorated tool or gely formed Alabama grave-marker hints at links with Africa. frican religion was also suppressed: the slave readily embraced hristianity because it seemed to be the key to the white man's power. In the successive evangelical waves of the Great Awakening of the Revolutionary years and the Great Revival of the early nineteenth century, generations of slaves were converted in great numbers by the Baptists and Methodists, whose fundamentalist religion they readily accepted. Too easily perhaps, as one verse fragment from the slave period acknowledged:

> White man use whip
> White man use trigger,
> But the Bible and Jesus
> Made a slave of the nigger.

Many early observers emphasised the overwhelmingly religious nature of Negro song. The church seemed to have had little difficulty, at least in the South, in reconciling itself with slavery and taught a doctrine of reward in the next life for the sufferings in this. An obsession with death colours many 'spirituals', as the religious songs were called, and a British minister, the Reverend David MacRae, was greatly troubled by 'the mixture of grief and gladness' in the Negro hymn, 'representing life as full of sorrow and death as a joyful release.' But the spirituals, which had been adapted from Wesleyan hymns and the 'Fasola' singing of the 'shape-note' hymnals and were developed independently by Blacks, had often another layer of significance. 'Crossing over Jordan' could mean death – but it could also mean escape from bondage. *Go Down, Moses* became a symbol of freedom.

> Go down, Moses, way down in Egypt's land,
> Tell old Pharoah 'Let my people go.'

An escaped slave and distinguished Abolitionist, Frederick Douglass, wrote drily that 'a keen observer might have detected in our repeated singing of

> O Canaan, sweet Canaan
> I am bound for the land of Canaan,

something more than the hope of reaching Heaven. We meant to reach the North and the North was our Canaan.' *Run to Jesus, Shun the Danger* was, he admitted, the inspiration for his own remarkable escape. Harriet Tubman, an illiterate field hand who escaped from slavery, as a 'conductor' on the Underground Railway guided 300 slaves to freedom.

Though the spirituals were apparently white in origin, the slave by his African means of expression and his ability to extemporise soon moulded them as something apart from the European tradition. He added tunes and themes of his own and invented new words. Thomas Wentworth Higginson, the generous-spirited white Colonel of a black regiment, wondered whether the songs 'grew by gradual accretion in an almost unconscious way.' He asked one Black, an oarsman, who 'dropped out a coy confession. "Some good sperituals," he said, "are start jess out o' curiosity. I been a-raise a sing myself, once."' Pressed by Higginson 'he began singing, and the men, after listening for a moment, joined in the chorus, as if it were an old acquaintance, though they evidently had never heard it before. I saw how easily a new "sing" took root among them.

> O, de ole nigger-driver!
>   O, gwine away!
> Fust ting my mammy tell me,
>   O, gwine away!
> Tell me 'bout de nigger-driver,
>   O, gwine away!
> Nigger-driver second devil,
>   O, gwine away . . .'

The chorus came in on the refrain of '●, gwine away!' in unison. He noted that its secular character was unusual, that nearly all the songs he heard were religious, and this is borne out by most other early collectors. Apparently the expressive needs in song were met by the spirituals which, in the slow, chanted 'long-meter' form were infinitely sad and poignant, and in the faster 'shouts', sung as a group shuffled counter-clockwise, African fashion, were joyous and exuberant. The 'shouts' in the 'praise-house' were permitted, for these were Sunday services for the slaves. But the spirituals overlapped with the work songs, which were being sung by the labouring gangs in the fields and so black song both at work and in praise took a leader-and-response pattern, with the gang-leader or the preacher outlining the theme and the whole assembly joining in with the response. Steady rhythms in gang labour ensured that the work progressed at an even pace and also, when axes or hoes were to be used, avoided accidents by co-ordinating movements. Work songs were to be heard across the sluggish waters of the bayous or the creeks and inlets of the Sea Islands raised by the boatsmen; they accompanied the beating of rice and the 'chopping out' of weeds in the cotton rows; they marked the tread of the roustabouts on the gangplanks of the riverboats as they loaded them to the top deck level. In the blazing heat of a summer sun or under the humid haze of the lowland swamps, where every movement is an effort, the gangs, which might number a hundred or more, toiled rhythmically to the beat of a song. To the white planter, the sounds of the work song floating to the Big House were an assurance that his slaves were fully employed; to his visitors it was picturesque, and Congressman Daniel C. DeJarnette, listening to the slaves singing could pronounce in 1860 that 'there is more humanity, there is more unalloyed contentment and happiness among the slaves of the South, than any labouring population on the globe.'

An image of happy, contented, 'child-like' slaves was a balm to a sore spot on many a conscience. Conditions varied widely on the plantations and though some were indescribably cruel and the barbarities practised on some slaves unparalleled until Auschwitz, there were others where conditions were bearable. Mary Reynolds, once a slave on a Louisiana plantation had 'seed them put the men and the women in the stock with they hands screwed down through the holes in the board and they feets tied together and they naked behinds to the world,' while the overseer beat them with a whip until the flesh was cut to the bone and the 'Massa' looked on. But she also recalled that the Master would let the slaves cultivate their own patches. Some Saturday evenings would be set aside for washing she said, and 'when they'd git through with the clothes on Saturday evenings, the niggers which sold they goobers and 'taters brung fiddles and guitars and come out and play. The others claps they hands and stomp they feet and we young-uns cut a step round.' On a Texas plantation James W. Smith remembered that the Master 'wanted them to have a good time. There am dancing and singing mostest every Saturday night. He had a little platform built for the jigging contests. Colored folks come from all around, to see who could jig the best.'

'Frolics' and 'jigs' were a justification of the view that the slaves were happy with their lot. Some slaves did attain skill as musicians and if the drums were banned in Mississippi, the drumming in Congo Square, New Orleans was long a tourist attraction. Thomas Jefferson, himself a planter, wrote in his *Notes on the State of Virginia* of the banjor, the ancestor of the banjo, which was an authentic importation from Africa. More popular than the banjo-player, though less remembered in popular folklore, was the fiddler. Generations of Scots and Irish settlers brought their jigs and reels to the South and gifted slaves played for the dances. Square dances and French *contre-danses* were learned by the slaves, whose own 'Calinda' and 'Pas-ma-la' were part French and part Ashanti. African dances frequently place emphasis on hand and body movements while the feet shuffle in rhythm; others are more athletic with leaps and unlikely steps. Combined with the European dance forms, they made an eccentric 'plantation dance,' sometimes a shuffling 'sand dance' and sometimes a high-stepping 'walk-around.'

It was the curious step of a deformed black stable-hand in Louisville which gave the idea to Thomas Dartmouth Rice to 'Jump Jim Crow':

> First on de heel tap, den on de toe,
> Ebery time I wheel about I jump Jim Crow
> Wheel about and turn about an do jis so,
> And ebery time I wheel about I jump Jim Crow

ran the words of Rice's ditty which gave an inglorious phrase, synonymous with segregation, to the nation. Like the dances of Dan Emmett and the Virginia Minstrels a little later in the 1840's, Dan Rice's *Jim Crow* of 1828 was based on a black original and was probably performed with more truth to the prototype than were the ministrel show parodies of later years, or the songs sentimentalised in the 'Plantation Melodies' of Stephen Foster.

From all this it may be seen that black traditions of music, song and dance had a long history extending far back in slavery and to an African heritage. Vestiges of Africa remained in their arts where they were permitted to do so, and in the Gullah dialect of the Georgia Sea Islands, and in scattered fragments through the South, may be heard African words and phrases. The ability of African Americans to adapt their music, to create anew, to improvise words and themes is evident in innumerable reminiscences and reports. All this has relevance to the blues and has had, in some way, an influence on the shaping of the music, its content or its function.

But the blues did not exist in slavery, at least in a form which can be identified with those which constitute 'the blues' as a music with its own character. In the years after the Civil War, the methods of gang labour largely disappeared as the plantations were broken up into small farms. Group work songs of the slavery kind might have disappeared but for the maintenance of the plantation system on the Southern penitentiaries. In conditions similar to slavery large gangs of field workers, under the watchful eyes of heavily armed guards, wielded their picks, raised their hoes, brought down their axes to similar leader-and-chorus work songs and in a manner which recalls that of African work gangs. Such a gang, recorded in 1939 by John A. Lomax on the Clemens Prison farm unit at Brazoria, Texas, still retained the long-drawn out responses from the labourers who completed the line begun by the leader, Clyde Hill.

> Captain I'm due to be in Seminole – *Ooooklahooma*
> Captain, I'm due to be in Seminole – *Oooklahooma*
> Oh in them long – *hot summer days*
>
> Black gal, if I never more – *seeee – youuu*
> Black gal, if I never more – *seeee – you*
> Oh in them long – *hot summer days.*

Its song style was age-old and yet the form suggested a link with the blues. In other work where co-ordinated labour was essential for safety or combined strength, work songs survived until recent times – on the railroads for example, where, to the calls of the straw boss, crews of 'gandy-dancers' straightened tracks distorted by heat. (The gandy-dancers' tools were made by John Gandy.) But elsewhere the group work songs were displaced by the lonelier field hollers, just as other aspects of black traditions were replaced after the Civil War.

Though the changes took place, they were not immediate and the blues was not the direct outcome of Emancipation. It has to be seen in the context of a revolution in African American music as a whole which took place at the end of the century. This period witnessed the last phase of many traditions and the beginning of new ones, although in the process of displacement many of the older elements survived in the new forms. Why this took place is complex but, as the earlier traditions were rooted in slavery, so the new ones, too, were related to a social upheaval.

A decade after the Civil War it was clear that Reconstruction had failed and by 1877 the last troops quit the Louisiana state house and the great experiment was at an end. It spelled disaster for Blacks; in the early 1870s they were playing their part in the political life of the South, but within a matter of years they were effectively disfranchised. In 1883 the Supreme Court declared the

Fourteenth Amendment was unconstitutional and deprived them of appeal in law. How many died in trying to exercise their political rights is unknown; estimates range from hundreds to thousands, but the steep rise in the number of lynchings was no coincidence. They may not have arisen directly from political acts, but violent Whites were making certain of their 'supremacy'. In 1890 Mississippi made it constitutional to disfranchise Blacks; Louisiana and South Carolina followed in 1895. In the space of the next fifteen years five more southern states had adopted new constitutions specifically aimed at limiting their power, and other states made similar statutory provisions.

As early as 1865 an experiment at segregating the railroads was made in Mississippi and, after Reconstruction, was resumed in 1888. Other states rapidly followed her example and as the century came to a close fourteen states had passed laws requiring segregated facilities. In 1896 the Supreme Court approved the segregation laws provided that 'separate, but equal' facilities were available. It seemed a deliberate cynicism, for in every accommodation Blacks were provided with poor, often filthy and squalid facilities. At the same time the nation as a whole was suffering a succession of economic strains. The depressions of the early 'nineties, the low prices for the harvests and the flow of gold from the country caused much hardship. Grover Cleveland's attempt to save the gold standard led to a humiliating personal defeat. Massive labour strikes in 1894 and outbreaks of violence threatened the nation and an army of jobless men took to the highways. 'No modern society' commented *The Railway Age* 'has been so disorganised as was the USA in 1894, never was human life held so cheap; never did the constitutional authorities appear so incompetent to enforce respect of the law.' Instead they took repressive measures against the workless and Blacks suffered still further as a Populist backlash supported the Democrats in establishing a one-party system of white supremacy in the South.

Four-fifths of the black population was living in rural areas still and of the remainder, three-quarters were living in urban areas of the South. Job opportunities were controlled by the kinds of labour for which Blacks were acceptable: logging, turpentine production, menial jobs in the steel and oil industries, levee-grading and ditch-digging, railroad maintenance, and, always, cotton cultivation. African Americans had been promised forty acres and a mule when the War was over; they didn't get them but the plantations were broken up into small farms. Those who couldn't purchase farms could rent them, or they could work a 'share': in return for their 'furnishings' of a mule, equipment, a hut and basic foods, they could work a plot of land, paying off their debt with their labour and giving half their produce to the landowner. A new system of slavery, share-cropping peonage, came into being. Labour costs were further cut by the iniquitous system of 'convict-lease' in which teams of chained convicts were hired out to plantation owners; no one bothered if they were sick, beaten, mutilated or dead.

Dire though the effects of this period of economic and social stress were upon the African American, the ultimate result was to impress upon him a sense of his own identity. Isolated by restrictive legislation, cut off from white society, he began to revitalise his own culture. The doors of the white churches were being closed to Blacks; they were barred from many entertainments; the schools were inadequately staffed and barely furnished. Thousands accepted the subordinate position thrust on them, admittedly, but far more significant were the actions of the militant. Education advanced with the opening of subscription schools from within the black community; new churches and new entertainments were established. If Booker T. Washington represented a policy of conciliation, W. E. DuBois concerned himself with *The Souls of Black Folk* and began a courageous programme of fighting back. Among the black folk themselves something of the new spirit was reflected in the emergence of new arts.

In 1895 a minister from Lexington, Mississippi, Reverend C. H. Mason, founded his Church of God in Christ in Memphis, Tennessee and a year later a cook began his own Church of God in Oklahoma – forerunners of the Pentecostal and premillenialist sects which revolutionised black religious music. At much the same time the cakewalks which had formalised the plantation walkarounds were being examined again by a number of Missouri pianists: Tom Turpin's *Harlem Rag* was published in 1897 and two years later, with the appearance of Scott Joplin's *Maple Leaf Rag*, the astonishing boom in ragtime music was bringing syncopated dance to the St Louis World's Fair, to Chicago and the East. Though the social conditions were somewhat different down the Mississippi River in New Orleans the first sounds of jazz were emerging. Perhaps the earliest of jazz bands was that led by the guitarist Charlie Galloway in 1894, though he was known to have had a band even earlier in 1885. In the mid-'nineties Buddy Bolden is credited with having improvised a 'blues' on the cornet, presumably a field holler played instrumentally, and the development of New Orleans jazz out of the marching music of the city took place around the turn of the century.

Its origins were of a folk character, but folk music of a more traditional kind, the ballad of the Anglo-Scots heritage, was also undergoing a process of change and rebirth. In the example of *John Henry*, a new and essentially black folk hero was born, and in the wake of that great ballad came a spate of others which told the stories of *Frankie and Albert*, *Eddy Jones*, *Ella Speed* or *Duncan and Brady*, based on dramatic events which took place in unknown saloons and dives at much the same time.

• It was this period of social upheaval which seems to have inspired a revolution in the culture of African Americans and which gave rise to the gospel song of the Sanctified and Pentecostal churches, the piano syncopations of ragtime, the polyphonic collective improvisation of the New Orleans jazz band and the narrative ballad of the black hero. It was also the period which inspired, from the fusion of a number of elements both traditional and innovatory, the beginnings of the blues. •

Cottonfield Hollers

When the blues began, the countryside was quiet. Loudest of the sounds to break the stillness was the roar of a steam train as it traced its way through the lowlands, leaving a smudge of smoke against the blue sky. A brief moment of excitement as it passed, a shrill whistle, dipping and wailing like a blues and it would be gone. It's said that the engineers tuned their steam whistle 'quills' to play a blues but it probably just sounded like this to the field hands who knew the hour by the regular trains. So, along the big rivers, did the whistles of the riverboats and the cries of the leadsmen 'heaving the lead line' as they continually called the soundings to the pilots. 'Stack-o-Lee's up the river, Big Katie Adams' in the bend . . .' sang the field hands who could recognise the different boats by their whistles and steam calliopes.

There was little else to listen to. No airplanes overhead, no automobiles lifting clouds of dust from the dirt roads, no television aerials on the cabin roofs, no tractors and mechanical cotton-pickers, no transistor radios to place on them. All these came, eventually, and each in some way left its mark upon the blues by improving communications or changing labour patterns. But that was much later. In the early years of the blues, their counterparts were the creaking of wagon axles, the groaning of gang planks, the cries of occasional street vendors – the tamale man, the charcoal man or the blackberry woman. Or perhaps the blind guitarist on the commissary steps.

Left to himself, a man would sing to his mules at daybreak, urge on his team with a yelling instruction to each animal, chant to the beat of his own hoe. A new pattern of farming had evolved after the War with the dissolution of the big plantations. But the methods of sowing, weeding and harvesting the crops remained essentially the same, even if the sharecroppers and tenant farmers now had to organise their own time. Gang labour was largely obsolete but if a farmer was ever to work himself out of debt peonage, he had to raise a large family, every one of whom, as soon as he was big enough to reach the lowest bolls, was expected to work in the cottonfields. The South's failure to realise the dangerous implications of its one crop economy meant that Blacks were still massively employed in cotton cultivation. Their cabins were scattered over the plantation or ranged before each man's 'share' at intervals with the long rows stretching to the horizon or the distant belt of cottonwood trees. A lifetime of work for himself and his family might mean that a man at his death still owned not a stick of his cabin, not a piece of furniture, not a mule or a tool.

Cotton grows in a warm and humid climate, agreeable in the early part of the year, sultry and exhausting in the heat of summer, much the same at night as in the day. Planting takes place around April and the first shoots appear a week or so after. They are stripped of unnecessary growth and the weeds were formerly removed by the endless process of 'chopping out' with the hoe, while between the rows the earth was kept open by ploughing and the stand of cotton supported by banking up. The latter part of July was a slack, hot month with a brief lay-off until the cotton was ready for picking. Picking was hard work, for the cotton clings tenaciously to the boll. Every man, woman and child was employed and droves came from the nearby townships, from the schools; the larger homes of the Whites emptied of house-servants. All worked from 'cin to cain't' – from the first glimmer of dawn light when one can see, until the setting of the sun when the picker can see no longer.

Singing while working had been a timeless tradition, but now the field hand did not have to co-ordinate exactly with his companions; he sang to his own speed, though other workers might pick up his call. 'Suddenly one raised such a sound as I had never heard before,' wrote Frederick Law Olmstead, 'a long, loud, musical shout rising and falling and breaking into falsetto, his voice ringing through the woods in the clear, frosty night air, like a bugle call. As he finished the melody was caught up by another, and then another, and then by several in chorus.' Such calls were called 'hoolies' or 'hollers' and they could be heard throughout the year in the farmlands, the plantations and equally, in the forests where the mill-hands and the muleskinners with their teams all developed them. On the railroads, section gangs were given instructions in hollers from the section bosses; in the levee camps, where immense banked revetments were raised to protect the lowlands from flood waters, the 'levee camp holler' was a familiar sound. The holler, in fact, replaced the group work song, and became in the process a constituent of the blues.

No holler can be readily described, for the singer takes pride in his embellishments, in his glissandi and 'bends', in his use of yodelling changes to falsetto and his slides to a lower note. A typical example was this 'arhoolie' or cornfield holler recorded by Thomas Marshall at Edwards, Mississippi in 1939. (Music Example 1 in Appendix.)

Oh . . . Oh . . .
I won't be here long; oh . . . oh . . . dark gonna catch me here;
Dark gonna catch me here . . .

Like most hollers it was modal in character and could be said to be sung in the Dorian mode, except for the G which is, in essence, decoration. But those qualities of black singing which James Weldon Johnson referred to as the 'curious twists and turns and quavers and the intentional striking of certain notes just a shade off key' resist musical notation. In the hollers as in the blues, they can only be implied and in lieu of first-hand experience can only be appreciated on record. Recognising this problem in analysis Dr Milton Metfessel and Dr Carl Seashore with a team of researchers devised a technique of 'phonophotography' at the laboratory of the Department of Psychology at the University of Iowa in the winter of 1924.

Phonophotography combined a 'portable sound photography camera', which recorded the music, converted the frequency of vibration, measured the time and filmed the singers. Notations as to text and phonetics were also taken and the 'pattern notation' plotted in a graph-curve against an even-tempered scale. In the following year they made a number of phonophotographic recordings of spirituals, work songs and blues, a *Cornfield Holler* being among them.

This graph-curve gives a strong visual indication of the use of vibrato, the swooping dips, the sudden climbs, the attack and release of the note which typifies the holler. The vertical intervals measure in seconds and Middle C is indicated by its frequency of 258.6 cycles per second.

To what extent are these characteristics peculiar to Blacks and how much may be ascribed to an African heritage? As has been seen, the work songs provided a continuity link with the traditions of Africa and some of these undoubtedly persisted in the solo work song and field holler. Reverend A. M. Jones described the character of melody

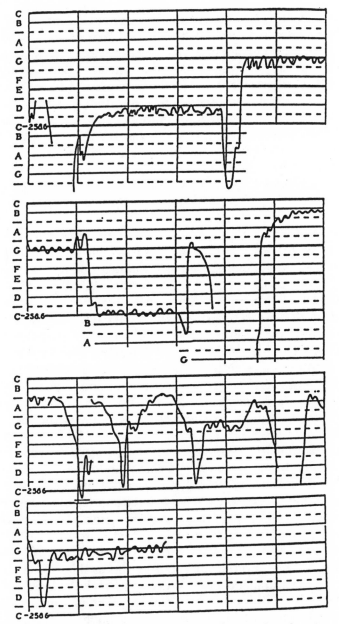

in African music as 'like a succession of the teeth of a rip-saw' in steep rises and gentle slopes in the tune. 'There is however a distinct feeling in these tunes of hovering over and around a central note or notes, round which the melody seems to be built or towards which it works.' Professor Kwabena Nketia has shown that there are several

such patterns which relate in part, though not exclusively, to the pitch
and tone elements in African languages. These qualities which affect
meaning no longer applied when the slaves learned English, but
vestigial variations of pitch and tone remained both in speech and
song, while other speech habits show tenuous African links. It was
Jones's view that African melody was 'in a strait-jacket' of meaningful
tones, though this in itself added variety to the songs, for each verse
'needed separate melodic treatment to make the tune agree with the
rise and fall of syllables.' But 'the liberty of melody is still further
restricted by the universal custom of singing only one note to each
syllable.' By using English, Blacks seem to have been freed from this
limitation and have been able to extend this embellishment of song
without the risk of altering meaning.

It is evident to the most casual listener that the blues, jazz,
ragtime, gospel song and other forms of African American music
have certain qualities that are not familiar, or not as marked, in
the western traditions of either formal or folk music. The 'Negro's
innate sense of rhythm' or 'his natural singing ability' are clichés of
writing on the Black American which have been endlessly repeated.
For the ethnologist, however, the problem of inherited and learned
abilities is a considerable one; whether in any way race may decide
innate abilities or whether culture may develop them remains a
crucial argument. The consensus of opinion argues for cultural
rather than racial influences on the development of a particular
ability shared within a social or ethnic group. As the distinguished
anthropologist Melville J. Herskovits wrote, with Afro-American
research particularly in mind, 'except in a sense so broad as to be
without significance' forms of behaviour 'do not arise from any
special innate capacity of the members of any particular society,
but are learned.' To Herskovits, the tenaciousness of culture under
the processes of cultural change is documented by 'such aspects of
musical conditioning as are to be inferred from historic continuity,
not only of rhythmic structure and tonal progressions of New World
Negro music but also of such subtle factors as skips, modes of attack
in singing, tessitura, and inner structure of melodic line.'

Such is the illogicality of segregation that in some States, even
one sixty-fourth part black blood was enough to classify a man as
'Negro', irrespective of the sixty-three sixty-fourths which were
'White', and this meant separate education, Jim Crow cars, 'Colored'
lavatories and all the humiliations of discrimination. It was under
these circumstances of rigorously enforced segregation that American
elements were learned and sustained, even among people whose

African heritage was fractional. So it comes as slightly less surprising that the archetypal Mississippi blues singer Charley Patton was moderately light-skinned and had long wavy hair of European type. Patton's music was at least part African, even if it was also part European; it demonstrated the processes of enculturation (the psycho-social mechanisms by which one generation passes on the behaviour patterns of the culture to succeeding generations) and acculturation (the confluence of those African elements with the Anglo-Celtic traditions). Blues is a late phase in both processes: the distant African heritage was still maintained through the work song to the field hollers, while the adoption of European harmonic structures led to the definition of the blues form. •

At the height of the cotton-picking season, there was little time for anything else but hard work during the day and the resting of aching limbs for a brief night, but during the rest of the year, when the sun went down, there was time for relaxation. At the end of the week the hands would go into town to bring produce to the market, to spend a little change, have a haircut and swap lies. The barber-shop became a traditional social and blues centre. Saturday night has always been the big night in southern rural communities; there were fish-fries and country suppers to the music of a string band or of a guitarist and fiddler by the river's edge when the weather was warm, and wilder pursuits in the hot, ill-ventilated 'juke joints.' On the Sunday, for the godly there was church, with services lasting on and off all day, the hoarse exhortations of the preachers leading to the lining-out of old spirituals or to the joyous sounds of the gospel song which was to become the successor to the shout. But that was Sunday. Saturday night was for good times, with the liquor flowing, the shouts and laughter of dancers rising above the noise of juke band or gin-mill piano, and sometimes the staccato report of a revolver fired in jest – or in earnest.

Reels, jigs, rags – where there was space, the dances were an acrobatic blend of square dance and jig, with movements imitative of birds and animals in the 'Eagle Rock' and the 'Buck and Wing', or the 'hoe down' with its exhibition dances in the centre of a hand-clapping ring. In the confined space of the juke the 'shake dance' demanded sinuous bodily movement; couples shuffled round in the rocking step of a 'slow drag' and danced close with a 'belly-rub'. The music for such juke joint sessions, which became longer in the July lay-off period before the new ground was broken in, drew freely from a variety of traditions: square dances of European origin, 'stomps' adapted from the old ring-shouts, popular tunes that had filtered through to the rural communities, narrative ballads. Ballads were popular at the close of the nineteenth century, rapidly replacing the roustabout songs and levee songs which had been the rage in the 'eighties. In 1876, Lafcadio Hearn had published in the *Commercial* of Cincinnati, Ohio, a number of roustabout songs which he had collected on the city's levee waterfront. They included Kentucky slave songs, work songs with alternating line and chorus, as well as verse and refrain songs with an Anglo-Scots origin: *Farewell, Liza Jane* and *The Wandering Steamboatman*. One of these, *Limber Jim*, had clusters of verses which moved freely between the songs of the period and had a hitherto unnoted asperity:

> Nigger an' a white man playing seven-up
> White man played an' ace; an' nigger feared to take it up,
> White man played ace an' nigger played a nine,
> White man died, an' nigger went blind.

Fifty years later Julius Daniels recorded in Atlanta, Georgia:

> Nigger an' a white man playin' seven-up this mornin',
> Nigger an' a white man playin' seven-up this mornin'
> Nigger an' a white man playin' seven-up
> Well nigger win the money but he scared to pick it up,
> This mornin' that' too soon for me.   .

– giving some indication of the persistence of traditional elements in black song which have been sustained through periods of change.
. Julius Daniels might have identified himself as a 'songster' – a singer and instrumentalist who, if not exactly professional, would nevertheless have gained a considerable local reputation as a musician and entertainer and would probably have developed an accomplished technique on the guitar. Such songsters, drawing broadly on all aspects of song and music traditions within the folk culture were to be found in black communities throughout the South at the close of the century, and in dwindling numbers continued to make their music during the period when the blues predominated. Others, calling themselves 'musicianers', concentrated on instrumental work, played for the dances and suppers and provided support for the songsters when they performed. Mississippi John Hurt, who was born in 1895, in Teoc, Mississippi, and Mance Lipscomb, a year younger, of Navasota, Texas were lonely survivors of the songster generation; it was their predecessors who popularised the ballads and did much to spread the blues.

Ballads may well have been derived from European sources but *Lady Isobel and the Elfin Knight* or *The Twa Brothers*, though popular in the rural regions of white America, would have had little significance to Blacks. It is true that versions of *Our Goodman* have been popular, even among blues singers, and such old ballads as *Young Maid Saved from the Gallows* have been collected. But far more prevalent have been the ballads of black folk-heroes. One of the oldest and most widely-known is the ballad of *John Henry*, which tells the story of a steel-driller employed in the Big Bend Tunnel on the C & O Line who competed with a steam-drill and died in the attempt. Its symbolism would have appealed strongly to those who could identify with the giant hero overcome by the impossible odds against him. The incident has been traced to the building of the tunnel in 1872 and the ballad, on the characteristic British structure of four or eight lines, was probably in circulation soon afterwards. It was often used as a 'hammer song' by workers who interpreted 'driving steel' as the hammering of spikes in railroad track-laying. The short lines and frequent pauses made *John Henry* an ideal work song and its remarkable longevity was partly due to this, and partly to its narrative and symbolic content.

> John Henry was a steel drivin' man
> Ca'(rrie)d his hammer all the time,
> 'Fore he'd let that steam drill beat him down,
> Lay down his hammer an' he died,
> Lay down his hammer an' he died.
>
> John Henry had a little girl,
> Her name was Polly Ann
> John was on his bed so low
> (She) drove with his hammer like a man
> Drove with his hammer like a man.

A phonophotographic record was made by Metfessel with the aid of Professors Odum and Johnson of a workman singing the ballad. It showed the rich variety of intonations in the singing. 'In Graph I alone, *John, Hen- ,ry, a*, the first tone of *steel, ca'd* and *-mer* are examples of circumflex. *Dri-* and *the* are rising. The second tone of *a, -vin, ham-* and *all* are falling intonations,' wrote Metfessel. An interpolated tone occurred at the beginning of the syllable of *time* and 'the circumflex-attack is represented twice, one on *Ann*, graph 4, and again on *man*, also graph 4. The upper limits of the circumflex are in each example a half-step below the note that follows.'

By the end of the century, a strong ballad tradition had grown with the simple harmonic progression of the British folk ballad and similar form, but approached with an essentially African American quality of singing. To a marked extent this trend in song was paralleled in white folk communities – among cowboys and lumberjacks for instance – where the legends of *Sam Bass, Cole Younger* or *Joe Mica* were told in ballad form. Sometimes the hero of black ballads was white, as was *Casey Jones*, and others, *Stack o' Lee* or *Delia Holmes*, seemed to have moved freely between the segregated racial groups. The fatal affray between *Billy Lyons and Stack o' Lee (Stagolee* or *Stackolee*) probably took place in Memphis, at least according to some reports. A Memphis songster, Furry Lewis, sang about thirty years after:

> I remember one September on one Friday night
> Stack o' Lee and Billy Lyons had a great fight,
>   Cryin' when you lose your money, learn to lose.

> Billy Lyons shot six bits, Stack o' Lee bet he passed,
> Stack o' Lee out with his .45, said 'You done shot your last'
>   When you lose your money, learn to lose.

> Lord a woman came a-runnin', fell down on her knees
> Cryin' 'Oh Mister Stack o' Lee, don't shoot my brother please'
>   When you lose your money –

Other reports place the shooting in St Louis where the murder of Al Britt by a woman named Frankie (Baker?) in 1899 gave rise to the best-known of these ballads, *Frankie and Albert*. Less famous, but very typical was the ballad of Morris Slater, from the turpentine pine woods of Escambia County, Alabama, who killed a dozen people between 1893 and 1895. 'I love you and do not want to kill you so do not come after me,' he wrote to Sheriff E. S. McMillan. But the Sheriff did come and he was slain by Morris Slater, 'Railroad Bill' as he was called, on July 3rd 1895. The man-hunt was on in earnest and Railroad Bill was ambushed and killed the following March. For Blacks, his battle against authority and the law officers made him a hero and a ballad was soon composed about him. Sang Will Bennett in 1927:

> Railroad Bill, oughta be killed
> He never worked and he never will,
>   I'm gonna ride my Railroad Bill.

Railroad Bill he took my wife,
Threatened to me that he would take my life
I'm gonna ride my Railroad Bill.

Goin' up on the mountain, take my stand,
.41 Derringer in my right an' left hand,
I'm gonna ride my Railroad Bill.

Buy me a gun just as long as my arm,
Kill everybody ever done me wrong,
I'm gonna ride my Railroad Bill.

Though Railroad Bill 'oughta be killed', there is grudging admiration for the bad man and soon the singer assumes the outlaw's personality. Like *Delia Holmes* with its 'She's Gone Delia, Gone' refrain, or *Frankie and Albert* and the celebrated 'He was her man, but he done her wrong', *Railroad Bill* followed the couplet verse with a single line refrain. It was sung in eight-bar stanzas but other versions, to a slightly different tune, would employ an eight-bar verse and a four-bar refrain as did *Frankie and Albert* or *Duncan and Brady*. Such ballads as *Ella Speed* or *Eddy Jones* often took an eight-bar form; others like *Po' Lazarus* or *Betty and Dupree* had a twelve-bar form. Generally they employed the simple chord progression of the English popular ballads: tonic, subdominant, dominant – in E, a much favoured key, the basic progression E, A, B7. But black singers and musicians favoured the 7th chords and a progression of E, E7, A7, B7, E would be used for a ballad like *Stack o' Lee*.

Though the influences on the blues are complex, the two major roots were the hollers of the field hands, freely structured and modal in character, and the ballads with their more disciplined eight and twelve-bar forms and conventional harmonic progression. For a long time the two inter-twined uncertainly, with the field holler readily apparent in the singing of country blues men. Robert Pete Williams, a paroled prisoner from Angola penitentiary in Louisiana, who was born in 1914 and did not start to play guitar until he was twenty, sang blues that were almost exclusively modal. But in general the years before the First World War saw the structure of the blues become more defined, eventually resolving inflexibly in a twelve-bar, three-line pattern which reflected the songster's couplet-and-refrain ballads. The tonality of the holler impressed itself on the blues even in its more rigidly structured form and this has given it a particular character. 'I have never heard an African singing the 3rd and 7th degrees of a major scale in tune' wrote A.M. Jones confirming the use of 'blue notes' in East African music with a confidence not shared

by all ethnomusicologists. It has been argued that the tendency to
flatten the 3rd and 7th in the major scale which is characteristic
of jazz and blues has resulted from the indecision that Blacks had
encountered in attempting to relate an African pentatonic scale to
the European diatonic. As many African scales are heptatonic or
gapped, and as European folk song is frequently pentatonic, this is
too facile an explanation; but the sound preference is nonetheless
there. The use of this 'blue tonality' is evident in a *Cottonfield Blues* by
Garfield Akers, the title significantly hinting at the qualities of holler,
and blues structure, which it demonstrates (Music Example 2).

> Ah well looka here mama, what in the worl' are you tryin' a do?
> I said looka here mama, what in th' worl' are you tryin'-a do?
> Don' know what makes me love you, you gonna break my
>   heart in two.
>
> I said if you don' wan' me what makes you wanna lie?
> I said if you don' wan' me mama, what makes you wanna lie?
> I said the day you quit me fair brown, sure as God tha's the day
>   you die.
>
> I'd rather see you dead, buried in some cypress grove,
> I'd rather see you dead mama, buried in some cypress grove,
> Than to have some garbage man mama, snatchin' up your clo's.

Garfield Akers' vocal was pitched like a holler, commencing high
with a strained extension of certain notes and falling at the end of
a line, except for a final upward curl. He accompanied himself on
guitar and a second guitar, played by his friend Joe Calicott, provided
a crotchet beat throughout the blues. As the blues progressed Akers
would hold a flattened third for two or even three beats, and as he
did so would 'bend' the second, D, of the scale by 'choking' the guitar
string – pushing it across the fret to form an E♭.

Basically, the field holler is the call of a man at work while the
blues is a song of a man at leisure. Being a song of leisure it can be
accompanied by the singer, and in this case, by his friend as well.
Joe Calicott was born in 1901 and lived in Nesbit, Mississippi;
Akers died about 1959, ten years before him. They were both small
boys when the blues was first being heard in the Mississippi Delta;
slavery had ended half a century before. Yet, in the shifting rhythms
of their playing, in the use of the flattened notes and the falling
vocal phrases there remains a glimpse of Africa. The tonality, the
calling quality is that of the holler and harmonically *Cottonfield Blues*
grapples with the form of the European-derived ballads and folk

songs. In its three-line, twelve-bar stanzas Garfield Akers' blues had the characteristic structure of the traditional blues verse, a structure which was apparently resolved during the first decade of the century and which was to some extent crystallised with the publication of Hart Wand's *Dallas Blues* and W. C. Handy's *The Memphis Blues* in 1912. In some ways Akers' song was typical of the blues and in some it was a-typical; the combination of vocal, rhythmic and formal elements had much in common with many aspects of the blues, yet the particular interpretation is essentially his own. And that, in itself, is typical of the blues.

Down the Dirt Roads

'One night at Tutwiler, as I nodded in the railroad station while waiting for a train that had been delayed nine hours, life suddenly took me by the shoulder and wakened me with a start.' The event which, quite literally, altered the life of William Christopher Handy and also, to a considerable degree, the course of the blues, was the playing and singing of a ragged, lean black guitarist. 'As he played, he pressed a knife on the strings of the guitar in a manner popularized by Hawaiian guitarists who used steel bars. The effect was unforgettable. His song, too, struck me instantly.

Goin' where the Southern cross the Dog.

The singer repeated the line three times, accompanying himself on the guitar with the weirdest music I had ever heard.' Tutwiler, Mississippi, has scarcely changed since that day in 1903. A few miles north of Parchman on Highway 49, it is deep blues country and you could probably still find a man who could sing about Moorhead, where the Southern Railroad crosses the Yazoo-Delta Railroad on the Illinois Central line – the 'Yellow Dog.'

It's one of the earliest dateable references to a specific blues and is important because of the evident folk character of the singer, the location, the idiom – which W. C. Handy later used in his *Yellow Dog Blues* – and the technique of playing the guitar. One of the many factors which influenced the character of the blues was the popularity of the guitar. C.F. Martin came to the United States from Germany in 1833 and started making guitars, but the rivalry of Orville Gibson's firm, which commenced making the big 'Gibson' in 1894, greatly affected output. Mail order guitars and guitar-making kits also increased the availability of the instrument, while the proximity to

Mexico and the presence of a Spanish-American population in Texas contributed to the popularity of the huge twelve-string guitars. To a considerable extent the guitar replaced the banjo and the fiddle, particularly the former which was little used by blues singers. The short, staccato notes of the banjo did not accord with the blues singer's concepts of accompaniment, offering neither long notes nor the warm and deep resonance of a guitar rhythm. Fundamentally a vocal music, the blues required a vocal quality from its instruments, effects which the guitar's flexibility permitted. A comparison between the solo blues recordings of the only two black banjo-players in the 'twenties to record in any quantity, 'Papa' Charlie Jackson and 'Banjo Joe' – Gus Cannon – with the guitar recordings of almost any of their contemporaries makes this clear. Both were bridging the songster and the blues generations and recorded a great many folk items, on which the abrupt, raggy banjo sounded appropriate enough. By choking the string a brief blue tonality could be obtained but this was far more readily achieved on the guitar.

Banjo playing in the folk idiom is notable for the use of open strings, achieved by retuning in a major or minor chord for different tunes. Banjo players often used different tunings for the various dance pieces that they played. Blues guitarists imitated them, developing 'crossed-note' tunings. This technique was applied to blues with considerable effect, the 'standard' guitar tuning of E-B-G-D-A-E being altered by raising or lowering the strings until the instrument was tuned to a chord. Not only did this allow, at the most elementary level, the opportunity to play a simple sequence by the use of the barre alone, but it also allowed considerable freedom in rhythmic patterns and finger-picking. Sometimes a single string would be altered – by lowering the bass E string to D for instance – and most guitarists developed tunings which they particularly liked. Several of the tunings had names but they were often inconsistently used and one singer's 'Crossed E' was another singer's 'Spanish'. 'Crossed-note' was a term often used to identify such retunings, presumably implying the use of the barre and the fact that the instrument was tuned to a chord. Some of the terms were significant in themselves, whether accurately applied or not – 'Spanish', 'Hi-wanna' (a frequent corruption of 'Hawaiian') and 'Sebastapol' suggesting possible derivations of such tunings or their currency and probable first appearance at the time of the Spanish-American War and the annexation of Hawaii, both of which occurred in 1898.

It is interesting that W.C. Handy attributed the use of a knife on the guitar strings as a link with the Hawaiian bars. By drawing his blade along the strings the guitarist could produce a whining sound like the cry of a human voice – or a field holler. As early as 1911 in the *Journal of American Folklore*, Howard W. Odum described the use of the knife in terms which exactly define the customary use among blues singers. The 'knife-song' he considered to be instrumental in origin and to derive its name 'from the act of running the back of a knife along the strings of the instrument, thus making it "talk" and "sing" with skill.' He noted that some 'musicianers' carried a piece of polished bone to slip over the finger to produce the same effect. Among blues singers a broken bottleneck, annealed at the break, was often used in this way, while others employed a brass ring. Some guitarists used the technique sparingly but others employed it almost exclusively, and its widespread distribution is indicative of the vocalised sound quality favoured by the blues singer.

Odum noted a large number of lines which were already current in the blues, and which, with rather surprising conservatism, are much employed still. As many appear to have pre-dated the blues, the specific move from one tradition to another cannot be traced. Of the many items in this early collection which show the blues, in all but name, to have been in wide circulation in the preceding few years, one may be used to show the processes of tradition, growth, change and mutation which took place before the form was crystallised. 'In the following song,' he wrote, 'which is sometimes sung with the knife instrumental music described elsewhere, each stanza consists of a single line repeated three times:

> I'm a po' boy 'long way from home,
> Oh, I'm a po' boy 'long way from home.
>
> I wish a 'scushion train would run,
> Carry me back where I cum frum.
>
> Come here, babe, an' sit on yo' papa's knee.'

Other lines quoted were:

> I ain't got a frien' in dis town.
>
> I'm out in de wide worl' alone.
>
> I wish that ole engineer wus dead,
> Brought me 'way from my home.
>
> Central gi' me long-distance phone,
> Talk to my babe all night long.

In the index it was noted that the song was collected from a visiting singer in Northern Mississippi, Lafayette County. Where the singer came from was unfortunately not shown. Fifteen years after the song was published, it was recorded in different parts of the South. The close proximity of the recording dates and the different tunes and words suggest that recording in itself was not the vehicle for dissemination. One of the oldest of the 'songsters', born in 1883, Gus Cannon (Banjo Joe) would have been at least in his mid-twenties when the song was collected only thirty-odd miles south of his home at Red Banks, Mississippi in the adjacent Marshall County. He was forty-four when he recorded it, playing knife-style on banjo, while the Georgia singer Blind Blake quietly accompanied on guitar.

> Been a poor boy and long ways from home
> Long ways from home,
> Been a poor boy and a long ways from home.
>
> I guess I'll have to catch the Frisco out – in this lan'
> Catch the Frisco out,
> Lord I guess I'll have to catch the Frisco out.
>
> I got 'rested, no money to buy my fine,
> Money to buy my fine,
> I got 'rested, no money to buy my fine.
>
> I cried 'Hello Central give me . . .
> Yer long distance 'phone,'
> I cried 'Hello Central, give me your long distance 'phone.'
>
> I cried 'Please ma'am give me Thirteen-Forty-Nine,
> Thirteen-Forty-Nine'
> I cried 'Please Ma'am give me Thirteen-Forty-Nine.'

His song then moved into the old New Orleans theme of *Bucket Got a Hole In It* with his slide banjo carrying some of the words. A few months earlier, in June that year, Barbecue Bob (Robert Hicks) a blues singer in Atlanta, Georgia, recorded a version, using a bottle-neck slide. Some of the verses were, as Odum had noted, simply repeats of a single line, others had four-line stanzas, and others took the customary blues form.

> I'm a po' boy, I'm a long way from home (2)
> I'm a po' boy, ain't got nowhere to roam.
>
> Honey, tell me what you gonna do
> Please tell me what you gonna do (2)

Ain't got nowhere to lay my worried head (3)
Some time I soon will be dead.

And the po' boy stood on the road and cried (2)
I didn't have no blues, just couldn't be satisfied.

Honey give me long, long-distance call (3)
I wanna hear from that bob-haired gal o'mine.

Hello Central, ring Six-O-Nine
Central, ring Six-O-Nine
I want to hear from that gal o' mine.

The following year still another version, again using a knife or other slide accompaniment was recorded, this time by a Texas singer, Rambling Willard Thomas. Its wistful theme and haunting slide was less closely related to the others but it was recognisably the same song.

Poor boy, poor boy; poor boy long ways from home.

I was down in Loosianna doin' as I please,
Now I'm in Texas . . . I got to work or leave,
Poor boy, poor boy, poor boy long ways from home.

'If your home's in Loosianna, what you doin' over here?'
Said 'My home ain't in Texas and I sure don't care'
Poor boy, poor boy; poor boy long ways from home.

I don't care if the boat don't never land,
I like to stay on the water, long as any man
Poor boy, poor boy, poor boy long ways from home.

Poor boy, poor boy, poor boy long ways from home.

And that boat came a-rockin' just like a drunken man,
And my home's in the water and I sure don't like land,
Poor boy, poor boy, poor boy long ways from home.

No irrefutable conclusions as to source may be drawn from a comparison of these songs; the time that had elapsed since it was first noted allowed for transmission in any direction. And as the original version was from a 'visiting stranger', it is as likely to have migrated to Mississippi as emanated from it. What is of value is the light it throws on the tenacity of certain lines or ideas, and the manner in which these have been moulded in to create new songs which have at least some relevance to the singers.

It is probable that the earliest blues were loose songs of similar character, which had certain unifying lines or verses but which were free enough to allow individual treatment by different singers. *Joe Turney*, a work-song ballad of a 'long-chain man' who brought prisoners to the Nashville jail from Memphis in the 1890s, became *Joe Turner Blues* and eventually, the root of Robert Wilkins' *Nashville Stonewall Blues*. *Must I Hesitate* or *Hesitating Blues* was collected widely in the field before both W. C. Handy and Smythe and Middleton from Louisville copyrighted it in 1915 – it became Sam Collins's *Hesitation Blues*. *C. C. Rider*, with lines which relate to Rambling Thomas's *Poor Boy*, was another early theme recorded by Ma Rainey as *See See Rider*. Among the songs noted by Howard Odum before 1910 were *Ain't Nobody's Biz-Ness What I do* and *Make Me a Pallet on the Floor*, themes which were widely adopted and long recalled by large numbers of singers. These early blues would have appealed particularly to the songsters – a number appear in the singing of such representatives of that tradition as Henry Thomas, Jim Jackson and Huddie Leadbetter (Leadbelly). They could be sung as songs, but they left much room for extemporisation. For the field hands, the one and two-line songs were easily adaptable to hollers – and the blues slipped into being. A fragment of a river song, 'I thought I heard the Katy Adams blow . . .' was applicable to a local train, the 'Katy' on the Missouri, Kansas, Texas line, or the 'K.C.' on the Kansas City Southern: 'I thought I heard the K.C. when she blowed . . .' 'I thought I heard the Katy whistle blow . . .' and a line could be added after a repetition or two, 'she blows like my woman is on board' or 'she blows like she ain't goin' blow no more . . .'

For the truly inventive singer, the new blues offered him a means of self-expression. Most of the ballads and folk-songs had been about other people, or heroes, or exterior events: a disaster like the sinking of the *Titanic* or the coming of the boll weevil. But through the blues a man could sing about himself as he did in the fields; he could be his own hero. He could brag a little, he could make up a story about himself, he could wish himself into a situation – leaving home for better conditions or where there were no responsibilities. Or he could tell of the unhappiness of yesterday and work it out of his system. The blues was a way of singing and playing; it was a kind of song, and as always, it was a state of mind. The blues singer didn't reason himself into a different frame of mind, he sang himself into it. And when the blues had gone there was still the blues to sing, to amuse himself, or his companions, or to entertain at the local juke.

One of the characteristics of the blues is that it is almost invariably personalised – blues singers nearly always sing about themselves – but there are also groups of singers who show certain common features in song or instrumental technique, in choice of melody, idiom or verse. Small 'schools' of blues singers emerge, often dominated by a major personality with a markedly individual or original turn of phrase or manner of delivery, who has his immediate disciples. This tendency to group into schools has led to a largely fruitless search for regional or state 'blues styles', although the territories represented are often extremely local. Blues singers might well be divided between those who remain in one small region most of their lives, and those who are 'ramblers', who move freely and frequently between centres, following the migratory farm workers or tracing the highways to the larger cities. The mobility of the latter group affects both, for it is the 'visiting singer' who may bring a new idea, a new concept to a district and be avidly imitated, as he picks up the fragments that appeal to him during his temporary stay. So a singer like Whistling Alex Moore lived his entire life within an area of a few blocks in Dallas, Texas, while an inveterate rambler like Big Joe Williams, only a few years his junior, claimed with perhaps fifty per cent accuracy, to have worked in every state in the Union, even if St Louis was his base. A sharecropper might be obliged to remain in one spot in the hopeless attempt to work himself free of debt; one of his sons may determine never to be in that position, and with some talent for making music, try to live by it. Blues does not lay a regular pattern over Black America, but continually changes in emphasis and distribution.

One of the most important figures in the whole story of the blues is Charley Patton. Few other bluesmen sang with such fierce conviction and with such growling earthiness, and though the number of singers who were directly influenced by him is not large, he was the inspiration of a great many. Patton was born in 1891, near Edwards, Mississippi, one of twelve children who moved with their parents to Dockery's plantation near Cleveland. Cleveland lies in the heart of the Delta – the D-shaped lowlands that lie between the Yazoo and the Mississippi Rivers south of Memphis and north of Vicksburg. When he moved to Dockery's where his father rented lands, Charley Patton was in his early 'teens, and he was thirty-four before he left the farms. David Evans has established that an older musician, Henry Sloan, helped shape his music, and the small, lean, wavy-haired young man with the powerful voice seems to have learned some of the songsters' repertoire in the erotic *Spoonful*, the obscurely bawdy *Shake it and Break It* (*Don't Let it Fall, Mama*) and a fragmented version of the *Ballit of the Boll Weavil* which he called *Mississippi Bo Weavil Blues*. By the time he began to record, when he was over forty, his songs were mostly blues. Patton's themes were sometimes concerned with his own experiences, relating in *High Sheriff Blues* how he had been jailed for drunkenness in Belzoni. *Tom Rushen Blues* told a similar story which seems to have lost the Sheriff, Tom Day, his job. Many of his blues were about women, either directly or in metaphor, and his fame as a blues singer seems to have won him many. He made some recordings of religious tunes, too, but he was not a church-member. A number of blues mentioned local personalities who would have had immediate significance only to those who knew who they were; the fact suggests that Patton, even in a recording studio, was singing only for his immediate circle. A few blues suggest some concern with social events but the two-part *High Water Everywhere* which told of the havoc caused by the Mississippi floods and the heavy loss of life and property in 1927 was exceptional. He still sang it as one of the fleeing thousands rather than as a detached observer, and in all his singing, with its dark intensity, there is a sense of complete involvement.

> Lord the whole roun' country Lord, river is overflowed
> Lord the whole roun' country, man it's overflowed (2)
> I would go to the hilly country, but they got me barred.
>
> Now the water now mama, done struck Charley's town,
> Well they tell me the water done struck Charley's town
>   Well I'm goin' to Vicksburg on that high mound.
>
> Ooooh-uh the water is risin', families sinkin' down
> Say now, the water was risin', airplanes all aroun'
> It was fifty men and children come to sink an' drown.
>
> Ooooh-uh Lordy women and grown men drown,
> Ooooh women and children sinkin' down
> I couldn't see nobody home an' was no one to be found.

Charley Patton had a reputation for 'clowning' when performing, and he prided himself for his professionalism in satisfying his audiences. But his inner personality seems to have been released when he was away from the joints and house parties and in the recording studio.

For some six years Patton lived in the small community of Merigold, outside the all-black town of Mound Bayou, but when he started recording, he moved near Clarksdale on Highway 61 where he joined a raw country fiddle player, Son Sims. Sims had been in the army during the First World War but Patton, at thirty, had not been in the services. There is little doubt however, that the War played a large part in spreading the blues, throwing men from different states and regions into close association and giving cause to sing the blues.

John Jacob Niles, as a pilot in the United States Air Force served in many theatres of war and made a collection of the songs of black troops. 'True, they sang some music-hall ditties,' he noted, 'but after all, those colored regiments were recruited from every corner of the United States – there were Harlem negroes, Texas negroes, negroes from south-side Chicago, negroes from North Carolina.' Apart from the semi-professional singers there were the 'natural-born singers, usually from rural districts, who, prompted by hunger, wounds, home-sickness, and the reaction to so many generations of suppression, sang the legend of the black man to tunes and harmonies they made up as they went along.' He wrote at length of an orderly named Elmer from Mississippi for whom 'the wire, the trenches, and the dud bombs, were of little or no importance, when compared to the agonizing thought of sea travel. On the way to France Elmer had suffered from a new kind of blues – the deep-sea variety.' His lyrics 'varied with the particular kind of misery he had come down with, but the blues were always of the deep sea.'

The Great War brought Blacks from many states together: the men of the 369th Infantry returned with the Croix de Guerre. Though a decade had elapsed since the War, fragments of blues relating to service overseas, in France and in Germany, appeared in many recorded blues, emphasising the importance of the confluence of blues currents which occurred at the time. Charley Patton's *Down the Dirt Road Blues* (*Over the Sea Blues*) appears to be one of them (Musical Example 3).

I'm goin' away to where I know (2)
I'm worried now but I won't be worried long.

My rider got somethin' she tryin' to keep it hid (2)
Lord I got somethin' to find that somethin' with.

I feel like choppin' chips flyin' everywhere (2)
I been to the Nation, Lord but I couldn't stay there.

Some people tell me these overseas blues ain't bad, (2)
It must not have been them overseas blues I had.

Ev'ry day, seems like murder here (2)
I'm gonna leave tomorrow, I know you don't didn't want me here.

Cain't go down that dark road by myself (2)
I don't carry my rider, gonna carry me someone else.

Patton's low, growling voice is not based on a called holler but is held with deep chest tones to a closer range. But his vocal line displays the flattened 3rd and 7th, especially in the descending phrases, the 3rd being natural when the voice is rising. The simple accompaniment is on a fundamentally rhythmic framework which achieves its impetus by the anticipation of the beat in the vocal and its variety by tapping the box and the occasional use of full chords.

A great many blues singers were either taught by Charley Patton or came under his influence at Dockery's. Jake Martin, who had also been born near Edwards, in 1886, joined him in 1916. The following year he went into the Army but returning in 1919 settled on Dockery's plantation where he remained for nearly thirty years. Better known are the names of Willie Brown, who came to the nearby town of Drew at the age of about twenty in 1911, and Son House, whose association with Patton and with Brown commenced almost twenty years later. Brown had a rasping, abrasive voice and had developed a dramatic guitar technique on his *Future Blues* in which the bass strings were plucked hard from underneath and snapped back on the fingerboard. There was a certain rough irony in his verses but his constricted throat and forced, dramatic singing had no hint of humour when he sang on *M & O Blues*:

> Now, it's all you men, ought to be shamed o' yo'selves
> Goin' roun' here swearin' fore God you had a poor woman
> by yo'self.
> I started t' kill my woman till she lay down 'cross
> the bed (2)
> An' she looked so ambitious till I – took back
> everything I said.
>
> An' I asked her how 'bout it, Lord an' she said 'Alright' (2)
> But she never showed up at the shack last night.

It was the opinion of many who heard them that Willie Brown was a better guitarist than Patton, the pupil excelling his master. But Patton's voice and guitar quality permeate Brown's playing and singing. Though other Delta musicians were less awesomely fierce than these, a great many adopted a style in which the vocal, adapted from the holler, took a more harmonically structured line but was accompanied by a rhythmic pattern that was more modal in conception. In effect, the accompaniment was within a single chord, or constructed on a group of notes within the mode. The tension established by the meeting of the two contributed much to the strange and dramatic beauty of the Delta blues.

One of the blues men who was profoundly influenced by the singers in the fifty-mile long Sunflower County, was Tommy Johnson, who himself became a powerful figure in the blues of Mississippi. Like Dick Bankston and Mott Willis, Tommy Johnson came from Crystal Springs, south of Jackson and out of the Delta region. Will Dockery had opened up his plantation in 1895, one of several in the Delta which had been developed with resident hired hands as an alternative to the sharecropper system. David Evans's exhaustive researches have revealed that Tommy Johnson moved to Drew with his brother Ledell about 1917, and Willis followed a couple of years later. Though Johnson could play guitar it was under the tutelage of the Dockery musicians that he developed one of the most distinctive and complete sounds to come out of Mississippi. Johnson's warm but relatively high pitched voice had a vibrant quality, his vocals sliding easily into humming, or employing falsetto syllables with effortless transitions. Most of his blues seem to have been based on verses already traditional and their beauty derived from a perfectly resolved form in which the planned accompaniments were indivisible from the total sound. Such themes as *Cool Drink of Water Blues* and *Maggie Campbell* were learned by innumerable singers and always performed in imitation of Johnson's style, while his walking bass accompaniment to *Big Road Blues* was widely copied.

Closest to Tommy Johnson was Ishman Bracey who was born in 1901 and who worked as a water boy carrying water to the 'gandy-dancers' on the Illinois Central line. His singing was strongly nasal and had a rapid vibrato with a phrasing which often recalled the hollers of the field workers from whom he learned to play guitar. The high opening notes and long, humming cadences which occurred in the middle of the first line of each verse of his eight-bar *Trouble-Hearted Blues*, had a pronounced field call sound. Other blues singers in the Jackson region, like the brothers Charlie and Joe McCoy, or the large Chatman family, were somewhat in the shadow of Johnson and Bracey, or developed a more melodic, lightly swinging music suited to dancing. North of Jackson on Highway 49 a small and very local tradition grew up which had its best-known exponent in Nehemiah 'Skip' James, who was born in 1902 on the Whitehead plantation. His friend Jack Owens lived in Bentonia, Mississippi, where he was born in 1904. He grew up with 'Skippy' James and played blues in the same local style. James learned at the age of eight from Henry Stuckey and Rich Griffith of an older generation of musicians. He developed a very personal, introverted form of blues with an unusually high falsetto as on his *Cypress Grove*. Skip James also learned in an Arkansas sawmill to play piano, and his tumbling, flurried figures on *22–20 Blues* were quite distinctive and little related to the pianistic styles of blues which were emerging at the time. A complex and secretive man, James was embittered by the neglect of his talent. By the time recognition came, in the mid-1960s, it was too late for him to gain any satisfaction from it.

Falsetto singing was also the trademark of Sam Collins, a blues singer from far south on Highway 51, McComb in Pike County. Known as 'Crying' Sam Collins he had a wailing holler-style which was echoed on his elementary but appropriate guitar accompaniment; one string and often the whole instrument was out of tune by conventional standards but the tonal preferences which make every African instrument have its drone notes and vibrators, seem to have persisted in Sam Collins's conceptions. A singer, perhaps from the same region, King Solomon Hill, refined Collins's approach and gave a chill clarity to his own falsetto singing by the close relationship of the guitar line. Both Collins and Hill used the slide extensively but Hill, though more derivative as a composer of blues lyrics, perfected the use of the guitar as an extension of the voice.

Mississippi has produced a multitude of blues singers with diverse talents and with varying degrees of originality in their creation of blues themes and development of instrumental accompaniments. Further particularisation is tempting, but probably unnecessary, for what was remarkable was the totality of creative inspiration. Though many Mississippi blues singers are now recognised as great folk artists, they were underprivileged members of the community in their home districts, subject to exploitation by 'The Man', the white landowner who at 'settlement' time evaluated the crop, and subject to the rigours of a hard life growing cotton in the fertile, black Delta lands. Within the state, and particularly the Delta region, a web of lines of influence may be traced. The sheer crudity of segregation in Mississippi, the barbarity of the measures to enforce it, the rich and yet despairing landscape with its low, red clay hills and the monotony of the flat bottomlands combine to give the state a perverse fascination. It is occasionally beautiful, but mostly it was elemental, cruel even, stifling in its feudalism. That a folk music of such stature and dignity took root and thrived in this soil continues to thrill and astonish, and for this reason perhaps, the view of Mississippi as the birthplace of blues and the epitome of the whole music is seldom questioned. And perhaps, when all is told in the story of the blues, this may be true. But blues is not a music of state and county lines or river boundaries, but of a people. While the blues was taking shape in Mississippi other traditions were emerging elsewhere.

Froggy Bottom to Buckhead

At the time when Tommy Johnson was in the Delta, Henry Sloan was considering leaving Dockery's and Charlie Patton was the undisputed master of the Delta blues, Walter Boyd the self-styled 'King of the Twelve-string guitar players of the world' was going to a dance. He was crossing the river bottoms near New Boston in Bowie County, Texas, close to where the state lines of Texas, Arkansas and Oklahoma meet. One of his companions, Alex Griffin, began to kid another, Will Stafford, about his girl. Somehow the guitar-player, Walter Boyd, came into the discussion and Stafford drew a pistol. Boyd was quicker and shot him through the forehead. On December 13, 1917 Walter Boyd, alias Huddie Ledbetter, alias Leadbelly, was charged with murder and assault to kill. Six months later the prisoner, who had already escaped once, was sent to the Shaw State Prison farm with a thirty-year sentence.

Leadbelly was a rough, tough, arrogant man, at least then. No one challenged his skill as a twelve-string guitar player, though his neck and body bore the scars from attacks challenging his claims on women. He was then thirty-three years old and in his prime; he had earlier spent a year on the Harrison County chain gang for assaulting a woman and, when he escaped, had assumed the name of Walter Boyd to avoid re-arrest. In the preceding years he had led an eventful, violent life and absorbed every kind of ballad, reel and folk song. Like his contemporary, Henry Thomas, and Mance Lipscomb, ten years or so his junior, Leadbelly was a songster, and he had the songster's pride in the breadth of his repertoire. He had been born some thirty miles from Shreveport, near the Caddo Lake, in 1885. His father bought sixty-eight acres of land when Huddie was ten; he grew up to the smell of the brushwood burning in the lake bottoms.

Jim Fagin and Bud Coleman were the old-time guitarists from

whom he learned the first rudiments of his music and even as a boy he carried a Colt revolver to the country 'breakdowns' in the bottom-lands, along with his guitar. He was envied for his sexual prowess which he exercised at the age of sixteen in the notorious joints of Fannin Street, hung on the side of a steep hill in Shreveport's red light district. It was there he heard the 'barrel-house' piano players whose use of heavy 'walking bass' figures was the inspiration for the powerful rhythms which he employed in his songs. Leadbelly sang and played every kind of theme that he heard in his restless life, from cowboy songs like *Old Chisholm Trail*, ballads like the popular Texas theme of *Ella Speed* to children's game songs, ox-and mule-driver's hollers and low-down blues. The man who taught him, more than any other, to sing the blues was Blind Lemon Jefferson.

Blind instrumentalists play a large part in the story of the blues. Unable to make a living handling the plough or the hoe, they frequently resorted to music, with an extra sensibility from their deprivation of another sense and with the time in which to practice frequently making them among the foremost of singers. Lemon Jefferson was born in 1897 near Wortham, Texas between the Trinity and the Navasota rivers about eighty miles south of Dallas. It is sad and wasted country today but then it was good farming country in the Texas cotton belt. In Jefferson's blues there are so many references to sight that it seems likely that he was partially sighted at birth, even if he was unable to join his brothers and sisters in the fields. He must have heard them, picked a little cotton perhaps, for his voice was coloured with the cries of the field-hands and the intonations of the work songs. He was still a youth when he was playing on the streets of Wortham for coin, and he was independent enough to forgo having anyone to lead him. Leadbelly once claimed to have known Lemon in Dallas in 1904; on another occasion he claimed to have known him for eighteen years. Both seem unlikely but undoubtedly during the years before his arrest Leadbelly and Lemon did meet and, for a sustained period, they sang together in the bars of Dallas and on the steps of the railroad terminals. Sometimes they travelled to Silver City, a rough haunt now forgotten where there were 'lots of pretty girls', as he once explained. 'We like for women to be aroun' cause when women's aroun' that bring mens and that bring money. Cause when you get out there the women get to drinkin' . . . that thing fall over them, and that make us feel good and we tear those guitars all to pieces.'

A large-built man who ran to fat, Blind Lemon's full features barely hint at the sensitivity of his singing, but seated defiantly and unseeingly before a camera he revealed something of his independence. When he sang it was with a deep pathos, a feeling that stemmed from the being of a man forever in darkness. His voice was high, lean and had a cutting edge that severed pretence and bared the soul. With a natural command of nuance, he employed a range of vocal devices, striking a note with unerring accuracy, soaring up to it, letting his voice swell and fade, falling in cadence like a train whistle at night. Unlike that of Mississippi bluesmen, Lemon's singing, close to the holler, did not have an insistent beat; instead he would suspend the rhythm or hold a note to emphasise a word or line. By 'hammering' on the strings – using a quick release which produced a succession of open and fretted notes – by choking the strings and by dextrously picked arpeggios, Lemon used rapid phrases which extended the vocal line. For him the guitar was another voice and he frequently used imitative phrases – the rapid chatter of needles for the unexpected line 'I've got a gal 'cross town, she crochet all the time.' His words were almost always autobiographical:

> I stood on the corner and almost bust ma head (2)
> I couldn't earn enough to buy me a loaf of bread.
>
> Now gather roun' me people, let me tell you true facts, (2)
> That tough luck has struck me and the rats is sleepin' in my hat.

But sometimes he would project himself into another man's situation with rare poetic insight; as when he sang on *Hangman's Blues*:

> The mean old hangman is waitin' to tighten up that noose (2)
> Lord I'm so scared I'm tremblin' in my shoes.
>
> The crowd aroun' the courthouse an' the time is drawin' fast (2)
> Soon a good-for-nothin' killer is goin' to breathe his last.

Many of Jefferson's unusual turns of phrase passed into blues lore – 'I got somethin' to tell you make the springs cry on your bed', 'I'm standin' here wondrin' will a match-box hold ma clo's?' 'I walked from Dallas, I walked to Wichita Falls'. Leadbelly learned from *Black Snake Moan* which exemplified Lemon's style. Sang Jefferson, with vivid sexual imagery (Music Example 5).

> Eeeeeheh, ain't got no mama now (2)
> She tol' me late last night 'You don't need no mama nohow'
>
> Mmmm-mm, black snake crawlin' in my room (2)
> And some pretty mama better get this black snake soon.

> Oohoo, that must've been a bed bug, you know a chinch
> cain't bite that hard, (2)
> Ask my woman for fifty cents, she said 'Lemon, ain't a
> child in the yard'
>
> Well – wonder where that black snake's gone (2)
> Lord that black snake mama, done run my darlin' home.

Each line of Lemon's vocal would be answered by a fragment on the guitar – a simple phrase or a rapid arpeggio, but on this blues he did not accompany himself while singing, and suspended the beat for the verse. In Jefferson's blues the old leader-and-chorus form of call and response was echoed in the construction of vocal and answering phrase. This was a form used by a number of Texas blues singers, who worked in Dallas at much the same time.

Dallas in the early part of the century had a rapidly expanding black population, in 1900 around ten thousand, which doubled in a score of years. A considerable shift in the population occurred through the voracious pest, the boll weevil, whose devastation of the cotton crop at the turn of the century had put many Negro farmers out of work. It first appeared in Texas in the 1890s. By 1905 it had also ravaged crops in Mississippi and caused widespread disaster. Incoming Texas Blacks concentrated in the run-down areas of Dallas and desperately sought employment or lived off the women, who could still get work as domestic help to the Dallas rich.

> I been walkin' all day, an' all night too (2)
> Cause my meal ticket woman have quit me and I can't
> find no work to do.
>
> I pickin' up the newspaper an' I lookin' in the ads, (2)
> An, the policeman come along an' he 'rested me for vag.

'Boys you ought to see me in my black and white suit,' commented the singer, Rambling Thomas, drily. He was one of the Texas arpeggio school of guitarists, working from Dallas to Shreveport. Shreveport had half its population Black and, since Leadbelly was there, had a flourishing blues tradition. Many Shreveport singers made the trip along Highway 80 to Dallas and were to be found gathering in the Central Tracks region, along the railroad lines near Elm Street. Here could be heard Rambling Thomas, Blind Lemon, Texas Alexander and even Lonnie Johnson. Lonnie Johnson came from New Orleans, where he was born in 1899. In spite of the popular view, New Orleans has not had an important part to play in the story of the blues, the

transition there being from the songs of the field and the dance
into jazz. One of a large and talented family, Lonnie worked in a
lumber yard, but from childhood played guitar, fiddle and a little of
other instruments. He travelled to England with a stock company to
entertain the troops in 1917 but the decimation of his family, probably
by the Spanish 'flu epidemic, saw him rambling through Texas and
up to St Louis. He had a smooth and accomplished guitar technique,
too polished and jazz-inflected for the rougher forms of blues, but his
musical skill made him popular with the record companies. In Dallas
he represented the 'professional' singer and was chosen to accompany
Texas Alexander.

Alger Alexander was a field hand and a rugged man who saw
much of the inside of the Texas penitentiary system. He did not
play an instrument but only sang – a personal, tweed-textured holler
which did not employ falsettos but moaned in long, sad cadences.
Lonnie Johnson followed with slow finger-picked notes, uncertain
where Alexander's freely-formed blues might take him. They were
frequently transpositions of the songs Alexander sang in the levee
camp and on the section gang:

> Oh nigger lick molasses, and the white man licks 'em too
> Oh I wonder what in the worl' is this mess' gang gonna do?
> Oh nigger lick molasses and the white man licks 'em too.

> 'Water boy, water boy, bring your water round
> If you ain't got no water, let your bucket down
> Water boy, water boy, bring your water round.'

> 'Oh capt'n, capt'n, what time of day . . . ?'
> Oh he looked at me . . . and he walked away.

His blues concluded with the low humming moan which often ended
his syllables. To the renters and 'croppers who had left the farms and
bottom land plantations for the city, the voices of Blind Lemon,
Rambling Thomas or Texas Alexander were singing for them,
sharing their own experience and predicament. Crowds would
cluster round them on Central Tracks and the coins would clatter
– nickels and dimes – in their hats and tin cups. Money was scarce,
and few Blacks owned property. Small denominations passed hands
for home-brewed liquor and as winnings in street-corner crap games,
or paid admission for a party. In the 'chock-houses', where a crude
form of alcohol cost a matter of cents, pianists hit the keys in a
rough-and-ready combination of ragtime and blues: 'barrelhouse',
as it was called, after the rudest of joints where barrels supported a

plank for a bar. Alexander Moore was one, born in Dallas in 1899 and making a living during the day by leading his mule-drawn junk cart; at night he rolled out the blues in the innumerable bars and joints down in the Froggy Bottom, where his words reflected the violent life of the population and the folkways of the people from the country.

> I shot at my woman because I was tired of so much
> bull corn (2)
> I said policeman jumped me, run me like a rabbit from
> a burnin' barn.
>
> She had red flannel rags, talkin' 'bout hoodoin' po' me (2)
> I believe I'll go to Froggy Bottom so she will let me be.

The vast expanse of Texas is divided into broad strips, the piney woods and the tangled, primitive undergrowth of the Big Thicket giving way to the bottom lands of the cotton-growing, farming districts of the Trinity, the Navasota and the Brazos Rivers. Beyond the blacklands strip, from San Antonio to Fort Worth, extend the Great Plains. This area had been slowly opened up to cotton cultivation and singers like Texas Alexander followed the migrant workers into West Texas for the cotton-picking harvest. But the bulk of Texas blues singers were to be found in the eastern third of the state, still an immense area, which largely concealed a rich variety of traditions, little recorded and little researched, but represented on record by such singers as Gene Campbell, Little Hat Jones and Funny-paper Smith. It's about 180 miles to Shreveport or Texakarna from Dallas, nearly 250 miles to Houston and still further to San Antonio. In the mid- and late-1920s when the first recordings of the southern blues forms were being made, only a small number of location recordings were made in San Antonio; the rest were in Dallas. As the talent scouts tended to draw on the available material or came from the Chicago and New York headquarters by rail for brief periods of 'getting up talent', the recorded examples are a heavily conditioned picture of the blues at the time.

This problem applies not only to Texas, of course, but elsewhere in the states of the South; later, some discussion of the recording patterns will be made but it's sufficient to mention at the moment that Shreveport was almost half-way between Dallas and Jackson, Mississippi, and Jackson was as close to Shreveport as it was to Memphis – 220 miles. But it was nearly 250 miles from Jackson to

Montgomery or Birmingham, Alabama, whereas the average distance
of these cities from Atlanta, Georgia was around 160 miles. For the
recording men on their infrequent field trips, Memphis, Dallas and
Atlanta were adequate centres. With talent scouts in each centre,
and one placed in Jackson, they had the south 'covered' – for the
commercial business of supplying enough talent for recording. But
the outcome of this was that Alabama was largely neglected by
the location recording units and even by the talent scouts, their
best-known singers from Alabama having either moved to Chicago
or to Atlanta, Georgia. Alabama's grinding poverty scarcely permitted
the conditions in which the blues could move from the field holler
to a recreational and, to some extent, performance art. In many ways
Alabama, like Arkansas or the Sea Islands, was too primitive and too
under-developed to have made this transition and its folkways were
of the plantation kind. The cultural entity that isolation permitted to
remain intact in the Sea Islands did not survive the fragmentation of
divided, stratified, segregated black life in Alabama. Between 1915
and 1916 a large number of work songs, gang labour songs and blues
fragments were noted in manuscript collections in Auburn, Monroe
County, Alabama, and in adjacent areas. They were published a dozen
years later by Newman Ivey White and they show that the blues, of a
field holler kind or in work song form was commonly heard. Forty
years after the notes were made, the field trips of Harold Courlander
and Frederic Ramsey Jr showed the blues in a similar state, with many
of the older song traditions which had otherwise largely disappeared,
fading but still intact. Their recordings suggest a retardation of the
processes which formed the blues elsewhere.

A singer who came from Alabama to Atlanta, Georgia, was
Barefoot Bill, raised in Greenville, south of Montgomery, who
had a hard, shouted tone in his singing. Barefoot Bill seems to
have been obsessed with themes of crime and punishment, half
his recorded blues have some reference to violence. His voice
dropped in a series of long steps from a highish opening note
which had an immediate attack and little or no inflection. Against
the stark vocal he played a rhythmic pattern which had a train-like
impetus, the alternate bass and treble notes giving a syncopated
lift to the movement of the blues. Coming from a region lying
between Mississippi and Georgia, Barefoot Bill appears to display
some qualities in common with the singers from both of the better
documented regions. But this is probably an illusion, supported by
the chance evidence of a few recorded sides. There is, incidentally,
some indication that he lived in Atlanta for several years and if this

were the case he could have been under some influence from the major singers in the region.

Atlanta, Georgia, was an important early recording location and was singularly well-chosen. Not only did it occupy geographically a strategic position for access to a large part of the rural South, it had also witnessed an astonishing growth rate, attracting people from the rural areas over a sustained period. The black population was concentrated on the west side of the city and to the south-west with large areas having over nine-tenths of their population 'colored'. There were over 35,700 Blacks in Atlanta in 1900 and in ten years they had increased by sixteen thousand; there were ten thousand more by 1920 and after the War a further dramatic increase occurred so that by 1930 the population exceeded ninety thousand. This meant that a rapid influx of rural Blacks to the city had kept the folkways alive and also easily accessible. It should be noted in passing that Birmingham, Alabama, had a population less than half that of Atlanta in 1900 but had exceeded it by 1930 – the availability of talent is not necessarily reflected in what is known about the music of the state. In Birmingham a third of the total black male population were labourers; in Atlanta the number was less – a quarter of the total, and a larger proportion could obtain work in service jobs. This meant that there was a little more money to be dropped into the tin cups of the street singers, a little more time to develop a musical skill to a point where a man might even earn a living by entertaining as a blues singer or songster. But it was a strictly segregated society – on the heights of the bald dome of Stone Mountain the Ku Klux Klan burned their flaming crosses, held their Klonventions and cruelly, brutally maimed and castrated Blacks who they considered were getting 'uppity'. On Decatur Street or Auburn Avenue however, the Klan seemed remote. These were the 'main stem' in Atlanta's segregated sector, bright, colourful with the lights of theatres, the music of the joints and the jostling crowd around Shorter's Barber Shop. Here the bluesmen gathered, here Peg Leg Howell would sing to the passers-by and the crowds queuing outside Bailey's 81 Theatre.

Joshua Barnes Howell was born in Eatonton, Georgia, in March 1888, the son of a Putnam County farmer. He worked on the farm until 1916 when he was shot in the leg by his brother-in-law during an argument. His leg had to be amputated and he was unable to do the heavy farm work; he got a job instead at the local fertilizer plant, though this could have been little easier. By the time he was thirty-five, he was tired of the country and moved to Atlanta hoping to make a living out of his guitar playing, singing, and selling moonshine whiskey. It was the latter business that cost him a year in prison in 1925, but at least it provided him with the theme for a blues. 'Peg Leg', as he was called, adapted the songs he had heard in the field. 'I learned many of my songs around the country', he told George Mitchell, 'I picked them up from anybody – no special person. Mostly they just sang, didn't play anything.' He had learned to play the guitar himself in 1909 – 'didn't take long to learn. I just stayed up one night and learned myself.' His blues are of special interest because they clearly represent the transition from old songs, work songs and ballads, to blues. His *Rolling Mill Blues* derived from the white mountain song *To the Pines*, his *Skin Game Blues* was based on the falls of the 'pikers' in playing the gambling game of 'Georgia Skin', and others had verses that link with many old themes. How confused and probably irreclaimable the origins of traditional blues themes may be is indicated by some of the verses in Peg Leg Howell's blues. From *Rock and Gravel Blues*:

> Honey, let's go to the river and sit down, (2)
> If the blues overtake us, jump overboard and drown.
>
> It take rocks, it takes gravel, to make a solid road (2)
> It takes a lovin' fair brownie to satisfy my soul.

or from *Turtle Dove Blues*:

> I weep like a willer, moan like a turtle dove (3)
> Said life ain't worth livin' if you ain't with the one you
>   love.
>
> If I had wings like Noah's turtle dove, (3)
> I would rise and fly, 'light on the one I love.

– can be gleaned verses which were collected by John A. Lomax from a woman named 'Dink' who was working with her man in a levee camp on the Brazos River, Texas, having come there in a team imported from Mississippi, a year or two before Peg Leg Howell had begun to play guitar.

It is apparent from many blues that there are currents which flow in regional traditions that are not shared elsewhere, but others show a cross-fertilisation which makes disentanglement almost impossible. Peg Leg Howell's *Rolling Mill Blues* has its counterpart in Charlie Lincoln's *Chain Gang Trouble*, suggesting that *To the Pines* was very much a local theme. But Lincoln's blues has the 'Capt'n' verses of the chain gang which have been collected throughout the south and, as has been shown, appear in the singing of Texas Alexander. Convicts wearing stripes and shackled in gangs were leased for plantation, construction and road work. Lincoln's song with its single line verse has, in its sad tones, the authentic sound of the road gang.

> The train run off nine miles from town and killed li'l
>   Lula dead
> Her head was found in the drivin' wheel, her body
>   have never been seen.
>
> I cried, I moaned, I cried I moaned, I asked
>   'How Long, How Long.'
>
> I asked my Capt'n for the time o' day
>   Then he throwed his watch away.
>
> How Long, How Long, How long 'fore I can go home . . .
>
> I rise with the blues and I work with the blues
> Nothin' I can get but bad news.

Charlie Lincoln (or Hicks) had a rich voice with a rough complaining voice, somewhat blurred and indistinct. Howell's solo recordings were accompanied with a delicately phrased guitar but Lincoln's were powerful and full-toned. Unlike a number of the Atlanta singers, Howell played a six-string instrument; Lincoln, like his brother, Barbecue Bob, favoured the big twelve-string. He did not play it as Leadbelly had done with a full and resonant thrumming of the strings but with a combination of the swelling bass and clear treble which the instrument can also offer. Leadbelly tuned his guitar with the top three pairs of strings in unison, the fourth and fifth pairs an octave apart and the sixth pair two octaves apart; the Atlanta guitarists probably used the more standard practice of tuning with the top two pairs in unison and the remaining four pairs in octaves. It is necessary to tune a twelve-string much lower than a six-stringed instrument but Leadbelly's tuning was exceptionally low, and much lower than that of Lincoln and Barbecue Bob. The higher tuning, while still retaining the sonorous notes of the bass strings, enabled them to use bottle-neck or brass ring on the top string – often on the first of the top pair only – with a stimulating contrast of light, whining notes against driving bass rhythms. This effect delighted the brothers who recorded a couple of two-part themes, *It Won't Be Long Now* and a 'hokum' *Darktown Gamblin'* in which the exhilarating effect of the twenty-four strings of their two instruments and their deep, brassy voices singing in unison can be heard.

Raised in a farming district, Lithonia, twenty-odd miles from Atlanta, the two brothers came to the city in 1920. Robert Hicks was eighteen years old, his brother was a few years his senior. Though Charlie had a little more experience and taught his brother to play guitar when he was still a boy, his own work was a shade rougher and deeper. Robert's playing was a little more proficient but they both cultivated a style where the accompaniment fell into patterns of rhythm and treble bottle-neck, broken by fractional pauses. In Atlanta, Robert got employment as a yard-hand and later worked as a janitor at the Biltmore Hotel. In the mid-'twenties, both brothers were cleaning car windscreens and serving barbecue'd ribs at a drive-in stand in the comfortable suburb of Buckhead. It was there that they were heard by Dan Hornsby and invited to record, with Robert making his first title in 1927 as 'Barbecue Bob', and calling it *Barbecue Blues*. It had the slightly aggressive, confident manner of all his sides, and underlying it, an elusive bitterness.

> Woke up this mornin' gal, twixt midnight and day (2)
> With my hand on my piller where my brownie used to lay.
>
> I know I ain't good-lookin', teeth don't shine like
> 　　pearls (2)
> So glad good looks don't take you through this worl'.
>
> Gon' starch my jumper mama, iron my overalls (2)
> My brown done quit me; God knows she had it all.
>
> I'm gonna tell you now gal; like t' gypsy tol' the Jew (2)
> If you don't want me – it's a cinch I don't want you . . .

Both brothers lived fast and carelessly; the smiling Barbecue Bob died only a few months after his last recordings were made, at the age of twenty-nine; his brother went to prison soon after, dying there in 1963, his long sentence almost certainly being for murder. Their form of blues was the influence on the obscure Willie Baker and the better-known Curley Weaver. The latter soon teamed up with another Atlanta singer, Blind Willie McTell, who made his name in the 'thirties. Like Charlie Patton or Tommy Johnson in Mississippi, or Blind Lemon Jefferson and Texas Alexander in Texas, these were the men who gave shape to the Georgia brand of blues and impressed its sounds in wax. One may lay undue emphasis on the recorded singers and omit those who might have been more influential, more important in those localities never visited by the talent scouts. Their approaches to their music could have been very different and equally individual. But the recorded singers are representative, and they have left sufficient testimony to their originality and creativity to assure us of their significance in the story of the blues.

It is easy to speak of the intensity of the Mississippi singers, the high and lonely, relaxed singing of the Texas bluesmen or the confident assertiveness of the Georgia artists. The broad generalisations may have an element of truth; detailed study reveals the subtler shades within the cruder colours of the blue end of the spectrum. If Barbecue Bob and Charlie Lincoln, Curley Weaver or Willie McTell were less introverted than the Texas singers in their blues, the general principle does not hold for Peg Leg Howell. At least – not in his blues. When he was singing other kinds of song, Peg Leg was the most extrovert of entertainers. Blues is a means whereby a man may give expression to his feelings, but it is also entertainment, and if blues is that which blues singers care to sing, then Peg Leg Howell – and his Gang – indicate another strain in a varied music.

Bed Slats an' All

I can shake it east, I can shake it west
But way down South I can shake it best,
   Doin' the Georgia Crawl
   Oh – Georgia Crawl
   We don't need nobody tryin'
   To do the Georgia Crawl . . .

A little country dance played by a guitarist and a fiddler with voices as rough as a plank road, Henry Williams and Eddie Anthony. They were members of Peg Leg Howell's 'Gang', a small band which included Ollie Griffin playing banjo or Jim Hill on mandolin when they went out to the country balls. Eddie Anthony scraped an 'alley fiddle' with raw, searing sounds to the encouragement of comments from the rest of the group as they sawed through *Beaver Slide Rag* or *Peg Leg Stomp*. Some of their tunes were hill-billy themes such as they played for white dances – *Turkey Buzzard Blues* was simply a version of *Turkey in the Straw*.

Dance tunes figured prominently in the playing of another guitarist, Blind Arthur Blake, who came from Tampa, Florida, to work in South Georgia and the East Coast towns. He had a light and swinging guitar technique which was more relaxed than that of many of the Atlanta guitarists and was eminently suited to the rag and dance themes. 'Now we gonna do that old country rock . . .' he announced on *West Coast Blues* (which was intended to be *East Coast*), and on *Southern Rag* he stated that he was going to play a little 'Geechee music' – meaning the music of the Gullahs of the Sea Islands.

Such tunes were popular among the older musicians and indicated the kind of functions for which they often played. William Moore from Rappahannock County, north of Richmond, Virginia, who was born in 1894, used to play an *Old Country Rock* whose very title hinted at the kind of music that the blues was displacing. He used the blues techniques of 'choking' the strings to produce a whining sound which showed his awareness of the new music. 'Sister Ernestine . . . show your papa how you rock . . . mighty fine boys, rock it . . . rock it till the cows come home', he commented as he played. Such dance tunes were not localised to one region but were known all over the southern states. Walter 'Buddy Boy' Hawkins, who is believed to have been born around 1890 in Blytheville, Arkansas, recorded a dance tune which he called '*A*' *Rag* and which, he observed, he had brought back with him from Jackson, Mississippi. In Mississippi itself John Hurt played similar tunes for country suppers; his *Spanish Flangdang* was typical, and the title, one of several variants of *Fandango*, give some indication of the date and source of the dance and the guitar tuning which was used to play it. Hawkins's '*A*' *Rag* in fact, has a marked Spanish flavour.

In Texas, where the dances were subject to may ethnic influences, Mance Lipscomb played the *Buck and Wing*, a plantation dance with bird-like steps and flapping arms, the *Buzzard Lope* with hunched shoulders and loose-limbed slides, the *Hop-Scop* which was danced in 'stop-time', with suspended rhythm, and the *Heel and Toe Polka* which hinted at European origins. Most blues guitarists of an older generation, or songsters and musicianers played for such balls for both white and colored people, who danced similar dances. Henry Thomas, 'Ragtime Texas', called out the sets of his *Old Country Stomp* while strumming his guitar and playing his pan-pipe 'quills'.

> Get your partners, promenade, promenade aroun' the hall
> Fall in this side the hall, take yo' partners – Promenade.
>
> Miss Jennie eat, Miss Jennie talk,
> Miss Jennie eat with knife and fork.

The playing of the 'quills' is an indication of Thomas's generation. 'A Pan's-pipe of but three reeds, made from single joints of the common brake cane, and called by English-speaking Negroes "the quills". One may even at this day hear the black lad, sauntering home at sunset behind a few cows that he has found near the edge of the canebrake whence he has also cut his three quills, blowing and hooting, over and over,' wrote George W. Cable in 1886.

Henry Thomas's quills were a rarity by the time he recorded them, and there are few other examples. Big Boy Cleveland, a singer who

may have come from the Memphis region, played a *Quill Blues* in a
gentle, pastoral fashion; significantly his only other issued title was a
blues played to guitar. In the 1960s however, the venerable Willie
Doss from Mobile, Alabama, showed that the memory of the quills
had not quite disappeared. In the context of the dance though, the
harmonica was an instrument that had more volume, was more
versatile, and came ready-made. It seems likely that the 'French
harp' as the blues singers called the harmonica, superseded it. And
if Willie Doss was any indication of a local Alabama tradition of quill
playing, it is perhaps not too surprising to discover that there was,
in Alabama, at least one traceable blues tradition in the harmonica.
In his *Fox and Hounds*, an imitative piece descriptive of the chase,
Henry Thomas showed a further link, for the harmonica is frequently
used for such impressionistic pieces. This suggests a reason why the
popular fiddle was also displaced, with only a few musicians – like
Eddie Anthony, Milton Robie or Rob Robbins – recording on it.
The *Fox and Hounds* was a typical show-piece among fiddle players
too – and the harmonica seems to have assumed the role of both.

'Mocking the trains' and mimicking a 'fox chase' are standard
themes for most harmonica players, the instrument lending itself to
both the copying of the chuffing of locomotives and the wails and
howls of animals. DeFord Bailey, a diminutive harmonica player from
Nashville in Tennessee, where there also appears to have developed a
strong school of harp players, included in his repertoire such themes
as the *Dixie Flyer Blues, Pan-American Express, Old Hen Cackle* and
Fox Chase which exploited the novelty aspect of the harmonica to the
full. For this reason perhaps, he earned unexpected fame as a featured
entertainer on the otherwise all-white hill-billy show, *Grand Ole
Opry*. William McCoy, another harp-player, who came from Dallas,
Texas even combined the two techniques in one piece entitled *Train
Imitations and The Fox Chase* as well as doing vocal mimicry with
his *Mama Blues*. It was the vocal element which appealed to the
Alabama harmonica players for although George 'Bullet' Williams,
who is believed to have come from Selma, recorded both a train
theme, *Frisco Leaving Birmingham*, which imitated its trip to Tupelo,
Mississippi, and a hunt theme, *The Escaped Convict*, he also played
an accompaniment in a vocalised style to the singing of an unknown
blues artist on *Touch Me Light Mama*. But the vocal technique on the
French harp was cultivated most effectively by Jaybird Coleman.

Burl Coleman – nicknamed the 'Jaybird' – was born in Gainesville,
Alabama, in 1896 and later lived in the town of Bessemer near
Birmingham. His technique was close to the field holler with a

sung vocal line and then an interpreting response on the harmonica. Though he separated his words carefully he sang into the reeds on alternate verses of *Mean Trouble Blues* half masking and distorting the sound. Coleman's records do not suggest the fact that he was noted for his comic entertainment, or make it credible that he was popular with the Ku Klux Klan, who actually managed him in 1929.

Both Jaybird Coleman and George 'Bullet' Williams have been rumoured as having played with the 'Birmingham Jug Band'. This group had three guitarists – known as One-Armed Dave, Doctor Scott and Po' Joe Williams. Bogus Ben Covington played harmonica and was noted for a ditty that began 'I heard the voice of a pork-chop say "Come unto me and rest".' This he sang on the streets, pretending to be blind – hence the name of 'Bogus Ben'. A man known only as 'Honeycup' played the jug, and one with an equally anonymous name of 'New Orleans Slide' played the washboard. The folk names of the musicians recall those of the 'Razzy Dazzy Spasm Band': 'Stalebread' Lacoume who played a home-made cigar-box fiddle, zither and banjo; Willie 'Cajun' Bussey who played harmonica; Charley Stein who played rattles, gourds, cowbell and an old kettle; a 'bull-fiddle' player named Chinee who made his instrument from a half-barrel; Emile 'Whiskey' Benrod, a whistle and kazoo blower, and the totally anonymous 'Warm Gravy'. This was a group of white boys, organised by Lacoume when he was only twelve years of age in 1897. They were one of the sights of New Orleans for a score of years and once played to Sarah Bernhardt. Perhaps because they were white they attracted more attention than the small black boys whose 'second line' bands followed the brass of the jazz bands on parade, but their ingenuity in making instruments and probably the kind of music they played, had its parallels in New Orleans among the black children.

It is not without historic significance that many of the early jazz bands featured guitarists and fiddle players. Buddy Bolden's guitar players included both Brock Mumford and Charlie Galloway who were playing together in the New Orleans streets in 1885, before the first jazz bands appeared. Country guitarists like the twelve-string player Stonewall Matthews, who played with Kid Ory's Woodland Band in 1905 alongside violinist Raymond Brown, or early New Orleans men like the earthy Lorenzo Stall (or Staultz), whose singing of obscene songs and blues was one of the less heralded aspects of jazz, must have done much to bring blues and string band elements into New Orleans music. Few of the string bands are recalled in detail, but the Watson family from Pass Christian, Mississippi, had one of the better known.

In Mississippi itself the most prominent string band, that built around several generations of the Chatman family, had a history which extended well back into the nineteenth century. When Charlie Patton was fourteen years of age and still living in the Bolton region, a few miles from his birthplace at Edwards, he played guitar with Ezell and Ferdinand Chatman, stringed instrument musicians who had learned from their father. One of the Chatman musicians had eleven sons, all of whom played a number of instruments. 'My brothers were Lonnie, Edgar, Bo, Willie, Lamar and me, Sam Chatman,' recalled one of them, 'and Laurie, and Harry Chatman, and Charlie Chatman,' he listed, still forgetting a couple of his brothers. 'I played bass viol for them, and Lonnie, he played violin and Harry he played second violin. And my Brother Bo, he played clarinet and my brother Bert played guitar and my brother Larry, he beat the drums. And my brother Harry, he played piano, you see. And my brother Bo he played guitar too and he even used to play tenor banjo. And I played guitar. We just pick and play any instrument and play one to another.' They called themselves the 'Mississippi Sheiks' and they were famous from Atlanta to San Antonio, and throughout the Delta. Lonnie and Sam also recorded separately, as did Harry Chatman, while Bo Chatman, as Bo Carter, was one of the best known blues singers of the period. Their repertoire included country dance tunes, popular folk songs, occasional hill-billy items – even imitations of Jimmie Rodgers. And blues above all, harmonised, sung as solos or duets against guitars and fiddle. With their adopted brother Walter Jacobs (also known as Walter Vincent) they maintained one of the most appealing of traditions which was highly popular with white audiences as well as with black ones.

In Texas the Mississippi Sheiks had the novelty attraction of having come from another state, but there the competition was keen, for the string band tradition was strong, dominated by the vast Wright family, whose place in Texas, though unrecorded, was as important as was theirs in their own state. Up in north Texas, the Dallas String Band led by Coley Jones had its own territory, playing their *Dallas Rag* instrumental with mandolins, Sam Harris's guitar and Marco Washington's bass fiddle. As a counterpart to the Sheiks' 'serenading' of *Yodelin' Fiddlin' Blues*, they harmonised in rough and ready fashion with *I Used to Call Her Baby* but though they were well known for their blues in person, the recorded examples emphasise the novelty aspect of their entertainment. These were 'serenading' groups – they played in the streets to white crowds, at dance functions and wherever they could find employment, using their skill at mastering a variety of instruments to meet popular demand, and playing blues for black functions.

Such bands as these, with a family tradition of musicianship and a semi-professional approach to playing, even if they were born and raised and died on the plantation, had no real need for make-shift instruments. But nearly every blues guitarist has a story to tell of his 'diddley bow', a length of wire nailed to a fence, or of his first guitar or fiddle, made out of a cigar box or a polish tin or a length of plank, with broom-handle, a couple of old strings and a bottleneck to play it. For some folk musicians such home-made instruments were the only ones they ever played, and the ability to improvise, which so enriched their music, also enabled them to manufacture instruments out of unpromising material. Singers who liked to vocalise through a kazoo – a submarine-like toy with a membrane that imparts a buzzing tone to a vocal sound similar to that of a comb-and-paper – would add an oil funnel to give its volume direction. Jew's harps, even the occasional musical saw were played. Metallophones made from plough-shares and farm implements were known in slavery times and a similar inventiveness gave rise to other instruments. Some of these, it has been suggested, have an African origin. Harold Courlander, an ethnomusicologist with experience in the South, the Caribbean and West Africa, linked the 'wash-tub bass' with the African earth-bow. The earth-bow is a bow plucked over a hollow in the ground which has a membrane of skin to act as a resonator; the washtub bass is simply an inverted washtub with a broom-handle and string, the latter being held in tension and varied in pitch by pressure on the handle.

All the same, it is possible that the washtub bass arose from domestic ingenuity, though a folk memory may have encouraged this particular use. Another and related domestic item, the corrugated washboard or 'rubbing board', gave rise to the often noted 'rubbings songs' of washerwomen. Its surface gives a staccato beat when a fork or similar implement is drawn across the washboard and its potential as a rhythm instrument was not missed. A parallel with the African notched stick might be made, but it is as likely that its use arose from the rubbing song. Whatever the source, the washboard became a popular folk instrument, with cow-bells and other embellishments added. The player often wore metal thimbles on his fingers to obtain a crisp, rattling sound, satisfying to the blues ear.

More arresting was the 'jug', though a bottle or even a length of pipe would serve as well. By half-spitting, half-vocalising into it a player could produce a fruity, resonant sound not dissimilar to that of a tuba. Though many who used the jug could make a similar noise without it, the larger glass vessels and earthenware demi-johns did produce a full boom, the player altering the sound by blowing at different angles. Though only one wash-board or one jug was normally to be heard in a folk string band it often gave its name to the whole group as a 'washboard band' or 'jug band'. One such group in central Mississippi was led by James Cole, a fiddle player, and it included two or three guitars, sometimes a mandolin and occasionally a piano. This shifting personnel was typical of bands of this kind but the sound was consistently brisk and the addition of a washboard gave a crisp unifying rhythm.

To a certain extent there was an overall similarity among the string, jug and washboard bands which probably arose from the need to decide on a structure for the music. Solo musicians could be relatively free in their playing; for a group a more rigid form was necessary. This may account for the unison singing which was quite common in jug band and similar groups. Though it had a jug with a tuba-like volume, King David's Jug Band with clear-toned mandolin sounded somewhat similar to the Dallas String Band, but it was probably based in Cincinnati. Somewhat rougher in character was the Birmingham Jug Band, mentioned earlier, whose heavy blues character was strengthened by the harmonica player. The tunes derived from various aspects of the folk tradition; *Bill Wilson* was a version of *John Henry*:

> Bill Wilson had a baby boy
> You could hold in the palm of your han'
> Well the last word I heard that baby cry
> 'Gonna be your wagon-drivin' man, Lord . . .'

the verse being completed on the harmonica. *Kickin' Mule Blues* had its roots in white folk song but the handling was character-istically black jug band. Some of the string and jug bands seem to have been mainly rural, like the group led by the legendary Sid Hemphill in the Mississippi Delta, which is now a fading memory but was once famous, with the leader playing guitar, banjo, violin, harmonica and quills himself. A large number, however, are associated with cities, where there was probably an oppor-tunity for employment most weekends and where they could 'serenade' in the streets at night during the week. Walter Taylor led a small band in Louisville, Kentucky, which included John Byrd on twelve-string guitar, a mandolin, kazoo, and the leader on washboard. They recorded one of the most infectious of songs in the outrageous, but bowdlerised version of a bawdy-house theme.

> Say the monkey and the baboon sittin' in the grass
> The one said 'no', the other said 'yas'
> > I know a thirty-eight plug, beedle-ee-bum
> > I know a thirty-eight plug, beedle-ee-bum
> > Say, cain't nobody use it,
> > Mama caught a thirty-eight plug.

Louisville was the home of a number of jug bands who formed a kind of jazz out of their music. Phillips's Louisville Jug Band had the leader playing jug and kazoo and was primarily an instrumental group featuring a flute player and Hooks Tilford playing alto sax. Best-known were the many groups led by the violinist Clifford Hayes. His Old Southern Jug Band included two banjoes and Earl McDonald took solos on the jug. Later groups such as the Dixieland Jug Blowers produced some fine music including an earthy *Skip Skat Doodle-Do* which featured good violin and banjo and some dirty jug blowing. But basically Hayes was jazz-orientated; the Dixieland Jug Blowers showcased the New Orleans clarinettist Johnny Dodds on some titles and Hayes's Louisville Stompers dispensed with the jug and even drafted Earl Hines into the band. Another group which also recorded as early as 1924, led by Buford Threlkeld 'Whistler' was closer to the folk even though some of its themes were of a jazz character – *Jerry O' Mine* or *Hold That Tiger*, for instance. Whistler's Jug Band had the leader playing slide whistle on occasion and had a typical line-up of violin, mandolin, guitar and jug. A hundred miles away in Cincinnati, Ohio, Lafcadio Hearn had visited, in 1876, a roustabout's haunt on the corner of Culvert and Sixth Streets where he had heard a fiddle-and-banjo team play for the dancing. 'The musicians began to sing; the dancers joined in; and the dance terminated with a roar of song, stamping of feet, "patting juba", shouting, laughing, reeling.' A little over fifty years after, a jug band led by Bob and Walter Coleman produced music that may not have been dissimilar.

> I'm gonna tear 'em down, bed slats and all (4)
> Now if I find another mule kickin' in my stall,
> Mama gonna tear 'em down.
>
> Now she drinks sloe whisky, has her fun
> Says run like hell when the police come,

I'm gonna tear 'em down, bed slats and all (4)
Now if I find another mule kickin' in my stall,
Mama, gonna tear 'em down.

Traditionally, the river ports had been rowdy, lawless centres of entertainment. River boatmen and the roustabouts who loaded the vessels sought 'good times' when landing, and the ports of Cincinnati, St Louis, Memphis and New Orleans teemed with gamblers, prostitutes and those who lived off the earnings of the rivermen. Many were railroad centres also, terminals for the train crews and the end of the line for the migrants and hoboes who travelled on the Southern, the Illinois Central or the Missouri and Ohio. There was a time when the cotton wagons were driven into Canal Street, New Orleans, and a huge cotton market lay off Beale in Memphis. Country people could travel from the depth of the Delta in a matter of hours to sample the pleasures that Memphis had to offer. Small wonder that the dance halls flourished in Memphis for a century and that the older string bands led on to the jug bands; nor is it surprising with its proximity to the Delta that the jug bands of Memphis had the strongest blues flavour of any in the cities.

Brass bands, string bands – all kinds of music were popular in Memphis, but the earliest jug band, according to report, was Will Shade's Memphis Jug Band. Raised by his grandmother Annie Brimmer, Shade was known as 'Son Brimmer'. He was born in 1898 in Memphis and as a youth learned to play guitar from a man named Hucklebones. Later, Tewee Blackman taught him more and he formed a three-piece band to serenade on Beale Street. It was an older man in his sixties, called 'Lionhouse', whose playing on a whiskey bottle gave him the idea to play a jug, though he had already been impressed by the Clifford Hayes recordings of the Dixieland Jug Blowers, which he had heard. Shade himself played guitar, harmonica, jug and 'streamline bass' as he called it – a bass made from a garbage can. The Jug Band lasted to the mid-thirties and had a varying personnel with the sleek guitar of Will Weldon from Kansas City, Milton Robie's violin, Ben Ramey's kazoo and the raucous laughter of the Alabama guitarist, Charlie Burse being heard on many recordings. Though they travelled a lot, they always came back to Memphis, where they were exceptionally popular with the crowds on Beale. Shade's guitar playing was simple but his harmonica was highly effective with its squeezed notes and open blowing giving considerable expressive range. They played waltzes, the 'mess around', old minstrel show numbers like *He's in the Jailhouse Now*, river roustabout themes like *Bully of the Town* and even attempted a naive pop tune in *I'll See You in the Spring When the Birds Begin to Sing*. But their music was really the blues, blues of a slightly 'hokum' kind very often, with cheerful ribbing, veiled ribaldry and sometimes, on such a theme as *K. C. Moan* a melancholy, beautifully resolved completeness. Will Shade's wife, Jennie Mae Clayton swapped verses with him, on a typical exchange:

> Your teeth ain't pearls daddy, your lowdown eyes aren't
>   navy blue (2)
> You're three times seven and you know just what you gotta
>   do.

and he replied.

> I think black folks is evil, darlin', high yellers is worse (2)
> I'm gonna quit all of my black women, Lord and I'll play
>   safety first.

One of the longest-surviving jug bands was led by Will Batts, a violin player, and Jack Kelly, guitarist. Dan Sane, a well-known Memphis musician who had come up from Senatobia, Mississippi, also played guitar and it was 'Doctor' Higgs's jug-playing which gave the name to Jack Kelly's Jug Busters. There was a darker, brooding sound to some of their recordings and Will Batts's fiddle moaned the blues behind Jack Kelly's voice on *Ko-Ko-Mo*. In later years Will Batts's band played for the conventions held regularly at the Peabody Hotel in Memphis and occasionally included a musical saw player and a pianist in the group. Still another such band was led by Jed Davenport, a harmonica player who stayed briefly in Memphis between medicine-show trips.

But the greatest of the Memphis jug bands was led by 'Banjo Joe' – Gus Cannon. His first banjo was made from 'a bread pan my mama used to bake biscuits in' and had a raccoon skin head. His early life on an impoverished farm in Marshall County, Mississippi, was hard and unrewarding, but an Alabama banjo-player, Bud Jackson, taught him how to finger pick for dances and he earned a little money by playing up and down the country. Cannon was thirty-three when he found himself up in Ripley, Tennessee, working on a farm. It was there that he met a harmonica player named Noah Lewis, and his friend, guitarist Ashley Thompson, and with them he played for country suppers and weekend dances. That was in 1916, and it was eleven years before they got together to record. Cannon was back in Memphis and when the opportunity came up he collected his old companions from Ripley. Later he replaced Thompson with Elijah Avery, who played a six-string banjo, and played banjo himself while blowing into the 'jug' (actually, a kerosene can) fixed on a harness on his neck. They produced a sound which blended the rippling banjo of the country dances with the feel of the blues. Often they used a syncopated beat which gave a certain lift to the melody line, carried superbly on Noah Lewis's harp. It was Lewis who really made the band, his blues playing being unequalled at the time: Lewis had a strong voice and sang a blues from Tennessee which linked to the old *Joe Turner* blues-ballad:

> The judge he pleaded, the clerk he wrote it –
>   The clerk he wrote it – down indeedy,
> The judge he pleaded, the clerk he wrote it down,
> If you gets jail sentence, you must be Nashville boun'.
>
> Some got six months, some got one solid –
>   Some got one solid – year indeedy,
> Some got six months, some got one solid year
> But me and my buddy, both got lifetime here.

The form was one that Lewis seems to have liked and used it again on *Goin' to Germany*, a sad, wistful tune which dated from their first meeting. On such themes as *Minglewood Blues* and *Feather Bed* Cannon's Jug Stompers attained a quality of blues feeling that was unexcelled by any other recorded string or jug band. But to consider these groups solely in blues terms is to misinterpret their role, for they were primarily dance bands and entertaining groups who provided the volume of noise for the country 'breakdowns', who could play the waltzes and square dances that the older generation wanted and the blues for the slow drags that the younger folk demanded. They played for the 'white folk's balls' when they were asked, and were proud of it. They felt no hint of condescension when they were fetched to provide the music for the white planter's sons, but felt indispensable, conscious of their ability. They were 'musicianers' who could turn in a good show when wanted, who would sing a ballad, shout a river rouster's song, 'clown' with their instruments, josh each other with a 'hokum' number, send the shack throbbing with their dance reels and play the blues at any time. They made the link between the Saturday-night dance, the medicine show pitch and the minstrel troupe, by bringing the blues to all of them.

On vacant lots in southern townships the 'medicine shows' would set up their stages. A typical 'Southern gentleman' in Stetson and goatee beard would introduce a team of performers; a few girl 'hoofers' perhaps, or a jug band, or just a young man with his face nonetheless 'blacked up' with burnt cork, 'cutting the pigeon wing' to the stop time guitar of his accompanist. The doctor in the stetson would produce a bottle of miracle tonic, one of the troupe would take a swig and be galvanised into making a pass at the nearest woman as proof of its efficacy. The crowd would respond raucously and the bottles would start selling. There were no scruples about selling the medicines. In the south only a few thousand hospital beds had to serve several million black people. As the clinics to which Blacks could go for free treatment were a mere handful, the medicines which they sold were at least some kind of service. Many of the 'doctors' were totally unqualified and their medicaments worthless, but others sold preparations which did relatively little harm beyond acting as a violent emetic, and sometimes did good. To drum up interest and to soften crowd resistance, the doctor would promote a show, travelling with a small company and setting up for a brief stand in each community they visited. Such medicine shows gave employment to innumerable blues singers and songsters, and some of them spent most of their active years working the shows. Gus Cannon, for instance, in the years between working in Ripley and organising his Jug Stompers, had travelled every year with his guitar-playing partner Hosea Woods in one medicine show or another, starting out with Dr Stokey's show which began from his home on South Parkway in Memphis, travelling with Dr Willie Lewis, and Dr W. B. Milton – on whose show he met one Chappie Dennison who played a piece of plumbing pipe and gave Gus the idea to play a jug. He worked with Dr Benson and Dr C. Hangerson, explaining 'I worked with a man out of Louisville, I worked through Mississippi, I worked through Virginia, I worked through Alabama, I worked through Mobile, Gulfport, Bay St Louis – far as I been down, playin' my banjo on them doctor shows.'

One of the blues singers on Dr Willie Lewis's show was Walter 'Furry' Lewis, who was born in Mississippi in 1893 but had spent most of his life in Memphis. He had lost a leg on the railroad when he was seventeen and the doctor shows provided him with employment. Dr Willie Lewis's show was large enough to support a jug band and Will Shade, Gus Cannon, Furry Lewis and Jim Jackson entertained the crowds while the doctor sold his 'Jack Rabbit Salve'. Jim Jackson was an older medicine show entertainer, born in the 1880s in Hernando,

Mississippi. He sang the old minstrel show songs like *In the Jailhouse Now* or *Travellin' Man* which told wry stories about simple Blacks, or morale-boosting stories about heroes who outwit the Whites. His songs, uninhibited by taste or the perpetuation of stereotypes would raise a warm response from the crowds, for they played on the problems of the minority group:

> Well a white man gives his wife a ten-dollar bill
> He thinks that's nothing strange
> But a colored man gives his wife a one-dollar bill
> And beat her to death 'bout the ninety cents change.
>
> > Sing I'm goin' roun' the mountain charmin' Betsy
> > I'm goin' roun' the mountain Pearlie Lee
> > Now if I never see you again, Do Lord, remember me.
>
> Well a white man lives in a fine brick house
> He thinks that's nothin' strange,
> But we poor colored men lives in the county jail
> But it's a brick house just the same!
>
> > Sing, I'm goin' round the mountain etc.

Jim Jackson was a successful blues singer and his recording of *Kansas City Blues* was one of the most popular in the idiom. Another native of Hernando and superior guitarist, Robert Wilkins, claimed to have composed it and Jackson heard him singing the song in Memphis. Like Jackson, Wilkins, who was born in 1896, worked on the medicine shows and in later years he became a specialist in herbal remedies himself. Jim Jackson worked in the Red Rose Minstrels with the pianist Speckled Red, through Mississippi, Arkansas and Alabama. It was a medicine show 'where the man sold all kinds of medicine and stuff. One medicine good for a thousand things – and wasn't good for *nothin'*. A whole lot of pills, everything. He had a big show where there was a whole lot of women and I was playing pianner. Sometimes I was on the stage, trying to dance, and I could talk, crack a whole lot of jokes – me and Jim,' said Speckled Red. Many of the medicine shows were large affairs. There were the 'low pitches' where the Doctor worked from a box on the ground with an entertainer or two to help him; there were 'high pitches' where the Doctor travelled in a wagon or truck equipped with a board stage and a light running off the truck battery; and there were the regular 'shows' which were often large enough to travel in two or three railroad coaches and which set up a tent where they stopped for the night. The company might number up to twenty – white, colored and blackface comedians of either race, and they were expected to be versatile.

Some blues singers, songsters and musicianers worked with a medicine show for a brief period only, like Tommy Johnson who spent a while with Dr Simpson's show in the mid-'thirties. Others might spend most of their career with one company, as did Pink Anderson. He was born in Lawrence County, South Carolina in 1900 and at the age of fourteen he joined Dr W. R. Kerr's Indian Remedy show in Spartanburg, and stayed with it for thirty years. Some worked in one or two states only or travelled just in the lay-off season, picking up a few local entertainers in Memphis or Birmingham, but others travelled considerable distances. Frank Stokes and Dan Sane would go west each year with a medicine show in which the white singer Jimmie Rodgers was also featured, and they were well recalled in Fort Worth on their way to New Mexico and beyond. Pink Anderson, born in South Carolina in 1900, still played in a medicine show in the 'sixties, including in his repertoire many songs learned from the recordings of Jackson and Stokes.

Through the small travelling shows the music of individual singers and entertainers became known in other parts, and deep 'in the sticks', far from the main towns and theatres, their knockabout shows were welcome. They filled in the gaps until the big tent shows and circuses came to their part of the country, bringing with them a touch of show business sophistication.

Rabbit Foot and Toby Time

Many blues singers served their apprenticeship in the second companies of the big circuses – Miller's '101 Ranch', the Mighty Haag Circus or the Hegenbeck-Wallace Circus. Such second companies were often for black audiences only and were called the 'dirty shows' in the circus business itself. Sometimes they followed the main show, sometimes they made a separate tour, and following them would often come the medicine shows and entertainers. The 'grifters' and 'trailers' attached themselves to the main show with a subsidiary one of their own and it was often in such side-shows that the blues singers worked. Others just helped as canvas-men and roughnecks, getting no pay but their food, for raising the tents, and living on what they could earn from their playing on the side. Some of the circuses employed blues singers as 'kinkers' within the company, but the main employers of blues singers were the minstrel shows.

Banjo-plunking, eye-rolling, blackface comedians are one of the stereotypes that the Nigger Minstrel companies have inflicted on African Americans and it is therefore somewhat incongruous that all-black Minstrel shows have been so numerous in the past seventy years. Before the end of Reconstruction, a colored company of 'Nigger Minstrels' was formed, and the showman Colonel Jack Haverley was running Callender's Colored Minstrels by 1877. From these shows came a number of entertainers in black show business, one of the first being Billy Kersands who worked with Richard and Pringle's Georgia Minstrels before running his own company. At one time Jelly-Roll Morton worked as his straight man. Other shows followed: Tolliver's Circus and Musical Extravaganza; Hicks and Sawyer's Minstrels; the King and Bush Wide-Mouth Minstrels, in which Gertrude Saunders began her career; the Georgia Smart Set, and its follower and rival, the Smarter Set; Pete Werley's Cotton

Blossoms Show; Booker and Clayton's Georgia Minstrels and Sugar Foot Greene's Minstrel Show. The most celebrated were Silas Green from New Orleans, and the Rabbit Foot Minstrels.

Originally organised by a barber, Eph Williams, who had worked in Skerbeck and Williams's circus before starting a road show of his own, Silas Green opened up in New Orleans in 1910. Later the show came under the ownership of W. P. Jones from Athens in Georgia and he continued to operate it for forty years. 'Silas Green from New Orleans' went out on the road every year until it was absorbed in the Gooding No. 1 Unit in 1959, though the following year it was still showing at the Missouri State Fair.

Its chief rival was the Rabbit Foot Minstrels which were organised by F. S. Wolcott from his home in Port Gibson, Mississippi. It was the central location of both shows on the Mississippi that enabled them to draw so freely on blues singers, but they also featured a variety of acts. Wolcott's show had jungle scenes and olios, wrestlers, comics, jugglers and vaudeville teams as part of the show. The 'Foots' travelled in two cars and had an 80 by 110 foot tent which was raised by the roustabouts and canvas-men while a brass band would parade in town to advertise the coming of the show. Changing facilities were a canvas tent or a railroad car on all the shows, some of which were permitted to travel on the railroads in special cars and slipped into sidings as they reached their location. The stage would be of boards on a folding frame and Coleman lanterns – gasoline mantle lamps – acted as footlights. There were no microphones; the weaker voiced singers used a megaphone, but most of the featured women blues singers scorned such aids to volume. Few 'Classic' blues singers of note became famous without serving a tough apprenticeship in the tent shows, barnstorming from settlement to township to plantation, from Florida to Fort Worth, from North Carolina to New Orleans and from Missouri to Mexico.

Among the first and best remembered of these singers was Ida Cox, and she remained with the Rabbit Foot for many years, though she had travelled with both major companies. She was born in Toccoa, Georgia in 1886 and had been in minstrel shows since the age of fourteen. Her voice was hard and nasal, with a small range, and generally she sang in only one key. But she sang almost exclusively blues and blues-songs, and was greatly loved by the audiences who heard her in the townships of the Deep South. When she was playing in Indianapolis she picked up her pianist, Jesse Crump, whom she married and who travelled with her for many years. Her blues were aimed, with a wry humour, at her Southern audiences.

When I was down South, I wouldn't take no one's advice (2)
Well I'm going home – let the same bee sting me twice.

I'm goin' where the weather suits my clothes (2)
Down where there ain't no snow and the chilly winds
    don't blow.

I don't want no Northern yellow, no Northern black
    or brown (2)
Southern men will stick by you when the Northern men
    can't be found.

In later years Ida Cox formed her own travelling show *Raisin'
Cain*, and was still touring with her company well into the 'fifties.
She enjoyed a brief retirement and died in 1968 in Knoxville,
Tennessee.

A greater singer and almost without compare among artists of this
genre, was Gertrude Pridgett who was born in Columbus, Georgia
in April 1886. It was there that she made her debut in a local talent
show 'The Bunch of Blackberries' when she was fourteen, and only
four years later she married Will Rainey, who came through the town
with a travelling show. Under the name of Rainey and Rainey 'The
Assassinators of the Blues' they worked for a number of years before
separating. Gertrude Rainey was always known as 'Ma' outside her
hearing, but in person she preferred to be addressed as 'Madame'
Rainey, and in spite of her short stature, her regal bearing and the
esteem in which she was held, ensured the respect she wanted. She
first heard the blues, she told John Work, when she heard a young girl
singing a 'strange and poignant' lament in a small Missouri town in
1902. After this, Ma Rainey used a 'blues', which she claimed to have
named herself, as an encore. But in later years the blues dominated all
her work. She had a deep contralto voice and sang with great power
and feeling, in broad impressive sweeps of sound.

Sometimes Ma Rainey's songs were boisterous, but even the most
riotous had a melancholy underlying theme and her low-down,
meaningful blues were without rival on the tent shows. In the
course of many years she worked with the Rabbit Foot, with
C. W. Parks and Al Gaines' Minstrels and eventually formed her
own troupe to travel throughout the South. Ma Rainey was rarely
heard in the North, but everywhere in the South her squat build,
her bisexuality, her broad Puckish features, her necklace of $20–gold
pieces and her Eagle back-drop were known. 'The Mother of the
Blues' they called her, and as she stepped forward to the footlights

and soared into *Bo-Weavil Blues* or moaned her *Counting the Blues* she
was the maternal archetype of blues.

> Layin' in bed this mornin' with my face turned to the wall (2)
> Trying to count these blues so I could sing 'em all.
>
> *Memphis, Rampart, Beale Street* set 'em free (2)
> *Graveyard, 'Bama Bound*, Lord, Lord, come from stingaree.
>
> Lord sittin' on the *Southern* gonna ride all night long (2)
> *Downhearted, Gulf Coast* – they was all good songs.
>
> Lord, 'rested at midnight, *Jailhouse* made me loose my mind (2)
> *Bad Luck* n' *Boll-Weevil*, made me think of old *Moonshine*.
>
> Lord, goin' to sleep now for Mama just got bad news (2)
> To try to dream away my troubles, countin' these blues.

The montage of blues and dream images seems to have been drawn
from her years of experience, but if the meaning seems fragmented
the quality of her singing and the expressiveness of her delivery gave
it coherence. In 1934 she retired from the road, having bought two
small theatres as an investment. She died quietly at her Columbus
home five years later, to be survived by her brother Thomas, and
her sister Melissa Nix. Melissa 'Rainey' continued for a number of
years to sing in the Harlem cellar clubs and even in the 1960s, Lillian
Glover in Memphis was known as 'Memphis Ma Rainey'. But really
Gertrude Rainey was without a rival, save only for Bessie Smith.

According to a long-established story Bessie Smith was heard by
Ma Rainey in her home city of Chattanooga and taken into her show.
It has been established that both singers did work briefly in Tolliver's
Big Show but Bessie herself always credited an otherwise unknown
singer from Chattanooga, Cora Fisher, as her chief inspiration. Bessie
Smith was born in the city in conditions of extreme poverty in April
1894 and made her first stage appearance at the age of nine, at the
Ivory Theatre. Her next ten years were spent with the Rabbit Foot
Minstrels and the Florida Cotton Blossoms, and in dives and tent
shows along the Gulf Coast. 1917 found her in Selma, Alabama
where she was heard by her future manager, Frank Walker, and a
couple of years later she was leading her own hip-shaking show at
the 81 Theatre in Atlanta.

Compared with Ma Rainey, Bessie Smith was closer to the
professional stage and, though she arrived 'tall and fat and scared
to death' in New York early in 1923, she soon made the metropolis
her home. Ma Rainey worked almost exclusively under canvas, but

Bessie Smith played the theatres appearing as much in Cleveland and Chicago as she did in Memphis or New Orleans. Whereas Ma Rainey liked a rough jazz band to accompany her, even a jug band, or had a blues guitarist like Tampa Red or Blind Blake, Bessie Smith preferred the legitimately trained Fletcher Henderson or the organist Fred Longshaw as her accompanist, and on record liked to be supported by contingents from the Fletcher Henderson Orchestra. It was Bessie Smith rather than Ma Rainey who moulded the jazz-blues style of singing, customarily called the 'Classic Blues', in which the inflections and expression of blues were brought to a popular song like *After You've Gone* or a ragtime number like *There'll Be a Hot Time in the Old Town Tonight*.

All the same, it was in the blues that Bessie Smith made her finest performances, her *Mama's Got the Blues* setting the form for a succession of profoundly moving compositions within the idiom. In a sense Bessie Smith's greatness seemed to lie in the complexity of her own personality. She was rough and brawling, addicted to alcohol, capable of startling gestures of generosity and also of jealousy, hurt and hurtful in turns. From her tortured being she produced a music which has been a measure of jazz expression and she remains now, as she was in her day, the 'Empress of the Blues'. Tall and statuesque where Ma Rainey was short and homely, she was beautiful even when she put on weight in her later years. In 1926 she sang

> I'm a young woman and ain't done runnin' roun' (2)
> Some people calls me a hobo, some calls me a bum,
> Nobody knows my name, nobody knows what I've done.
> I'm as good as any woman in your town,
> I ain't no high yeller, I'm a deep yeller-brown
> I ain't gonna marry, ain't gonna settle down,
> I'm gonna drink good moonshine an' run these browns down . . .

Though it was sung in some truth, she did marry, living with a barely literate night watchman named Jack Gee with whom she had a tempestuous relationship. The Columbia executive, Frank Walker, became her recording manager, but her brother Clarance managed her frequent and exhausting tours of Southern theatres and under canvas. For most of her life Bessie Smith worked in the professional theatres but the decline of her career after the Depression and before her eventual, tragic death in 1937 were a sad indication of the decreasing interest in her kind of blues in the 'thirties. In the 'twenties however, she dominated the Classic blues and few other singers could compare with her. One who did was Clara Smith, who improved steadily in the course of her career, and who was also recorded and promoted by the Columbia Company. Billed as 'The Queen of the Moaners' she had a singing style close to that of Bessie Smith, who was no relation, and was the only singer with whom Bessie recorded. Those who saw her recall that she was a less dynamic personality and when she died in 1935 she was virtually forgotten.

That there was a great deal of talent that is scarcely recalled today was evident from the records of the period. Cleo Gibson's *I've Got Ford Engine Movements in My Hips* was a superb example but it was the only record she made. Except that she was named Cleothus Gibson, worked for a time in Atlanta and toured with her husband in the team of 'Gibson and Gibson,' nothing else is known about her. Another Southern singer of repute was Lillian Glinn from Dallas, Texas, whose *Shake 'Em Down* and *Atlanta Blues* were in the grand manner. She had the heavy contralto voice of the more impressive women singers of the day and toured to New Orleans and Atlanta, though she appeared most frequently at Ella B. Moore's Park Theatre on Central Tracks in Dallas. On a good day Martha Copeland from Pittsburgh was one of the best, in spite of being billed as 'Everybody's Mammy' and *Nobody Rocks Me Like My Baby Do* had the exuberance that was associated with the road shows. Mattie Hite was one of the most esteemed singers noted as much for her risqué words as for the quality of her singing, but she was exceptionally popular in Chicago and New York clubs and particular in the dance-halls of Atlantic City, New Jersey. Younger than these singers was Bertha 'Chippie' Hill who came from South Carolina in 1905, although her slate-like voice with its dark hardness leads one to believe in her line 'Pratt City, Pratt City that's where I was born' from *Pratt City Blues*, the town being a suburb of Birmingham, Alabama. As a child she went to New York and her extreme youth earned her the name of 'Chippie'. She sang at Leroy's Harlem Cabaret and Mule Johnson's Cellar before moving to Chicago to sing for seven months with King Oliver at the Plantation, her tough voice being appropriate to the blues-inflected playing of the orchestra. For a while she toured with Ma Rainey but at the age of 24 retired to raise a family of seven children. An automobile accident damaged the sight of one eye, and after a brief comeback in the late 'forties she was killed by a passing car in May 1950.

New Orleans jazz bands provided work for a number of singers, although the formal structure of the tunes often reduced the chances of singing the more free forms of blues. In New Orleans itself there were a few singers, including Esther Bigeou, who sang with Armund

J. Piron's Orchestra and with whom she recorded her *West Indies Blues* in 1923. A cousin of Paul Barbarin, she toured the theatres until the Depression, when she retired in New Orleans and died about 1936. A year younger was Edna Hicks, like Esther Bigeou a somewhat light-voiced singer, who was born in 1895 and toured the shows in 1920, scoring a conspicuous success at the Lyceum in Cincinnati in 1920. Her *No Name Blues* was billed as 'A Barrel House Blues' by Gennett Records – it was hardly this, but she had a good voice and her death in 1925 in an automobile accident robbed the Classic blues of a promising singer. Her sister, Lizzie Miles, was Esther Bigeou's age and after singing in church as a child began to work with the jazz bands. She also sang with Piron and King Oliver, her 'gumbo French' verses giving an appropriate local piquancy to her work. Lizzie Miles toured with the Alabama Minstrels and the Cole Brothers Circus, but in her early years her voice tended to be thin. Disillusioned, she retired from singing for several years but made a comeback in the 'fifties when her voice had matured, and she sang vigorously with white Dixieland Bands like that of Sharkey Bonano. In the main she was not a blues singer and did not compare with the lesser-known Ann Cook, who was born in Franzenville, Louisiana, in 1888 and who sang with Louis Dumaine's Jazzola Eight, with whom she recorded *He's the Sweetest Black Man in Town*. Perhaps in repentance, for she had a formidable reputation, Ann Cook turned to the church in the 'fifties and died in 1962. Apart from songster Richard 'Rabbit' Brown, New Orleans did not produce any significant male singers in spite of the rise of its jazz bands, though mention should perhaps be made of 'New Orleans Willie' Jackson, who sang in blackface and attracted people to Brown's Ice Cream Parlor with comic renditions of opera tunes. He was called 'The Big Boy with the Blues' but his recordings were mediocre.

A stronger vein of Classic blues singers was to be found west of the Mississippi. The versatile Thomas family which had already produced George Thomas, the composer, also had two of its talented members in Sippie Thomas, later Sippie Wallace, and Hociel Thomas. Born in 1898, Sippie Beulah Wallace had a warm-toned voice which earned her an instant success when she came to Detroit in her brother's footsteps. Her *Special Delivery Blues*, and *Suitcase Blues* had a pleasantly relaxed feeling and she sang with the slightly moaning sound of many of the Texas singers. Her sister, Hociel Thomas, who was born about 1908, had a tougher voice which was not always appropriately matched to the bands with which she recorded; *Fishtail Blues* was one of her best recordings and when she made a brief comeback in the 'forties, now married and known as Hociel Thomas Tebo, she rolled out her *Tebo's Texas Boogie* to reveal an unexpected talent as a pianist in the Texas tradition.

Spurred on by the success of these singers a younger girl, Victoria Spivey, who was born in Houston in 1906, made her way up to St Louis and demanded from the promoter Jesse Johnson the chance to record. She accompanied herself on piano on her own *Black Snake Blues* which, with her *T.B. Blues*, became one of the best-known and most frequently recorded of blues compositions of the 'twenties. Victoria Spivey's *Bloodhound Blues* was one of a group that she made with the forceful Luis Russell Orchestra, and her moaning voice had a bite of its own. Victoria was invited to play a part in the King Vidor all-black film *Hallelujah*, and was one of the few Classic singers to work regularly after the Depression. Jesse Johnson's wife, Edith Johnson, who was a little older, was herself a good singer and occasional pianist. Her *Nickel's Worth of Liver* was an original song in the hard-voiced style of the St Louis singers. It was her husband who discouraged her from following the career further.

New Orleans and St Louis were strong jazz centres and the bands offered opportunities for the women singers who did not play an instrument, to obtain work. To the west of St Louis, Kansas City was the centre of a blues-based form of jazz which swept the country in the 'thirties and gave the impetus to the big orchestras of the swing era. As might be expected, Kansas City had a number of blues singers. The most important of them was Lottie Beaman, a broad, massive woman known as 'The Kansas City Butter Ball'. In the 'twenties she was in the complex of activity around the Merritt label owner Winston Holmes, with whom she recorded a couple of duets, with the latter making bird whistle noises. This was the kind of song that her hearers remember most clearly, though she was a fine singer of blues including *Rollin' Log Blues* and *Red River Blues* for which she was famous. Later, Lottie Beaman married the vocalist Sylvester Kimbrough and they made an effective team supported by Paul Banks's orchestra. Another good, though relatively little-known Kansas City singer, was Laura Rucker, who played her own piano when she wasn't being accompanied by Cassino Simpson, and who sang in the mid-'twenties at Elmer Bean's Club on 18th and Paseo, and later at Meyer's Chicken Farm. She moved to Chicago later and adjusted herself to the jivier style of the mid-'thirties, singing to the drumming of Baby Dodds at the Tin Pan Alley bar in the early 'forties.

Another Kansas City singer who also played piano was Julia Lee, born there in 1902. She played violin in her father's string band as a child and was featured in the 'Novelty Singing Orchestra' of her brother, George E. Lee, when she was only in her 'teens. Julia Lee was a good singer with a swinging style, capable of adapting herself to the changing character of Kansas City jazz. In 1933 she got an engagement at Milton's Tap Room and remained there for over a decade with only occasional trips to Hollywood and Omaha. This insularity made her far less known than other singers of her generation who toured the theatre circuit or who worked extensively with the touring jazz bands. In the 'forties however, she sang with Jay McShann's Kansas City Stompers and Tommy Douglas's Orchestra and moved to Hollywood for a couple of years for a successful period singing with her 'Boy Friends'. Her *Julia's Blues* and *Young Girl's Blues* were in traditional vein and offset the banality of *I'm Forever Blowing Bubbles*. In 1949 she returned to Kansas City and continued to work with her band until shortly before her death a decade later.

For the most part it was the jazz-blues singer who survived the Depression and those in Kansas City who brought the blues to a blues-inflected jazz, most of all. A year younger than Julia Lee, Jimmy Rushing was the most prominent of these singers. He was born in Oklahoma City in 1903 and his family were all musical. He learned to play the piano and travelled over the mid-west playing in barns and for country dances, working his way down to Dallas and eventually to the West Coast. He joined Walter Page's Blue Devils after his return from California, where he had played in night spots and sung for a couple of years, touring with them in the mid-west. In 1929, Page went bankrupt and Jimmy moved over to the Bennie Moten band in Kansas City. It was with Moten that he began to make his name, and subsequently, when Moten died in 1935 and William 'Count' Basie took the band over, Rushing remained with the orchestra for fifteen years. Jimmy Rushing's blues 'shouting' was ideally suited to a Kansas City jazz orchestra; he had a punching vocal style which had great rhythmic drive and he used his voice as if it were a front-line instrument. His words were unimportant; he sang endless repetitions of a small vocabulary of verses drawn from the tradition:

> Don't the moon look lonesome shinin' through the trees (2)
> Don't your house look lonesome when your baby packs her
>   trunk to leave.
>
> Sent for you yesterday and here you come today (2)
> You can't love me baby and treat me that-a-way.

– and his final choruses of 'we're gonna rock this joint' would be repeated riff fashion to exhaustion. But singing in his high voice, shaking his 250 pound frame, phrasing out the words across the beat, he was the epitome of the jazz-blues singer. Known affectionately as 'Mister Five by Five', Jimmy Rushing created a form of singing which was taken up by a number of other male singers in the mid-west including Walter Brown from Dallas, who sang with Jay McShann's Kansas City Orchestra in the 'forties, and Jimmy Witherspoon, a much younger singer, who was born in 1923 in Gurdon, Arkansas, and who spent the war years with the Merchant Marine. While in Calcutta, Witherspoon sang briefly with the band led by Teddy Weatherford, and on his return to the United States decided to follow a blues singing career. In California he met up with Jay McShann who had lost Walter Brown, and began singing with the Orchestra. His 1947 recording of *Ain't Nobody's Business if I Do* made his name and he sang with many other bands, touring widely but becoming increasingly more inclined to popular song performed in 'ballad' style.

Far earthier than Frankie 'Half-Pint' Jaxon, these singers were more directed to jazz than to the blues groups. Jaxon however, was something of an anomaly. Though he was born in Montgomery, Alabama, in February 1895, he was raised in Kansas City, yet his feminine, shrill voice had none of the Kansas City vocal quality. As early as 1910 he was touring with a show run by Hattie McDaniel's father – Hattie McDaniel was herself a blues singer who eventually became better known on films as a stock 'Mammy' figure and as 'Aunt Jemima' for a popular brand of cakemix. Two years later, Jaxon was at Bailey's Theatre in Atlanta, Georgia and made his way via the Carolinas and Philadelphia to Atlantic City, where he was a hit as a female impersonator. In Chicago in 1917 he began working with the arriving jazz bands and later sang with King Oliver, Freddie Keppard and Ollie Powers at the Sunset Café, the Plantation and elsewhere. Frankie Jaxon joined Bennie Moten in 1930 after working with Tampa Red and Cow Cow Davenport a short while before, and even singing with Tampa Red's Hokum Jug Band. Later he sang with the Harlem Hamfats and thus moved from jazz band to show business to hokum Chicago band with considerable ease.

In general, the singers with the jazz bands of the 'twenties, like Mae Alix or Lillie Delk Christian, were rather vapid and colourless in their voices, with little affinity to blues. Alberta Hunter, who was born in Memphis in 1895 and ran away to Chicago at the age of eleven, was one of the girls who had the thin, melodic but rather featureless voice characteristic of many lesser singers who came within the Classic blues. When only fifteen she was singing in Dago Frank's, a notorious Chicago dive on Archer Street, and stayed until it was closed down. Her big break came when she sang for King Oliver at the Dreamland and soon after she was booked in the Broadway show *How Come*. By 1929 she was singing in Europe and was soon booked for the spectacular *Show Boat*. After a comeback she died in 1984.

This course was typical of a particular kind of singer with sweet voice and agreeable looks who was directed to the world of show business. Ethel Waters was one of these and though her *Shake That Thing* was a song that had been popularised by Papa Charlie Jackson, hers was a performance that had most of the sting taken out of it. Ethel Waters was born in Chester, Pennsylvania, in 1896 and as 'Sweet Mama Stringbean' had a successful career on the vaudeville stage, commencing her act with the statement that she 'ain't no Bessie Smith' and bearing out her claim with her sweet singing. It was this which eventually earned her engagements in *Blackbirds, Rhapsody in Black* and *Africana*, some of the spectacular all-black shows which were the rage in the 'twenties. Later she had a successful career in films like *Cabin in the Sky* and *Pinky*. Of similar inclination was Edith Wilson who recorded with Johnny Dunn's Jazz Hounds in the early 'twenties and was a sensation with the *Hot Chocolates* and *Hot Rhythm* shows, in which she starred with Florence Mills, and in the *Blackbirds* show.

Many of these singers were among the first black artists to record and they were probably chosen partly for the relative purity of their voices and partly because they had become successful singers on the vaudeville stage. Lillyn Brown for example, came from Atlanta, Georgia, where she was born, the daughter of an Indian, in 1885. Billed as an 'Indian Princess' she toured with the Queen City Minstrels as early as 1896 and later sang in Florida, Memphis and Chicago. She claimed to have been the first to sing blues on the professional stage – at the 'Little Strand Theatre' in Chicago in 1908 but when she recorded at the age of thirty-six in 1921 and her voice should have matured, it was disappointingly lacking in blues feeling. Generally singers of this kind tended to gravitate to the East coast resorts in New York or Atlantic City. Lucille Hegamin was also born in Georgia, in Macon in 1897, and went to Chicago with her husband and their Blue Flame Syncopators in 1914. They worked for a couple of years on the West Coast in Seattle before eventually coming east to play the theatres and clubs of Philadelphia and Washington.

First of the 'Classic blues' singers to record and thus to set the style for the other companies was Mamie Smith, who was born in Cincinnati in 1883 and toured as a young woman with Tutt

Whitney's *Smart Set*. By 1919 she was working at the Orient on 135th Street in Harlem and later toured extensively with her band, dressing herself in an ermine-trimmed costume as befitted a singer who could command $1500 a week. Though her *Crazy Blues* had a phenomenal sale and her records sold in prodigious quantities, she was not an exciting singer by the standards of Bessie Smith or Ma Rainey. She died in 1940, three years before her namesake, Trixie Smith, whose voice was somewhat piping but had a certain edge, which gave an agreeable quality to her *Railroad Blues*. In 1922 Trixie Smith won the first 'Blues Singing Contest' at the Inter-Manhattan Casino with her *Trixie's Blues*, singing against Alice Leslie Carter, Daisy Martin and Lucille Hegamin.

Daisy Martin, Alice Carter, Mattie Hite, Katie Crippen, Mary Stafford and many others sang in the celebrated night-spots in the wide-open resort of Atlantic City, particularly with Charlie Johnson's Orchestra at Rafe's Paradise. Such dance-halls provided work for the singers who made their way to the east, but the principal sources of employment were the theatres. This made the blues and jazz-blues into a performance art for a listening audience and contributed to the subtle change of character in their work. The Western Vaudeville and B. F. Keith-Orpheum Circuits booked in acts for black audiences who could watch from the 'peanut galleries' in the segregated theatres, but there was a need for a specifically African American theatre chain. This the Theatre Owners Booking Agency provided.

As early as 1907 F. A. Barrasso of Memphis organised a circuit of a small number of Southern theatres for black audiences and the success of the venture led his brother, A. Barrasso, to organise a Theatre Owner's Booking Agency in 1909. That year an Italian, Sam Zerilla, opened the Pastime Theatre on Beale Avenue in Memphis and some while later the Pacini Brothers followed with the Beale Avenue Palace, the largest black theatre in the South at the time. There were nightly shows and Thursday nights were set aside for Whites and Blacks at separate performances. A feature of the presentations were the 'Midnight Rambles' – late shows in which blues were especially popular, and these became a regular feature of T.O.B.A. theatres throughout the South. The initials of the T.O.B.A. were soon said to stand for 'Tough on Black Artists' (or Arses) for the conditions of changing and performing were often poor and the pay was exceptionally low. Nevertheless the T.O.B.A. circuit was always advertising for talent, offering regular employment for stock companies who could be sure of engagements at every one of the forty-odd places on its circuit. The Lyric in New Orleans, the Lyceum in Cincinnati, the Dream in Columbus – which was owned by Ma Rainey – the Koppin in Detroit, the Park in Dallas and the Monogram in Chicago were among the major theatres, and the 81 Theatre on Decatur Street, Atlanta was the most notorious. Run by the 'boss' of the city, Charles P. Bailey, a vindictive 'cracker' in the recollections of those who worked on the circuit, it was on the main stem of Atlanta life. But the artists who worked there had to obtain passes from Bailey himself to be out after dark and many contended that T.O.B.A. stood for 'Take Old Bailey's Advice'.

In spite of the cramped conditions in many theatres, the T.O.B.A. gave employment to literally hundreds of blues singers and entertainers of all kinds and was run with increasing efficiency after it was taken over in 1921 by a Nashville Jew, Milton Starr, and his partner Charles Turpin, a St Louis ragtime pianist. Starr owned the Bijou in Nashville and Turpin the Booker T. Washington in St Louis. These were added to the circuit, and the Washington ran a blues singing contest – won eventually by Lonnie Johnson – for eighteen weeks in 1925. Almost all the Classic blues singers worked the 'Toby Time' as they called it, at some stage in their careers and its rigorous schedule of one-week stands gave them a hard but professional testing-ground. Though the T.O.B.A. had theatres in places from Jacksonville, Florida, to Little Rock, Arkansas, from Kansas City, Missouri, to Bessemer, Alabama, it had no theatre in New York. But here the Lincoln Theatre run by Joe Bright, the Seventh Avenue Lafayette Theatre and the Alhambra were principal theatres for black artists. The Howard Theatre owned by the Howard brothers and managed by a veteran minstrel showman from Texas, Rufus Byars, was the main theatre in Washington, D.C.

Apart from the chorus girls, the 'Brownskin models' and 'Sepia Lovelies', apart from the comedians and tumblers, jugglers and snake-charmers that regularly formed part of the stock companies, the blues singers were among the main attractions. Particularly popular in black vaudeville were the husband and wife acts, and that of Dora Carr and Cow Cow Davenport was the first of these to record. Generally they exchanged lines in banter and argument and, though frequently cliché-ridden, they often took a blues or near-blues form. The technique was brought to a state of refinement by Butterbeans and Susie. Jodie Edwards was born in Georgia in 1901 and his wife Susie in the following year. They were married on-stage at the Standard Theatre in Philadelphia in 1917 and made the rest of their career an unending comedy of regretting it. They toured with the Rabbit Foot, worked the T.O.B.A. and returned each year to their Chicago home on 35th and Calumet. Very occasionally they sang blues or blues exchanges but their singing was rich in blues inflection and timing. This was equally true of Leola B. Wilson, the wife of Wesley 'Kid Sox' Wilson who recorded blues with the guitarist Blind Blake. As Coot Grant and Kid Sox Wilson, she and her husband were on the stage together for more than twenty years, during which they wrote over four hundred songs. Among them were the last titles that Bessie Smith recorded, including the immortal *Gimme a Pigfoot*.

Another team of similar character was that of George Williams and Bessie Brown. Both singers recorded solo blues as well as working together. George Williams's voice was relatively 'straight' by blues standards, but a phonophotographic comparison of the interpolated tones in the syllables 'day' and 'ball' in his *Chain Gang Blues* with similar tones in Bessie Smith's *Cemetery Blues* and in *Anyone Here Want to Buy My Cabbage* by the Texas singer Maggie Jones, gives an indication of the blues inflection as he attacked a note.

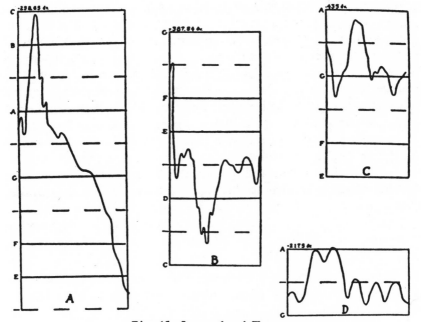

Fig. 65. Interpolated Tones.
A. Chain Gang Blues. Columbia. 14049-D. Sec. 75. *Ball.*
B. Anybody Here Want to Try My Cabbage. Columbia.
14063-D. Sec. 77. *Way.*
C. Cemetery Blues. Columbia. 13001-D. Sec. 73.
D. Chain Gang Blues. Columbia. 14049-D. Sec. 22. *Day.*

If George Williams's voice seemed more appropriate to the stage, it is nonetheless interesting to note that the one-man band Sam Jones, who called himself 'Stovepipe No. I' and who played a stovepipe, guitar and harmonica, sang a folk version of George Williams's *A Woman Gets Tired Of One Man All the Time*. Both singers were from Cincinnati. Vocal exchanges seem to have fed back into folk blues, or were an integral part of them with some notable examples being recorded by Howling (Funny Paper) Smith with Magnolia Harris and Dessa Foster.

George Williams and Bessie Brown worked at the Cotton Club in Indianapolis some years after their kind of act had normally gone out of favour. This was the comfortable club where Jesse Crump and Nina Reeves had worked and where later, Leroy Carr played. A few years after Carr's death, the duets were revived by Champion Jack Dupree and Ophelia Hoy. Orphaned as an infant, Jack Dupree had been born in New Orleans in 1910 and was raised in the Colored Waif's Home. Leaving at the age of fourteen he learned to play piano from watching the playing of a Rampart Street barrelhouse pianist named Drive-'Em-Down. After a few years with Kid Green's Boxing School, Jack Dupree turned to making a living from piano playing. He hoboed north and, when he hit Indianapolis, decided to stay. A born entertainer with a wit as rugged as his piano playing, he was a great success at the Cotton Club and his partnership with the young Ophelia Hoy, in the best tradition of vaudeville exchanges, was favourably compared with that of Butterbeans and Susie themselves.

But in a sense they were an anachronism. The closing down of the theatres, the cessation of recording as a result of the Depression, and the disbanding of the road shows and circuses, often permanently, hit the Classic blues singers and the vaudeville entertainers hard. Many retired, never to return to the stage. Others joined the minstrel shows and stock companies that were still active until they too were stranded. Today, nothing remains of the Classic blues but old recordings and yellowed press-cuttings.

Struttin' that Thing

In 1905 the only black theatre in Chicago was the Pekin on 26th and State; in fact its proprietor, Robert T. Motts proclaimed it as 'The Only Negro Theatre in the World'. Motts had succeeded 'Mushmouth' Johnson as Chicago's gambling king. When the police attempted to limit his operations in that area, he opened up the Pekin as a new venture to present cakewalks, ragtime piano contests and vaudeville entertainment. Motts died in 1911, and Henry 'Teenan' Jones took over; he came from Alabama and had been a club operator for sixteen years before he opened his Elite Café on 31st and State. This was soon to become the hottest corner in the black world as the Big Grand Theatre opened up, to be followed by the Vendome Theatre, the Phoenix Theatre and the Lincoln Theatre as well as Clarence Williams's Music Stores – later taken over by Erskine Tate – and the Jackson Music Shops. A few blocks further down on 35th and State were the Monogram Theatre, the Fiume Café, the States Theatre, the De Luxe Café, the Washington Theatre, the Dreamland Café and another Elite, No. 2 operated by Teenan Jones. These intersections witnessed the full flood of New Orleans jazz, rocked to the sounds of Erskine Tate, King Oliver's Creole Jazz Band, Sugar Johnny, Tony Jackson, Lovie Austin and scores of others. In these, and innumerable nightspots and theatres scattered over the South Side, the professional blues singers and jazz singers also worked and for a dozen years from the end of the First World War, almost every name in black jazz and show business was to be heard in the entertainment centres along and around State Street.

All this is well documented, colorful jazz history, frequently retold. It owed much to the futile, corrupt regime of William Hale 'Big Bill' Thompson, the Republican Mayor of Chicago, who, incredibly, was voted in on a reform platform but made it possible for Chicago to flourish as a 'Wide-Open' City. Exploited by the gangland empires of Johnny Torrio and (after Torrio had retired with five garlic-tipped bullets in his chest in 1925) of his successor, Al Capone, the South Side was a warren of speakeasies, brothels and 'hole-in-the-wall' dives. It was also the home of a hundred thousand African Americans.

Back in 1850 there had been a little over three hundred in Chicago; they trebled in the next decade, more than trebled again in the next. Until the end of the century, the population continued to double every ten years, and, by 1900 the black population in the city was ten times that of fifty years before. Much of this growth reflected the movement out of the South of workers who were freed of the restrictions of the plantation system, but the increase in anti-black legislation and discriminatory laws hastened the process as the twentieth century began. It also intensified the increasing hostility within the city itself and racial disturbances were on the increase. Soon Blacks, who had been scattered over the city, found themselves inexorably pressured into a ghetto area which ran due South along State Street. During the First World War the stopping of immigration had caused a labour shortage which Southern African Americans could meet. Steel mills and stockyards provided opportunities for work and the militant *Chicago Defender* urged them to quit the South. 'Have they stopped their Jim Crow cars? Can you buy a Pullman sleeper where you wish? Will they give you a square deal in court yet?' challenged the editor, Robert S. Abbott, himself a migrant from Georgia. 'If you can freeze to death in the North and be free, why freeze to death in the South and be a slave?' he asked a year later, in 1917.

> 'Some are coming on the passenger
> Some are coming on the freight,
> Others will be found walking,
> For none have time to wait'

the paper rhymed. The blues singers echoed the words more succinctly in many 'migration' blues. Sang Cow Cow Davenport a dozen years later, when the migration was still in full spate:

> I'm tired of being Jim Crowed, gonna leave this Jim Crow town.
> Doggone my black soul, I'm sweet Chicago bound,
> Yes, I'm leavin' here, from this ole Jim Crow town.

> I'm goin' up North where they say, money grows on trees
> I don't give a doggone, if ma black soul leaves,
> I'm goin' where I won't need no B.V.D.'s.

Lord well, if I get up there – weather don't suit –
Well, I don't find no brown; got to tell that bossman of mine,
Lord I'm ready to come back to my Jim Crow town.

Cow Cow Davenport was a pianist and he came from Alabama. Of the 109,000 Blacks in Chicago in 1920, over 90,000 had been born in other states, and most of these were Southern. To Illinois, which had a total black population of 182,000 in the census for that year, nearly sixty thousand came from the Upper South and another sixty thousand from the Lower South. So it's not surprising perhaps, that among the 20,000 from Mississippi, the 23,000 from Georgia and Alabama, let alone those from Louisiana, Arkansas and as far away as Texas, there were many blues singers.

At the Dreamland Cabaret in the mid-'twenties, one could go to hear Ollie Powers singing with Mae Alix, and press on to the Monogram Theatre to catch Alberta Hunter from Memphis singing with Lovie Austin at the piano. Or there was the chance to hear Bertha 'Chippie' Hill with her abrasive voice singing with King Joe Oliver at the Palladium Dance Hall. Most of the spots were open to white people and as yet they weren't eyed with the suspicion that they were 'slumming' if they mixed with the predominately black crowds on State. But in the tiered, galleried, wooden frame houses along the Illinois Central tracks it was different; and it was different too, in the tenement blocks both on State and off. A caller who went on down from the Grand Terrace Theatre on South Park Way to hear Earl Hines might have been tempted to look up No. 4005 in the hopes of hearing Blind Blake, though he would not have been welcome at the old brownstone houses. He would have been less so if he had tried to find Pine Top Smith at 4435 Prairie Avenue where a gang of boogie-woogie piano players lived; and a caller at the Mecca Flats who tried to locate Jimmy Blythe in the huge and complex tenement block on 34th and State would have been discouraged. Built in 1891 as a model apartment house for a hundred and seventy-five families, it was now vastly over-crowded; two thousand people were reported to have been living in congested squalor when it was eventually torn down. *Lovin's Been Here and Gone to the Mecca Flat* – the title of a Blythe composition – was an indication of a hopeless quest. Not that anyone would have attempted it – the blues singers at the Mecca Flat or in any one of the numberless apartment houses, tenements, kitchenettes and 'hot-beds' were known only to their own circle, and if they were recorded, it was almost by accident. Blues guitarists from Mississippi and Tennessee, pianists from Louisiana and Texas and Kentucky came with the tide of migrants who continued to flood into Chicago. Especially, for some reason, the pianists.

Blues pianists on the whole have received far less attention than the guitarists although they are probably almost as numerous. It's true that Mississippi, on the Illinois Central line straight to Chicago probably did not produce many of them, and hence, among the large numbers of Mississippi men who went North, the guitarists seem to predominate. But elsewhere there were strong piano blues traditions. As the guitarists grew out of the songster and string band heritage, so the pianists appear to have emerged from the ragtime and 'barrelhouse' blend of ragtime and blues. Ferdinand 'Jelly Roll' Morton, the jazz composer and pianist from New Orleans recalled many who would appear to have played both blues and ragtime – Josky Adams who played an early version of *See See Rider*, Sammy Davis, 'one of the greatest keyboard manipulators in the history of the world', a recommendation which suggests that his playing may have been more legitimate, the dope addict Alfred Wilson and gambler Albert Cahill. 'At that time, back in 1901 and 1902, we had a lot of great blues players that didn't know nothing but the blues,' said Jelly Roll, introducing a theme by a sporting house pianist named 'Game Kid' who was 'ragged as a pet pig' but 'the best in the section when it came to playing blues'. He recalled Buddy Carter who also played the honky-tonks, 'Charley King from Mobile, Alabama; Baby Grice and Frazier Davis from Pensacola, Florida; Frank Racheal, supposed to be the tops from Georgia; and Porter King, a very dear friend of mine and a marvellous pianist now in the cold, cold ground, also from Florida.' Whether all of them were blues pianists or not, the large number that Jelly Roll remembered and their widespread distribution is evidence enough of a strong tradition along the Gulf Coast. His memories were filled out with 'Florida Sam', 'Skinny Head Pete', 'Trigger Sam' and 'Brocky Johnny', who were certainly barrelhouse pianists in the last years of the nineteenth century.

Morton was born in Gulfport, Louisiana in 1885 and was playing in the 'sporting houses' of New Orleans when he was seventeen, in 1902. His recollections of the Gulf Coast pianists, many of whom would have been older than himself, give an indication of the popularity of the instrument for the blues, or what he remembered as the blues, at this time. He left New Orleans in 1903 and after working in various townships in Texas, Mississippi and along the Gulf Coast through Alabama, he made his way up the river via Helena, Arkansas, to Memphis, Tennessee. There he heard in the Monarch Saloon, the formidable Benny Frenchy. The Monarch, built by Jim Kannane,

BACKGROUND TO THE BLUES

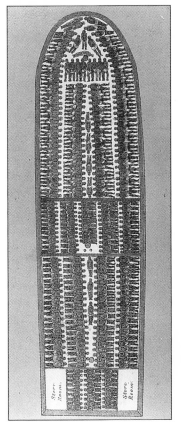

CREDIT SALE OF A CHOICE GANG OF 41
SLAVES!
COMPRISING MECHANICS, LABORERS, ETC.
FOR THE SETTLEMENT OF A CO-PARTNERSHIP OF RAILROAD CONTRACTORS

BY J. A. BEARD & MAY, J. A. BEARD, AUCT'R.
WILL BE SOLD AT AUCTION, AT BANKS' ARCADE, MAGAZINE STREET,
ON TUESDAY, FEBRUARY 5th, 1856,
AT 12 O'CLOCK,
A VERY VALUABLE GANG OF SLAVES,

Belonging to a co-partnership, and sold to close the same. The said slaves comprise a gang of 41 choice Negroes. On the list will be found a good Blacksmith, one superior Bricklayer, Field Hands, Laborers, one Turner, one Cooper, and a first rate woman Cook.

LEWIS, a black man,	aged	32	good field hand and laborer.
SHELLY,	do	26	do do
PHILIP,	do	30	fair bricklayer.
HENRY,	do	24	fair cooper.
JACOB BATES,	do	22	good field hand and laborer.
BOB STAKELEY	do	35	do do
COLUMBUS,	do	21	do do
MARTIN,	do	25	do do
GEORGE,	do	30	No. 1 blacksmith.
WESTLY, a griff,		24	a fine turner and bricklayer.
NELSON, a black man,		30	a good field hand and laborer.
DOCK,	do	28	do do
BIG FRED,	do	24	do do
LITTLE SOL,	do	22	do do
ALFRED, a griff,		28	do do
SIMON, a black man,		21	do do
WATT,	do	30	do do
JIM LEAVY,	do	24	do do
JIM ALLEN,	do	26	do do
FRANK GETTYS, a griff,		26	do do
JERRY GETTYS, a black,		23	do do
BILL GETTYS,	do	23	do do
GRANDERSON,	do	24	do do
LITTLE FED,	do	23	do do
FRANK HENRY, a griff,		23	do do
EDMOND,	do	21	do do
ANDERSON, a black man,		24	a No. 1 bricklayer and mason.
BOB SPRIGS, a griff,		25	a good field hand and laborer.
ELIJAH, a black man,		35	do do
JACK,	do	30	do do
REUBEN,	do	28	unsound.
STEPHEN,	do	22	a good field hand and laborer.
YELLOW JERRY, a griff,		26	a good teamster.
BIG SOL, a black man,		26	a good field hand and laborer.
BILL COLLINS,	do	28	do do
JESS,	do	26	do do
JUDGE,	do	30	do do
JERRY CARTER,	do	28	do

LOUISA, a griff, 38 years, a good Cook and seamstress, and an excellent servant.
ROBERT, 13 years old, defect in one toe.
JASPAR, 74 years old, an extra No. 1 laborer, driver and coachman.
The slaves can be seen four days previous to the day of sale. They are fully guaranteed against the vices and maladies prescribed by law, and are all selected slaves.

TERMS OF SALE—One year's credit for approved city acceptances or endorsed paper, with interest at 7 per cent. from date, and mortgage on the slaves if required ACTS OF SALE BEFORE WM. SHANNON, NOTARY PUBLIC, AT THE EXPENSE OF THE PURCHASER.

After the sale of the above list of Slaves, will be sold Another lot of Negroes, comprising Field Hands, House servants and Mechanics. A full description of the same will be given at the sale. The slaves can be seen two days previous to the sale.

The rate at which slaves were imported in the 1850's exceeded that of fifty years before in spite of the ban on the African slave trade in 1808.

Loading plan of the lower deck of a 'Guinea-man' slave ship.

(*Left*) Slaves on Edisto Island in Charlotte Forten's day.

THE OLD PLANTATION HOME.

Currier and Ives depicted plantation life as pastoral and carefree.

Slaves on a rice plantation in the South-East. Their calls and work-songs were a means of regulating the labour of field hands and impressed visitors to the work plantations. Early nineteenth-century drawing.

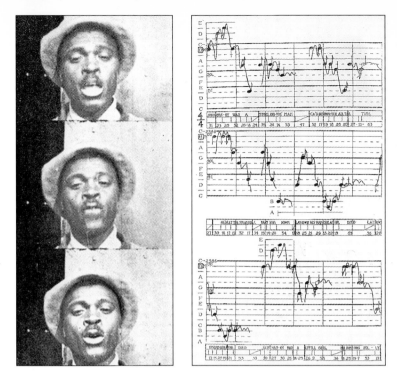

(*Left*) A workman sings *John Henry*. Close-ups of quick sound-shifts: top – the vowel *ah* of *time*; centre and bottom – *f* and *o* respectively of *Fore*.

(*Right*) Phonophotographic record of the vocal line during the singing of *John Henry*. (Recorded by M. Metfessel)

'Hollers' and work songs lightened the burden of the cotton-picking season.

(*Left*) Fra–fra musicians in Ghana sing praise songs for their chief with the same inflections as African-American field hands.

(*Right*) Banjo player and dancer about 1890.

(*Right*) An early circus poster illustrated the exaggerated elegance of the house servant's ball.

(*Left*) 'Blackface' minstrels parodied black banjo, tambourine, fiddle and bones players.

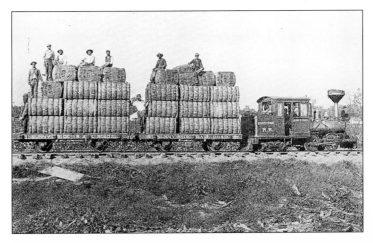

(*Right*) Railroad cars on the Sunnyside line loaded with 500lb cotton bales.

(*Left*) Associated with music for 'the Master', the fiddle declined in popularity.

(*Below*) Young guitar and mandolin players, Detroit, Michigan, 1902.

LOVERS OF THE MUSE.

(*Above*) Riverboats on the Ohio by the levee at Cincinnati, soon after Lafcadio Hearn collected the songs of roustabouts.

(*Right*) Guitarist with the black crew of a Florida riverboat c.1900.

(*Above*) *Original Rags*, the first published composition of Scott Joplin, appeared in March 1899.

(*Right*) Irving Jones was a black composer whose songs fed back to the rural singers.

(*Right*)
Joe Calicott,
from Mississippi,
who sang in a
holler style.

DOWN HOME BLUES

(*Left*) Louisiana mule-skinners harnessed their teams, and urged their animals with shrill 'hollers'.

(*Below*) A waterboy refreshes workers in the cotton fields.

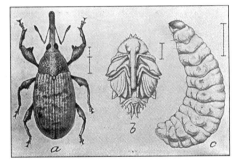

(*Above*) The cotton boll weevil as recorded by *Insect Life*, when it first appeared in Texas in the 1890's. By 1905 it had also ravaged crops in Mississippi and caused widespread disaster.

(*Right*) Black sharecroppers were subject to exploitation by 'The Man', the white landowner who, at 'settlement' time evaluated the crop, and took his share.

Black convicts working deep in the Georgia woods were chained at night in mobile pens. A bucket beneath the pen served as a latrine; armed guards stood by. Trustees worked as dog handler and cook, while another was permitted to play his guitar.

(*Right*)
Convicts in the Angola Penitentiary, Louisiana, sing a 'cutting song' as they wield their axes, in a manner which recalls that of African work gangs.

(*Left*)
A family string band in Mississippi playing guitar, mandolin and cello.

Huddie Ledbetter (Leadbelly). His
criminal record transcript listed
'Homicide'; Aslt w/i to murder; Fel.
Assault'.

Leadbelly learned about life from the
women of Fannin Street in Shreveport,
Louisiana, who, as he recalled later 'nearly
killed him'. Fannin Street (*left*) is still
regarded with apprehension.

(*Right*) Black
homes in Atlanta
in the 'thirties.

'Papa Charlie' Jackson, banjo playing songster, travelled to Chicago from New Orleans.

(*Above right*) One of the last of the songsters, Mance Lipscomb of Navasota, Texas.

(*Left*) Songster Jim Jackson from Hernando, Mississippi worked with the medicine shows.

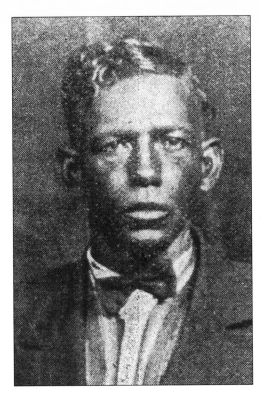

(*Left*) Charley Patton's fiery blues were heard in joints around Dockery's Farms (*above*) in the north of the Mississippi Delta.

Best known of the Crystal Springs singers were Tommy Johnson (*bottom left*), and his friend Ishman Bracey (*bottom right*).

(*Left*)
Blind Lemon Jefferson, about the age of thirty.

(*Below*) Advertisement for a record by Willard 'Ramblin' Thomas, a fellow Texan.

Frank Stokes of the Beale Street Sheiks, who worked most of his life in the medicine shows.

Walter 'Furry' Lewis of Memphis, Tennessee sang ballads.

Blind Blake came from the East Coast. Unable to work in the fields blind children turned to music for their living.

Blind Willie McTell, seen here in Atlanta in 1926, played a jumbo-size Stella twelve-string guitar.

(*Above*) Peg Leg Howell (*right*) and his gang, Eddie Anthony (fiddle) and Henry Williams on an Atlanta street.

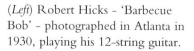

(*Left*) Robert Hicks - 'Barbecue Bob' - photographed in Atlanta in 1930, playing his 12-string guitar.

BLUES ON STAGE

In the river towns, black string bands played in the saloons; this one played in an open-air barrelhouse in St Louis at the turn of the century.

Cannon's Jug Stompers. Gus Cannon with banjo and paraffin can 'jug', Ashley Thompson, guitar, and Noah Lewis, harmonica.

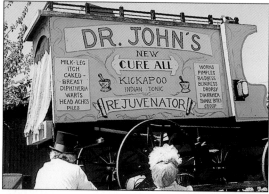

(*Above*) The Mobile Strugglers, a string band, playing in Montgomery, Alabama, in the 'fifties.

(*Centre*) A 'high-pitch' medicine show wagon.

(*Below*) A 'low-pitch' medicine show, Huntingdon, Tennessee.

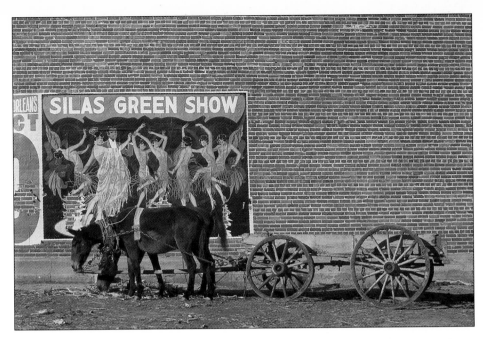

The Silas Green Show from New Orleans was considered one of the most
musical entertainments 'on the road'.

String and jug band veterans – Bo Carter of the Mississippi Sheiks,
Will Shade, who led the Memphis Jug Band, and Gus Cannon.

(*Above*) Gertrude 'Ma' Rainey on stage accompanied by the Georgia Jazz Band which included Georgia Tom Dorsey, piano, Al Wynn, trombone, and Ed Pollock, trumpet.

(*Right*) Viola McCoy from Memphis, was a popular singer at the Lincoln, Lafayette and Alhambra Theatres, Harlem.

(*Above*) Butterbeans and Susie (Edwards) were a celebrated Vaudeville team.

(*Right*) Esther Bigeou from New Orleans.

(*Below*) Entertainers wanted advertisement from the *Chicago Defender*.

(*Right*) Ida Cox, who worked for over fifty years in road shows, including her own 'Raising Cain' company.

Edmonia Henderson,
known as 'The Melodious Blues Singer'.

Lottie Beaman,
the 'Kansas City Butterball'.

(*Right and bottom right*)
Lillian Glinn on record and in retirement.

(*Below*) Lizzie Miles returned to
New Orleans in the 1950's.

(*Above*) Now a church, the Lincoln Theatre on West 135th Street, Harlem, where Bessie Smith headlined several shows.

(*Right*) Bessie Smith. In performance she would include popular songs of the day, as well as blues and blues-songs.

(*Left*) Frankie 'Half-Pint' Jaxon, a diminutive entertainer and female impersonator.

(*Below*) The Big Grand on State Street, Chicago, shortly before demolition.

Louis Armstrong, who accompanied many singers, discusses a recording session with W.C. Handy, composer of *St. Louis Blues* and *The Memphis Blues*.

UP FROM THE COUNTRY

The Great War brought Blacks from many states together and helped spread the blues.

A sawmill on the Mississippi below the bluffs at Natchez. Elzadie Robinson and Will Ezell were among the singers who worked in the camps and sang about them.

Segregation. Shreveport, Louisiana style;
'separate but equal'.

Logos of some of the railroads used by
bluesmen and migrants.

Cotton warehouses at the foot of Beale Street. The Illinois Central
railroad tracks in the foreground.

Nehemiah 'Skip' James learned from
an older generation of musicians.

Big Joe Williams, a rambler
from Crawford, Mississippi, played
a 9-string guitar.

Henry Brown, one of the St Louis school of blues pianists, playing a 44-key piano
in Pinky Boxx's Beauty Parlor.

Musically, Buddy Moss was a link between Blind Blake and Blind Boy Fuller.

(*Above*) Blind Gary Davis applied blues technique to gospel songs and played his 'holy blues'.

(*Left*) The influential singer Blind Boy Fuller. He played a steel-bodied National guitar with a circular diaphragm resonator.

(*Above*) Brownie McGhee was a guitarist but he also played piano and a 'jazzhorn'. In the 'forties he teamed up with harmonica virtuoso Sonny Terry (*left*) to form one of the most enduring partnerships in the blues.

(*Left*) Whistling Alex Moore. A junk-man by trade, he was an inventive pianist and a blues poet in the Texas tradition.

(*Below*) Black Ace, (B.K. Turner) migrated from the country to Shreveport. He played a steel guitar Hawaiian-style with a bottle for a slide.

(*Left*) Lonnie Johnson. A celebrated blues singer he also played guitar with Louis Armstrong, Duke Ellington and other jazz musicians.

(*Right*) 'Sleepy' John Estes sang blues about his experiences in his home town of Brownsville, Tennessee.

(*Left*) Edwin 'Buster' Pickens wore the forehead quiff which proclaimed that he was a barrel-house pianist. He played the sawmills and the joints along the tracks in Richmond, Texas (*below*).

was opened about 1909 as the finest black club in the South and was operated under the management of Jake Redwood, with the notorious two-gun bouncer Bad Sam, to keep some kind of order. Benny Frenchy played while the whores 'would run directly up to the wall and with a little bitty shuffle and clap their hands together and kick back their right leg. And they'd say, "O Play it, Benny, play it."' Morton had a poor opinion of Benny Frenchy as a pianist but W. C. Handy, who had an ear for the folk blues, heard and noted the figures which Benny Frenchy, Sonny Butts and Seymour Abernathy played with their 'eight-to-the-bar pre-influence' of boogie-woogie.

Morton's recollections were supported by other pianists – Richard Myknee Jones, for instance. Jones was born in New Orleans in 1889 and had been impressed by the boogie playing of a heavily-built pianist, 'Stavin' Chain' (obviously using the name of a folk hero) whom he heard in a railroad construction camp near Donaldsonville on the Bayou La Fourche south of Baton Rouge, Louisiana. And there was Clarence Williams, born in Plaquemine and four years his junior, who heard the blues as a young man in a turpentine camp near Oakdale on the Calcasieu River between Lake Charles and Alexandria. He was joined in New Orleans in 1911 by George W. Thomas, from Houston, Texas, who had composed the theme of the *New Orleans Hop Scop Blues* – in spite of its title – based on the blues he had heard played by the pianists of East Texas.

Morton's *Jelly-Roll Blues* was probably based on a folk theme – it was popular with Peg Leg Howell and his gang and appeared in the singing of other folk musicians – while Jones's *Trouble in Mind* has an eight-bar strain of some antiquity. Clarence Williams's *Michigan Water Blues* was based directly on what he had heard in Oakdale, and W. C. Handy used the Monarch pianist's right-hand figures in his *Beale Street Blues* which he published in 1917. These men, all highly influential in jazz, moved early to the North and the East, settling in Chicago and New York, or in Morton's case, in California, when *Beale Street* was being published. Their well documented movements were echoed by less established names whose direct contact with jazz was less, but who were more important in shaping the piano blues; many of them were in middle-western and eastern cities before the First World War.

While some of the blues pianists followed the route to Chicago and Detroit, others remained in the South to play obscurely in the backwoods and to follow a circuit which was an east-west movement rather than a south-north one. Many of them were 'professional' pianists by their own lights – making a rough living from playing wherever a piano was available to them. Though born later, in

1906, Little Brother Montgomery began to play the piano when he was only five years old, under the influence of many of these virtually anonymous blues pianists. His father ran a juke joint in Kentwood, Louisiana, close to the Mississippi border and deep in the piney woods. This was lumber country and the sawmill companies operated their mills in the region. The Montgomery juke was there to entertain the loggers off from their shift-work and Eurreal 'Little Brother' was able to 'hear real people play – such as Son Framion and a guy named Friday Ford. There was another player that was called Papa Lord God and one named Varnado Anderson.' In other sawmill towns he heard other pianists – Blind Homer, Blind Jug, and around Lake Village Arkansas, he came in contact with 'Burnt Face' Jake Facey, Joe Martin who 'died one Christmas I think, in 1923 or '22' and Son Young 'he got killed at Waterproof, Louisiana. He was a great piano player; Walter Lewis, he was another one. I ran across another guy they called Skinny Head Pete, he was good . . .' Little Brother's list of blues pianists that he had known, met and worked with seems inexhaustible. Few of them we shall ever know by their music, only by their names. But Montgomery, who was a superb blues pianist himself, gave some indication of their quality by his admiration for the men whom he recalled forty years after.

A pattern emerges from the succession of pianists whose shadows remain in the memories of a few veterans of the piano blues. Almost all of them worked in the company camps – the levee, turpentine and sawmill camps of the Piney Woods and forest belt of the South. In 1870 less than a tenth of the nation's lumber was produced in the South; by 1909 this had risen to nearly 45% and was approaching half the total production in the country by 1929 when Little Brother Montgomery was leaving the sawmill camps. In that year 2,670 millions of feet of lumber were cut in Mississippi, nearly as much in Louisiana, over two billion feet in Alabama and nearly 1,500 million in Texas. The industry was dirty and it was dangerous – casualties in logging were five times those in the iron and steel industry, and conditions were appalling: 'Across the railroad track from the depot and company store were about one hundred unpainted shacks for Negro workers. These are one room with a window at one end – not always glass but with a wood flap to let down. Each had one door on one of its sides. Set up on short lengths of wood piling in rows and fairly close together with ground around, quite bare and packed and garbage strewn. Hogs were under both white and colored workers' houses and no doubt mosquitoes were too because there was standing water about', wrote Charlotte Todes in a report for the Labour Research Organisation on a logging camp owned by the Great Southern, near Bogalousa, Louisiana. A single hydrant gave water and cooking facilities weren't provided. The logging camps, often far from towns, had 'barrelhouse jukes' to provide some kind of recreation facility for the workers. A piano was usually installed and drinks were purchased from the company. Conditions were similar in the other types of camp – those for turpentine workers, or for the men who 'graded' the levees and built up the banks of the rivers to protect the land against flooding. The camps were rough, beyond the law. Killings were far from infrequent and discipline could be brutally enforced without hindrance. Barbed wire fences often surrounded them; strangers were met with hostility. The entertainers in the camps were pianists who were known on the 'barrelhouse circuit' and travelled between camps, switching jobs with other pianists and following the railroads through the forest belt. Compared with the relatively static situation of the cotton-belt sharecropper, the position of the sawmill hand was a fluid one. As the forests were reduced to stump lands, the camps retreated deeper into the woods; their impermanence, their defences against intruders all discouraged the talent scouts and there was little attempt on the part of the recording companies to seek out the pianists of the camps.

Given that he knew where there was a piano to play the blues, a pianist had a certain mobility; he could not take his instrument with him as could the guitarist, but he was unencumbered, could 'hop a freight train' to the next town without preparation. A piano-player had already gained the independence that made such mobility possible; a blues guitarist might stay on the same plantation all his life, but a pianist who worked the camps, by the very nature of his career, travelled frequently. The Texas and Pacific, the Southern or the Louis and Nashville carried him from camp to barrelhouse to township and eventually to the city. Many pianists found that the cities, where the rows of juke joints and loan offices, clothing stores and saloons, leaned against each other for support, provided ample opportunities for work. Incoming migrants liked to hear the music they had known at home and the itinerant pianists who travelled in the 'blinds' – the 'blind' baggage cars – or 'on the rods', the perilous perch provided by the brakerods beneath the cars, found that the discomfort of hoboing was rewarded by a receptive audience in the city joints.

As a direct result of the migration, the black populations in the cities had increased dramatically. There were twenty thousand Blacks in Indianapolis in 1910 and nearer fifty thousand a decade later.

It was a constantly recurring pattern, though the growth rate in some cities was phenomenal, Gary doubling its black population twelve times in ten years. St Louis and East St Louis; Louisville and Indianapolis, Cincinnati and Cleveland – these were all target cities whose expansion was considerable. Some had substantial Black populations already and cities such as St Louis and Indianapolis had been centres for the somewhat earlier ragtime piano tradition; the pianists who came with the tide and those who were already there developed styles which showed a ragtime influence.

Within this period of urban expansion Chicago had a black population which had increased from 44,000 to over a hundred thousand – but the most remarkable increase was in Detroit which had some 5471 Blacks in 1910; eight years later, it had over thirty-five thousand, and by 1926 some eighty thousand. Hastings Street was the main artery of the black ghetto and it soon became famous as a resort for the piano players who came from the South. One of the first was 'Tupelo Slim' from Lee County, Mississippi; another was known anonymously only as 'Fishtail'; and still another was James Hemingway. They were all playing when Rufus Perryman, an albino Black from Georgia arrived in the city. Called 'Speckled Red' because of his pink and freckled skin, he had been born in Monroe, Louisiana, in October 1891 but was raised in Hampton, Georgia. At the age of ten he was brought by his parents to Atlanta and was still in his early 'teens when he moved to Detroit. His father, a field-hand, had little use for the near-blind boy and Speckled Red had to fend for himself. In Detroit, at Butch's Club on Reward and Division, he heard a pianist named 'Seminole' whose playing so mesmerised him that he recalled it vividly in dreams and learned to play Seminole's music from memory. It was clearly not the Paul Seminole whose fame as a ragtime pianist in Philadelphia and New York was legendary. Paul Seminole was born in the year that Speckled Red was listening to his namesake – 1904 – but it is probable that both came from Florida and used the Indian name. Speckled Red reversed the usual progression, taking a freight train to Memphis and spending the next twenty years playing in the sawmill and levee camps of the South, leaving everywhere the memory of his riotous, obscene barrelhouse piano version of *The Dirty Dozen*.

Another pianist to leave a profound impression where he played was Charles Davenport. He was born in Anniston, Alabama, in April 1894, the son of a preacher who sent him to a Baptist College to follow in his own footsteps. But Davenport had other ideas. He picked out pieces on the piano and was soon playing for the socials and suppers which were popular in Birmingham. A touring carnival show gave him an opportunity to travel and brought him in contact with Bob Davis, a barrelhouse pianist who taught him a lot. Davenport made his way to Texas where he picked up a theme called *The Cows* which later he considerably altered to develop a train imitation, the *Cow Cow Blues*. He worked in mining camps and brothels playing his theme, which earned for him the nickname of 'Cow Cow' Davenport. Davenport's technique was simple, alternating bass figures and treble figures rather than playing both concurrently on some of his most 'early' sounding pieces. With Dora Carr he formed the vaudeville team of Davenport and Carr, later doing similar duets with Ivy Smith, a better blues singer, to his own rough and ready piano accompaniment and earning enough to start his own road show. His stay in Detroit was well remembered as was his influence in Chicago. Later he settled in Cleveland, still another of the 'target' cities.

Two of the best-known pianists on Hastings Street were Charlie Spand and Will Ezell. Spand may have come from Georgia – a Charlie Spann in Atlanta was recalled by Georgia Tom Dorsey – but his brooding *Mississippi Blues* suggests otherwise. Lean and loose-limbed he played a stomping *Soon This Morning* with a powerful left hand.

> Soon this mornin' 'bout the break of day,
> Turned to my piller where my brownie used to lay
>   Oh soon this mornin', 'bout the break of day,
>   Turned to my piller, where my brownie used to lay . . .

With the guitarist Blind Blake he made a recording called *Hastings Street*. Murmured Blake: '. . . I know you want to go back to 169 Brady . . . I can't hardly rest . . . always tellin' me about Brady Street . . . wonder what's on Brady? Must be some of them marvellous mmm. .mmm. .mmm . . .' In the area bounded by Brady, Lafayette, Rivard and Beaubien streets between twelve and fifteen thousand Blacks were crammed in houses 'in very bad repair, many of them actual shanties' as the National Urban League reported, where the rents trebled in eighteen months. Other houses in the St Antoine District were 'unsanitary beyond redemption'; life wasn't easy; vice, crime and corruption were rife under the stress conditions. The joints and the men who played the blues in them offered some relief and a memory of the more pleasurable aspects of home. Will Ezell, a pianist from the sawmill camps, had worked with Elzadie Robinson, a strong-voiced woman singer in Shreveport, Dallas, Fort Worth, St

Louis and Chicago. Ezell's *Barrelhouse Man* was a sombre blues but the juke-joint atmosphere of his *Gin Mill Blues* and the medley of influences in his *Mixed Up Rag* showed his ability and the nature of the music he had brought with him from labour camps.

Of the innumerable pianists who worked between Detroit and Chicago undoubtedly one of the most memorable was Clarence Lofton, who was born in March 1897 in Tennessee and settled in Chicago. Like Davenport and others he was an entertainer, singing in his crackling voice, dancing, rapping on the piano lid, whistling and playing with his hands behind his back and his back to the piano. 'When he really gets going he's a three-ring circus', wrote Bill Russell. His *Streamline Train* was a typical railroad piece, strongly influenced by Davenport's *Cow Cow Blues* and like many of his themes had a powerful, rolling bass figure. One of his most celebrated was *Strut That Thing*, a fast romp, enlivened by his finger snapping off-beat syncopation, and vocal and instrumental breaks,

> Gettin' sick an' tired o' the way you do
> Kind mama, gon'a poison you
> Sprinkle goofer dust 'round your bed
> Wake up in the mornin' find you own self dead,
> Cause you should not do it at all,
>   Shouldn't do it at all,
>   Shouldn't do it all,
> I'm tellin' you lover,
> How to be struttin' that thing, night and day . . .

Lame from birth but apparently not inconvenienced in doing his dance, 'Cripple' Clarence Lofton made a living during the day polishing automobiles and played at his clubs at nights to the early hours. He died in 1957.

Some of the Chicago pianists were native born; Jimmy Yancey was one. His blues style was especially distinctive and its origins hard to ascertain. Born in 1894, he was already earning as a child of six in 1902, dancing the 'buck and wing' in the Bert Earl road show. Ten years in vaudeville even brought him to England, but returning to Chicago in 1913 he took a job as ground-keeper at the White Sox baseball park on 35th Street and developed his blues. Perhaps his vaudeville tours took him to New Orleans or Mexico for his playing always demonstrated the 'Spanish tinge' which Jelly Roll Morton had considered an important component of jazz. (Music Example 6.) Jimmy Yancey's bass figures sometimes had a tango and habañera rhythm which relate them to the music of the legendary

Doug Suggs and Little David Alexander. Doug Suggs was the same age as Yancey, being born in 1894 in St Louis where he was influenced by the playing of Claude Brown; later he moved to Chicago and also took a job at the Sox ball park, working as a porter. Contact between the two musicians must have helped develop their similar use of bass patterns, but Suggs, though less known in later years than Yancey, was an important influence on the younger generation of Chicago pianists.

It is noticeable that the first generation of blues pianists who were born in the 1890s showed distinct ragtime influences, while the second generation, born a decade later, were exclusively blues players. Most of them seemed to have met at some period in their formative years. Little Brother Montgomery came up to Chicago in 1929 after spending a period in Vicksburg, Mississippi, where he had worked and met pianists Robert Johnson and Ernest 'Forty-Four' Johnson a year or two his senior. Together they developed one of the most widespread of all blues themes, the *Forty-Four Blues*, Montgomery teaching it to a young clothes-presser, Lee Green. In turn, Lee Green passed the theme on to Roosevelt Sykes, who came from Helena, Arkansas, where he was born in the same year, 1906. Sykes was raised in St Louis but he visited his relatives frequently in West Helena and was greatly impressed by the pianists in the town, Baby Sneed, Joe Crump and Jesse Bell among them. Sykes moved up to Chicago in 1929 for a period, although he continued to make St Louis his main home, bringing with him the *Forty-Four Blues* and putting a number of country piano themes on record, both under his own name and under his pseudonyms of Dobby Bragg and Willie Kelly. Sykes, Montgomery, Green and Sunnyland Slim – Albert Luandrew – a Mississippi pianist a year their junior, had worked the levee camps and sawmill camps of southern Mississippi together for a number of years before they recorded but, with the exception of Sunnyland Slim who remained in Memphis, the others had all reached Chicago by 1930.

In a sense they were late comers. Blues piano had become highly popular in the tenements and the number of blues pianists was legion. Some it is true, may have had a very limited repertoire, but they did have the creative ability to reformulate the bass patterns and treble figures they had mastered to compose new blues – Jimmy Yancey himself only had about twelve basic themes although his musical invention within his restricted range was remarkable. The 'parlor social' and the 'struggle', the 'gouge' and the 'percolator', the 'skiffle' and the 'too terrible party' were all names for the function most commonly termed 'boogie' or 'house rent party'. In the height of the prohibition era these provided a substitute for open saloons, being mounted in back-rooms in ten thousand apartments all over the South Side. The house-rent party, a southern custom which was transplanted with equal effectiveness to Harlem, was a means of meeting the rent when money was low. Spending the last few dollars on jars of 'moonshine' and 'home brew', the host would engage a piano player – if he wasn't one himself – and throw a party for which admission was a quarter. It was in these parties that Montana Taylor, Romeo Briggs, Romeo Nelson, Charles Avery, Dan Burley, 'Mr Freddie' Shayne, Alex Channey and scores of other painists, known and unknown, played. They included the child prodigy, Hersal Thomas, whose appearance in Chicago and Detroit from Houston, Texas, at the age of fourteen created a sensation and profoundly influenced the piano players who heard his grumbling basses and highly poetic melodic inventions. They also included Clarence Pine Top Smith.

Pine Top Smith was from Troy, Alabama, where he was born in January 1904. He moved to Birmingham, in his early 'teens. Birmingham seems to have had a fairly strong piano tradition and Clarence Smith, lanky enough to be called Pine Top and with red hair – probably from a dietary deficiency in childhood – seems to have had a natural aptitude. He toured on the T.O.B.A. as an accompanist to Butterbeans and Susie and as a solo act – a few of his scarce records, like *I'm Sober Now* or *Now I Ain't Got Nothin' at All*, have marked vaudeville character. Pine Top seems to have been an eccentric personality but a highly likeable one, and he developed a smoothly rolling style of piano playing. He was playing at a honky-tonk in Sachem Alley, Pittsburgh, when Cow Cow Davenport was appearing at the Star Theatre on Wiley Avenue. Davenport, hearing of the young pianist, looked him up and encouraged him to go to Chicago with a dance-piece he was playing. 'Boy, look here, you sure have got a mean boogie woogie,' commented Davenport, alliterating the name of the style of piano played at the Chicago 'boogie' parties. It was 1924. Pine Top took his wife, Sarah Horton Smith, to Chicago and took the room on South Parkway in a building where, coincidentally two other piano-players, Meade 'Lux' Lewis and Albert Ammons, were also living. There he raised his two children and passed on much of his light, easily-flowing music with the effortless bass figures to the other two tenants: Lewis, who was from Louisville, where he was born in 1905, and his companion, Ammons, a thickset man with an exceptionally dynamic left hand who had not recorded, but was well-known on the South Side. They must have made a thrilling team. Then in December 1928 Pine Top Smith, put on wax his immortal *Pine Top's Boogie Woogie* and sang in his high, plaintive voice with marked Southern accents, his *Pine Top's Blues*. Five weeks later, on January 14th and 15th, he cut seven more titles, and they were to be his last. Two months after, to the day, he returned from a job and stopped in on a party on Orleans Street which was being held by the Odd Fellows Lodge in the Masonic Hall. An argument broke out between two of the members and guns were drawn. In the ensuing shooting affray Pine Top fell, mortally wounded with a bullet in his chest. He was buried in Restvale Cemetery and something of the spirit of the early Chicago blues was buried with him. But Pine Top had given a name to a whole piano blues tradition and there were innumerable piano players who were to develop it.

Walking the Basses

There's every indication that the blues is a music based on the express-iveness of the human voice: the use of the slide techniques and string 'choking' on the guitar, the playing of harmonica, fiddle, and even kazoo all bear this out. For the pianist though, there were problems, for the fixed notes of the piano, tuned to a European diatonic scale and with a purity which is alien to blues, made blues interpretation on the instrument extremely difficult. Though the 'out-of-tune piano' is a cliché of blues writing, and of blues imitation for that matter, the blues pianist does incline towards an instrument which produces a metallic, hollow sound, or where the notes sound a shade flat. Many blues pianists disliked the concert grand when they had the opportunity to play one, being unable to manipulate its impeccable tuning into the tone colour they required. Every African instrument has a drone, a vibrator or other device which produces a buzzing note or in some other way destroys a totally pure note. Such sound elements may be in the nature of the instrument itself, but if not, they will be added – a handful of beans or small stones will be put inside a calabash or in a drum, a length of chain will hang from the sanza 'thumb piano'. For the blues pianist the problem was often solved by the fact that the instruments were indeed out of tune, or the felt on the hammers was worn, but sometimes he would put newspaper behind the strings, even tacks in the hammers to alter the sound, and generally the front would be removed from the upright piano.

Such devices only changed the colouration and gave it an edge; the equivalents of the guitarist's 'mashing' of the strings was produced by startling dissonances, the deliberate meeting of notes that would be incompatible in any orthodox playing. Blues pianists 'crush' the keys, playing notes almost simultaneously but not quite – striking one a fraction before the one above so that the implied passing note hits the ear in a manner similar to the guitarist's slide. The technique is that of the pointillist, permitting the sounds to vibrate in the ear as the painter's spots of colour vibrate on the retina. Imitative passages are frequent in piano blues, particularly the evocation of the rhythms of trains, but the pianists seldom attempt to imitate the human voice. Instead the blues pianist makes equivalents, gaining his effects of anguish, sorrow or humour by the tone colour he achieves through discords, vibrant juxtapositions, tremoloes and bass figures.

Blues basses are the most distinctive aspects of the pianistic form. They are often repetitive and sometimes approximate the bass figures of the guitarists; the 'walking basses' in particular, can be achieved readily on both piano and guitar. It was these that Leadbelly heard in Shreveport in 1901, though they are by no means the only kind of blues bass patterns. Pianists like Clarence Williams, Fletcher Henderson or Eddie Heywood, in spite of their frequent accompaniments to classic blues singers, seldom used blues figures but rather the vamp of the music hall or the chords of the dance band. Blues pianists preferred configurations using the open octave and 5th, omitting the 3rd; they liked bass figures in straight crotchets or in triplets with fourth and eighth notes in triplet time, and they favoured the walking bass using spread octaves. The 'walk' could be effected in many ways, the pianist rocking from fourth finger to thumb up and down the scale in the most typical form; through using the 'catch-up' of alternating walk and chord, and numerous other variants.

Often the basics of the piano blues are very simple, as in the playing of Henry Brown. Born in St Louis in 1906, Henry Brown learned his style of piano blues from a man known only as 'Blackmouth' who played on Deep Morgan. 'He was a real old-times blues player and he'd stomp 'em down to the bricks there on Deep Morgan', recalled Brown, who also learned from another unrecorded pianist named Joe Cross. Brown's extremely economical blues was reflected in the playing of other pianists in St Louis, who seemed to favour the sparse phrases, as simple and uncluttered as Shaker furniture.

Brown's *Deep Morgan Blues* (Music Example 7) employs a bass figure which is heavily accented on crotchet beats, emphasised by the dotted rhythm. A very elementary bass with few note changes, it moves into a simple walking bass later in the piece. Other St Louis pianists like James 'Stump' Johnson or Walter Davis also liked these simple bass patterns. It seems to have been a matter of preference. Johnson learned to play piano from Son Long whom he claimed was the 'originator' of boogie-woogie and who was also from Morgan Street;

he could play a more complex theme when he wished. Walter Davis, though from Grenada, Mississippi, spent his life in St Louis and his many recordings used simple bass figures only, just a couple of solos on *Frisco Blues*, and *Biddle Street Blues* show more development.

Chicago in the late 'twenties had an extraordinarily large number of folk musicians who were experimenting with the bass figures of piano blues to create a 'powerhouse' music of great dynamism. Those who derived their music from Pine Top Smith, like Romeo Nelson, whose *Head Rag Hop* was closely modelled on *Pinetop's Boogie Woogie*, developed a running impetus in their playing. This seems to have been inspired by the rhythms of the railroads which rattled past their walls at second and third floor levels. Many imitated the 'rattlers' with urgent, rolling left-hand patterns and paralleled the clatter of points and the 'elevated' with their right hand tremoloes. One of the most famous of these railroad impressions was *Honky Tonk Train Blues* recorded by Meade 'Lux' Lewis when he was a driver for the Silver Taxicab Company. His fellow-driver, Albert Ammons who was born in Chicago two years later, in 1907, also played a forceful 'boogie woogie' although he remained unrecorded at the time (Music Example 8). In later years the bass patterns that he used became stereotyped and over-familiar through excessive repetition, but in the 'twenties they were fresh and original.

A happy accident in the rediscovery of Lewis's single title won recognition for both pianists, but others remained in total obscurity. One such player was Charles Avery, known mainly for his accompaniments to singer Lucille Bogan, and for his only piano solo, *Dearborn Street Breakdown*, a piece with a driving rhythm and an unusual bass figure that was somewhat more melodic in character than were many (Music Example 9). How inventive these obscure musicians were within their idiom is demonstrated by Wesley Wallace's solo, *Number 29*. Wallace came from Alton, Illinois and his recording, with spoken commentary, describes his trip as a hobo on the 'train they call 29 leavin' out of Cairo comin' into East St Louis.' His right-hand quavers hammer the sound of the bell and his momentum conveys the impression of the train that was travelling too fast for him to get off. 'She's lopin' now . . . I wanted to get off that train but she's goin' too fast . . . I hauled away and touched one foot on the ground . . . I feel like nearly knockin' my brains out.' He fell off and for a moment the rhythm was suspended as he explained 'this is the noise I made when I hit the ground', the right hand describing the rolling hobo tumbling down the bank. 'I'm rollin' now. I got up and waved my hand, told her goodbye. This way I keep walkin' on into East St

Louis.' Wesley Wallace's performanice was a *tour de force*, with the left hand playing triplets in 4/4 time, winding upwards from C to G. Later the pattern changed when the first C came on the first beat. The right hand played quavers and isolated crotchets in 4/4 over the bass; the quavers sometimes as triplets, sometimes in groups of two. And over this he spoke the commentary in a matter-of-fact a-rhythmic narrative.

Piano blues is essentially bi-linear with the bass figures rolling on inexorably and the right hand playing melodic sequences against them. In fact it is more true to say that both left and right hands are melodic-rhythmic and much of the strength of the music lies in the counter-rhythms and cross-rhythms that are set up. From an orthodox point of view, the discords are often extremely daring but they arise largely from the horizontal, linear conception of the music. This dual linearity which becomes tri-linear when the pianist sings, is very African in overall conception and though the orthodox tuning of the piano would seem to suppress African cultural survivals, the use of the piano by the blues artist would seem to be, nonetheless, a further expression of persistent Africanisms. Its suitability for the juke joints and barrelhouses of the levee camp and company town lay in its powerfully percussive nature. It was this which also made it ideal for the rent parties and clubs of the northern cities. 'Barrelhouse Buck' McFarland played in similar clubs. He came from the same town as Wesley Wallace and often worked with him and with Peetie Wheatstraw.

If the pianists initially made the strongest impact in the north, the cities attracted the guitarists no less than the piano players. Outside Chicago, a ring of cities had developed strong blues traditions, in particular, St Louis, Missouri, Louisville in Kentucky, Indianapolis, Indiana and, to some extent, Cleveland and Cincinnati in Ohio to the eastern part of the ring and Kansas City to the west. All were important railroad intersections or were strategically placed on migratory routes, while lines like the Baltimore and Ohio and the Louisville and Nashville linked them together. Although some singers remained relatively static, others moved freely between one city and another. William Bunch, who called himself 'Peetie Wheatstraw, the Devil's Son-in-Law and the High Sheriff of Hell' was one. He was born in Ripley, Tennessee, in 1902 but after a period playing in the Arkansas saw-mill towns moved up to St Louis. He played both piano and guitar with equal aptitude, although his guitar was seldom recorded. Peetie had a blurred, indistinct voice and a lazily arrogant delivery:

Don't tell all your women what Peetie Wheatstraw can do (2)
That will cause them to be suspicious and you know
   they will try him too.

I am Peetie Wheatstraw the High Sheriff from Hell (2)
The way I strut my stuff – well now you never can tell.

Peetie's frequent companion was Charley Jordan who came from
Helena, Arkansas. The bullet-headed, smiling Peetie and the balding,
taut-voiced Jordan made a tough team in the Third Avenue 'Valley'
sector, the red-light district which provided them with many
opportunities to play music. Charley Jordan played an uncorrupted
country style of blues guitar with an effortless, light technique. He was
known as a bootlegger of moonshine liquor, had several brushes with
the law and walked with a limp caused by a bullet in his ankle. Jordan
sometimes played with a gravel-voiced guitarist named Henry Brown
who, presumably to distinguish him from the St Louis pianist of the
same name, rather curiously used the pseudonym of the old white
minstrel show owner Hiram Patrick, 'Hi Henry'. Hi Henry Brown
came from Mississippi but his *Nut Factory* was about the prostitutes
'on Deep Morgan, just 'bout Sixteenth Street'.

Some draw a check, oh babe, some draw nothin' at all (2)
Well, they don't draw nothin' they husbands bust them
   in the jaw

Among other singers who came up from Mississippi to St Louis was
Henry Spaulding, whose unusual and much-remembered *Cairo Blues*
referred to a favourite haunt at the intersection of the Missouri and
the Mississippi at the southern-most tip of Illinois, where he stayed
before moving on to St Louis. Another was J. D. Short, a rough and
primitive singer from Port Gibson, Mississippi, where he was born
in 1902. 'Jelly Jaw' Short modelled his playing on the recordings
of the Texas singer, Funny Paper Smith, but his 'flailing' technique
lacked the subtlety of the western blues man. Theodore Roosevelt
Darby, a blind singer, also came from Mississippi. He was influenced
by Peetie Wheatstraw, and, like him, played both guitar and piano,
singing in a lighter voice. Though he was born in Shelby, Mississippi,
in 1909, Henry Townsend was raised in Cairo and moved as a youth
to St Louis where he worked with a boy of his own age, Sylvester
Palmer. He was greatly impressed with Lonnie Johnson's recordings
and his appearances at Jesse Johnson's De Luxe Club and the Booker
T. Washington Theater, but Henry Townsend showed little evidence

of it in his playing. His guitar work was accomplished and well-phrased but it did not have Johnson's sleek proficiency and his voice, high as it was when he first recorded at the age of nineteen, deepened with the years and had the tautness typical of a number of St Louis singers. Townsend played often with pianist Henry Brown and his rasping, 'gutbucket' trombonist partner, Ike Rogers, whose smears and slurs had something of the New Orleans tradition and not a little of the circus show. Henry Brown and Henry Townsend worked together as a piano and guitar team for many years in the clubs of St Louis and East St Louis, across the Mississippi River. Often Townsend accompanied Walter Davis, too, and they were joined frequently by the Mississippi-born Po' Joe Williams.

A close relationship seems to have existed among the St Louis musicians: Peetie Wheatstraw would play piano for 'Barrelhouse Buck' McFarland, a thick-voiced singer from Alton, Illinois, where he was born in 1903. He was not as accomplished as his friend Wesley Wallace, but was capable of playing on his own records. Roosevelt Sykes, who settled for a long time in St Louis, also played for many singers, including the bespectacled 'Specks' McFadden and 'St Louis Jimmy' Oden, a prolific composer of blues. 'There were just so many good piano players in St Louis in those days', commented St Louis Jimmy, explaining why he did not bother to develop his own playing. He and Sykes travelled extensively together, returning frequently to St Louis though they both eventually moved to Chicago. Piano and guitar teams were popular in St Louis – the brothers Aaron 'Pine Top' and 'Flying' Lindberg Milton Sparks, with a history of petty crime, were one such team, with the former on piano. A bald-headed guitarist who was jestingly referred to as 'Papa Slick Head' or 'Papa Egg Shell' – his name was Lawrence Casey – was often to be found in the company of Henry Brown; and there were many others. They frequently accompanied the women singers like Mary Johnson from Jackson, Mississippi, who came to St Louis in 1915 at the age of fifteen, or the locally born 'Little Alice' Moore and Jessie White. These girl singers tended to a nasal style of blues which, though not as pronounced as Ida Cox's singing, still imparted to it a tough and uncompromising quality. They sang at Charles Turpin's Jazzland Club on 23rd and Market or the Chauffeurs Club on Lawton and Jefferson Avenue. Mary Johnson's tough blues earned her the name of 'Signifying Mary'. Across the Mississippi River from St Louis lies the crude, unlovely town called East St Louis which had been the scene in 1917 of an appalling race riot when black labour was brought in to replace striking white workers. The scars remained, but for those who worked and lived in the squalor of its factories and disintegrating wood houses, there was some outlet in the joints and bars of Market and Main, and Main and Broadway, where, at Katy Red's honky-tonk for instance, Henry Brown, Roosevelt Sykes, Alice Moore and Peetie Wheatstraw might be heard.

Of all the border and northern cities outside of Chicago and Detroit, St Louis was undoubtedly the richest musically. Its active life continued throughout the 'thirties with some singers travelling extensively but making the city their base. Stump Johnson and Roosevelt Sykes, Walter Davis, Charlie McFadden and others all toured in Texas; Big Joe Williams was everywhere. Clifford Gibson, a fairly high-voiced, clear-toned singer with a clean guitar style came up from Louisville, Kentucky, to St Louis where he became well-established, though he returned often to Louisville; Peetie Wheatstraw and a lighter-voiced singer, Jimmy Gordon, who claimed to be his brother, also maintained close links with Louisville. In the mid-'thirties Peetie was playing regularly at Louisville's Tip Top Club, but even he was heard as far south as Texas. Like other river towns, Louisville, Kentucky had a long-established string band tradition. Its principal black sector ran back from the riverfront and downtown areas on the city's grid-iron plan. Developed from its string bands, Louisville had, as has been already discussed, a number of 'jug' bands which established a link between blues, string bands and jazz. One string band was led by E. L. Coleman, a violinist, and included Charles Washington playing banjo, and guitarist Sylvester Weaver. Weaver was a well-known artist with a relatively light voice and was an accomplished guitarist, recording a *Guitar Blues* and a *Guitar Rag* as early as 1923. He had mastered rag and, probably, slide styles and was a good accompanist, working with the local singer Sara Martin for many years. According to E. Simms Campbell, she 'had a flair for the dramatic. In a darkened theatre, with only candles on the stage, she would begin to wail in a low moan – "Man done gone – got nowhere to go." She literally surged across the stage, clutched the curtains in the wings, rolled on the floor, and when she had finished the audience was as wilted as she.' Her histrionics may have made up for a lack of vocal expressiveness; she was a popular singer, made many recordings but only in the last ones she made did she rise above the general level of 'Classic blues' singers. Among Louisville's pianists were Johnny Gatewood, who later moved on to Chicago's North Side, and Dan Briscoe, who was notorious in the Louisville underworld, according to Paul Garon's informants. Both men played with the Clifford Hayes groups, which also included

Earl McDonald who had an active jug band in Louisville until his death in 1948, when it was continued by his violinist Henry Miles. Louisville's black population was heavily concentrated in three zones, with one forming a strip only seven blocks wide and three times that in length, containing some 20,000 people. In this section near the central business district the decaying buildings housed a flourishing red-light district, a powerful criminal element and an active night life which supported many blues singers hardly heard on record, on whom there is little documentation.

Peetie Wheatstraw, who was popular in Louisville, seems to have been equally at home in Indianapolis, a hundred-odd miles further North. The Louisville and Nashville railroad runs from New Orleans by way of Birmingham, Alabama, through Nashville to Louisville, Indianapolis and on to Chicago by way of the Pennsylvania Railroad, so Indianapolis was a natural staging post for the migrants from Alabama, Tennessee and Kentucky. Its railroad links with St Louis and Cincinnati also ensured a free movement of migrants and easy access for the blues singers to other centres. It seems to have been a favourite stopping-off place for Texas singers, especially the pianists who were heading for Detroit. One of the early arrivals was Jesse Crump who was born in Paris, Texas, in 1906 and had travelled on the T.O.B.A. circuit before arriving in Indianapolis when he was still only seventeen. There he played piano for two girl singers Genevieve Stearns and Nina Reeves, and worked as entertainer and pianist at the Golden West Cabaret. Crump's work was in a vaudeville vein but he could play good blues and impressed Ida Cox, who sent for him through her manager, to come on to Chicago. It was a particularly successful partnership and they were married for some years, during which time Crump made many records with her.

More earthy than Jesse Crump was Arthur Taylor who had been born out west in Butte, Montana, in 1903, but who came to Indianapolis when he was sixteen. It is likely that he learned to play piano after his arrival, for his work was characteristic of the barrelhouse pianists of the south central and mid-western regions. Though his *Whoop and Holler Stomp* was marred by the mediocre vocal of his kazoo-playing 'Jazoo Boys', 'Montana' Taylor's playing was an indication of his fast, romping blues. Better-known as classics of the boogie-barrelhouse form were his recordings of *Indiana Avenue Stomp* and *Detroit Rocks*, which indicated, no doubt, the places where he played. Indiana Avenue was the main thoroughfare of a black Indianapolis where the best bluesmen in 'Naptown' − as Indianapolis was known to its residents − could be found. Here the

Golden West Cabaret was located and when Jesse Crump and Nina Reeves left, Montana Taylor put in a spell. Further down was the Paradise Club, which was operated by Dee Davis, and the notoriously tough Blackstone. Other joints where blues players worked in the 'twenties and 'thirties were located on Bright Street and Smith Street, in the red-light district on Tenth Street or, like Bolton's and Ran Butler's clubs, on Northwestern Avenue. It was possible to hear the country blues of Mississippi in the Bright Street taverns where Shirley Griffith played. Griffith had come up from Mississippi where he was born in Brandon, near Jackson, in 1908 and where he had heard and learned from Tommy Johnson and Ishman Bracey. He arrived at the age of nineteen and for a year or two before the Depression closed many of the joints, made a scratch living from his playing. Or there was the fluent guitar playing of Scrapper Blackwell to listen to.

Francis Hillman Blackwell was brought from Syracuse, North Carolina, by his grandmother when he was only three years old, in 1906. Part Cherokee Indian, 'Scrapper' was one of a musical family. 'There's sixteen children. Eight boys and eight girls. My sister played the piano', Blackwell explained to Theodore F. Watts who asked him if anyone else in the family played an instrument. 'Everybody,' replied Scrapper. 'My sister plays, my brother-in-law plays. My brother plays now, Hawaiian. And my father was a lead violinist. I got a brother a drummer. And another one a singer.' He made his own guitar as a child from a mandolin neck and cigar box and learned to play such themes as *John Henry*, *Bugger Burns* and *Bully of the Town*, picking up the blues as they became popular in Indianapolis. Scrapper Blackwell's *Penal Farm Blues* was on a familiar subject whose frequent appearance in the blues may have had significance as a symbol of injustice and oppression to his listeners. In his 'twenties he had a flourishing business 'Alky cooking' – making moonshine liquor – and only reluctantly recorded a few titles when he was approached by a young promoter named Guernsey who had come to Naptown from England to set up a record business.

> Early one mornin' on my way to the penal farm (2)
> Baby all locked up and ain't doin' nothin' wrong.
>
> Thrown in the dog wagon and down the road we go (2)
> Ah baby, ah baby you don't know.
>
> In to the office, then to the bath-house we go (2)
> And after a light shower, baby we change our clothes.

All last night oh baby it seemed so long, (2)
All locked up, ain't doin' nothin' wrong.

I tell you people, penal farm's a lonesome place (2)
And no one there to smile up in your face.

Oh baby, baby, won't you come back to me? (2)
My time is up, penal farm has set me free.

His blues had a logical progression, a story line which gave them clear shape, and a neatness of phrase which did not make them too self-conscious and detached from the folk forms but provided a certain originality in the lyrics. The recordings were made in Indianapolis, and Guernsey was ready to introduce Blackwell to another artist, the pianist Leroy Carr. It was an historic meeting. Carr was a couple of years Blackwell's junior and had been born in Nashville, though he had been brought to Indianapolis in 1912 by his mother. As a child he learned to play the piano at home and was still a boy when he ran away with a circus troupe. Later, and under age, he joined the Army and was stationed at Fort Huachuca in Arizona. He was still only seventeen when he was married in 1923. According to Duncan Scheidt, who has uncovered Carr's life story, he was sent to the State farm for a year for bootlegging. It seems likely that he was his own best customer, for Carr had a prodigious thirst. This he shared with Scrapper Blackwell and they struck up a lasting friendship. In 1928 they commenced a series of recordings which were of outstanding quality.

It would seem that Guernsey was the initiator of the guitar-piano partnership. Carr's piano playing was mellow and rolling, and his voice was bitter-sweet. As a singer Blackwell was less distinctive though a little richer in tone, but his guitar playing, with its contrast of chord sequences and single-string finger-picking, had an astringent clarity which compensated for Carr's softness. Together they made an incomparable team, with a driving movement and lilting swing which was extremely infectious. Neither was at his best alone; it was their perfect timing and effortless mutual support which made them. Most of their recordings were of blues that had been written by Blackwell with his sister, Mrs Mae Malone. They were carefully composed and far from casually planned but they had a rare and simple poetry. 'Hurry down sunshine, see what tomorrow bring . . .' 'I've got the blues before sunrise, with tears startin' in my eyes . . .' or 'In the wee midnight hours, just 'bout the break of day . . .' – the lines of their blues passed into the folk tradition and soon every blues singer knew *How Long How Long Blues, Blues Before Sunrise, Shady Lane, Mean Mistreater Mama* or *Prison Bound*.

Many trips were arranged for the two bluesmen and they appeared often in Louisville, Cincinnati, Nashville and St Louis. When they went to Chicago they stayed on Prairie Avenue at 4746 and being renowned for their records were soon known to the many bluesmen there. When the Depression temporarily ended their recordings, they played at the Booker T. Washington Theatre or Charles Turpin's Jazzland Club in St Louis, and were among the first blues artists to be recorded when money began to flow again. But it was a hard, reckless life and both men drank bad whisky in vast quantities; Leroy Carr's liver was deteriorating and he was suffering acute pain which he attempted to drown by drinking still more. On the night of 28th April 1935, he was attending an all-night party when he suffered a severe attack of nephritis. Reportedly he had earlier had a slight argument with Scrapper and the guitarist wasn't with him. By the morning he was dead and his old companion was heartbroken. Leroy Carr was one of the best loved of all blues singers and he was widely mourned.

It was a shock which Scrapper Blackwell never got over and, though he obtained work in an asphalt plant for a while, he soon succumbed to alcohol. He lived on for nearly thirty years before being murdered in an Indianapolis side-street, but though he recorded for a few collector labels his active life was virtually over. Many blues singers were profoundly influenced by the Carr and Blackwell team. One was Amos Easton – 'Bumble Bee Slim' – another was Bill Gaither, who called himself 'Leroy's Buddy'. Still another was Turner Parrish, and the influence of Leroy Carr is to be heard in the work of singers like Champion Jack Dupree, Rhinehart and Stubblefield, or Mercy Dee Walton, pianists who came from Louisiana, Alabama and Texas – far beyond the territory normally worked by Carr and Blackwell. Not only is it a testimony to the esteem with which they were held among other blues singers – it was also an indication of the potency of the recording medium.

Hard Time Everywhere

'Who first thought of getting out Race records for the Race? Okeh, that's right. Genuine Race artists make genuine Blues for Okeh . . . It's a cheerful day, folks for everybody,' bragged the General Phonograph Corporation when it published the *Blue Book of Blues* to introduce the singers on the Okeh label. Ralph Peer, recording manager to the firm, who had already conceived the term 'Hillbilly', admitted in 1938 that the company had 'records by all foreign groups: German records, Swedish records, Polish records, but we were afraid to advertise Negro records, so I listed them as "Race" records and they are still known as that.' How Perry Bradford persuaded Fred Hager to record Mamie Smith instead of Sophie Tucker singing his compositions *That Thing Called Love* and *You Can't Keep a Good Man Down* is a much retold story, especially by Bradford himself. He had 'greased my neck with goose grease every morning, so it would come easy to bow and scrape to some recording managers', he claimed in his autobiography but the important thing was that an African American woman had at last, in February 1920, been recorded. Sales were phenomenal, and secured for her another recording date in August that year when *Crazy Blues*, a Bradford composition on a traditional theme, was made. Mamie Smith, said Alberta Hunter, 'made it possible for all of us, with her recording of *Crazy Blues*, the *first* blues record.'

Okeh's success with Mamie Smith's initial issues, which were selling 75,000 copies a month, encouraged other record firms to employ black talent. In August 1920 the Arto firm recorded Lucille Hegamin, in March the following year Lillyn Brown recorded for Emerson and in May Alberta Hunter made her first sides for Black Swan, a short-lived company operated by black partners Harry Pace and W. C. Handy. In September 1921 Columbia followed with Edith

Wilson, still making no departure from the established principle that 'Blues' was sung by women vaudeville and jazz entertainers. Though the majority of these singers were southern-born, they brought little blues feeling to the songs which were 'composed' blues written by Perry Bradford, Clarence Williams, Spencer Williams and other professional writers. The companies addressed the audiences as they considered appropriate: 'we're tellin' you there's none finer or grander when it comes to warblin' mean and hot low-down ravagin' Blues until you don't know whether your sensations is your wigglin' spine or if your spine has got the wigglin' blues,' was the claim for Sara Martin.

It was not until Bessie Smith's recording of *Down Hearted Blues* in February 1923 that the authentic voice of the blues was heard on record. The composition was one which had been recorded by Alberta Hunter with her pianist Lovie Austin and Bessie Smith's version was deliberately designed to 'cut' her. Throughout her recording career Bessie Smith took the songs that had been made famous by other women singers and made vastly superior ones herself; it seems to have been a weakness in her personality that she always had to reassure herself of her own stature by 'carving' other singers. Only once did she apply her ruthless technique to 'Ma' Rainey and then she made *Moonshine Blues* and *Bo Weevil Blues*, the two themes that Rainey considered her 'signature tunes'. On this occasion she did fail to exceed her rival. Ma Rainey first recorded in the December of that year for Paramount, who had earlier made titles with two other southern women blues singers – Lottie Beaman and Lucille Bogan. She recorded prolifically with the company until 1928; Bessie Smith remained with Columbia until 1931. But though these major 'Classic' singers were extensively recorded, the potential of the southern rural singers, and particularly the male blues guitarists and pianists was slow in being recognised. As early as November 1923 Sylvester Weaver had made a few soli on guitar and in April the following year a *Barrel House Blues* was made in Atlanta by one Ed Andrews, singing and playing guitar. Yet it was not until August 1924 that Papa Charlie Jackson, the minstrel-show ragtime banjo player from New Orleans, opened up the market by recording his *Papa's Lawdy Lawdy Blues* and *Airy Man Blues* (actually, 'Hairy man'). There was a veiled sexual implication in the latter title; the next recording, *Salt Lake City Blues* was even more daring. Salt Lake City was Mormon, and Blacks, as was well-known, were unwelcome.

Goin' back to Salt Lake City, ain't no place for me (2)
Goin' back to Salt Lake City where the women won't
    let me be.

You have a wife in the mornin', Lord a wife at night (2)
And always a substitute to take her place (if) she's out
    of sight.

I'm leavin' here tonight if I have to ride the blinds (2)
Take a freight train special, tell the engineer 'Lose no time'.

Now the jinx all on me all over this town (2)
That's the reason why I'm Salt Lake City bound.

Papa Charlie Jackson was available in Chicago to make recordings of the Southern blues. But Paramount, 'The Popular Race Record' label operated by the New York Recording Laboratory, an improbable subsidiary of the Wisconsin Chair Company, was intent on getting new talent. 'There is always room for more good material and more talented artists,' it stated, introducing J. Mayo Williams, its black Recording Manager, and soliciting suggestions. Paramount's recording conditions were primitive, its record surfaces deplorable, but it discovered through its talent scout Arthur Laibley and others, folk blues singers of outstanding calibre. They were brought to Chicago and thence to Port Washington, Wisconsin, to record, but when Okeh and Columbia sought authentic blues talent, they employed scouts to seek out the artists and arrange for them to be on location – in St Louis, Memphis, Dallas, Atlanta, or New Orleans according to the tour. Columbia's tours commenced in November 1926 when Peg Leg Howell was first recorded and ceased with the last of Barbecue Bob's 56 recorded titles, when the effect of the Depression was felt, late in 1930.

It is obvious that many factors conditioned the availability of singers in the South – the recording units stayed only a few days in any of the principal cities on their tour and did not return for another year or so. With the reluctance of some to record, the unreliability of others, the taste and selection methods of the talent scouts – Dan Hornsby in Atlanta, R. T. Ashford in Dallas or H. C. Speir in Jackson, Mississippi, for example – the factors which decided whether an artist was ever heard on record or not were manifold. But to the talent scouts must go the credit for having discovered so many blues singers in the periods when they were being largely neglected by the folk-lorists. All the major recording blues singers of the 'twenties were located in the space of five years. Blind Lemon Jefferson was first recorded in 1926, Texas Alexander in 1927, Tommy Johnson in 1928, Charley Patton in 1929, Willie Brown and Son House in 1930. Jefferson's records sold in great numbers and revealed the extent of the southern market. He was, moreover, exceptionally talented, with a gift for original composition. From the recording point of view this was important for there was a demand for 'new' blues rather than repetitions of old ones. Even a singer like Tommy Johnson used a limited repertoire of traditional verses which he re-arranged when he sang. In performance this may hardly have mattered; on record it could have been spread very thinly indeed. Jefferson had the advantage also of having recorded first relatively 'early', i.e. in 1926, and had built up a large and appreciative audience. What might have happened in the 'thirties: whether his appeal would have faded or whether he could have adapted himself to changing tastes remains totally conjectural – for in 1930 Blind Lemon died of a heart attack in a snowstorm in Chicago. 'My friends,' preached Reverend Emmett Dickinson in a remarkable recorded sermon on the *Death of Blind Lemon* soon after, 'Blind Lemon Jefferson is dead, and the world today is in mourning over this loss. So we feel, our loss is Heaven's gain. Big men, educated men and great men, when they pass on to their eternal home in the sky – they command our respects. But when a man that we truly love for the kindness and inspiration they have given us in our upper-most hearts pass on to their rewards we feel there is a vacancy in our hearts that will never be replaced.'

Blues singers of the stature of Blind Lemon Jefferson became the new black folk heroes through the recording medium. Phonographs like the 1920s model Victor Talking Machine brought their voices into private homes. Recording had become the communication medium for African Americans both literate and illiterate. Though the *Defender* and the *Amsterdam News* reached large audiences, the blues records conveyed the feelings and experiences of ordinary men. It may appear that too much importance is laid on the recorded singer, and for the analysis of local traditions this is undoubtedly true. But the record industry brought the blues into countless homes, made the names of singers familiar in households; their music was shared for dancing and entertainment by countless thousands who might never see or hear them personally, and the content of the blues lyrics spoke for the black masses.

'Favorite hits you will enjoy,' ran the legend over such titles as *'Lectric Chair Blues* and *See That My Grave is Kept Clean* with no apparent humour intended. 'Whether you go on a "Blue Monday" or a joy-full Saturday night you'll find here exactly the record to please you, made just as carefully, and wonderfully, as all other Victor Records are – and by members of your own Race. And nobody needs to tell you that *they know how*,' a supplement advertising Tommy Johnson's *Maggie Campbell Blues* and the Memphis Jug Band's *Bob Lee Junior Blues* appealed. 'Blues that seem to know just how you feel,' ran the legend advertising Blind Willie McTell's *Mamma, Tain't Long Fo' Day*. Patronising they might appear, but six years had passed since *Mama Whip, Mama Spank*; *Sax-O-Phoney Blues* or *I Want a jazzy kiss* were being sung by Lucille Hegamin and Mamie Smith and the companies had a much clearer idea of what the black market wanted. Paramount Records asked for suggestions; they sold records by mail order. Victor tried crude caricature to advertise. Vocalion gave coupons with Memphis Minnie records, which could be exchanged for a portable phonograph.

But the market was really an illusion – there were many markets and the companies were trying to meet them all. In the most rural areas travelling salesmen were marketing victrolas and table model phonographs maintaining an after-sales service of records; in the cities the drug-stores and furniture stores sold the discs and lines formed outside them as the new releases appeared. So it was possible to meet local needs and increasing confidence was being placed in local black distributors – men like Jesse Johnson in St Louis, who was married to blues singer Edith Johnson and who operated the De Luxe Music shop. He was enterprising enough to hire a plane to shower leaflets announcing the latest issues on the baseball crowds and kept an eye open for fresh talent. It was possible to sell discs of locally recorded artists in their home districts, but outside their immediate areas there were problems – sometimes the extreme parochialism of the singers and their blues made them of little interest in other districts or in the North.

Newly arrived migrants provided a special market and one that became increasingly important. They required both a reminder of their home background and reassurance in their new and unfamiliar environment. They wanted to feel in touch with their friends and at the same time be urban and sophisticated. Lonnie Johnson was the sort of singer who met their needs. He had won the talent contest for blues singers organised by Jesse Johnson in St Louis in 1925 which earned him a seven-year contract with Okeh. His command of a number of instruments and unending stream of blues themes made him an ideal recording artist, while his clean, limpid guitar and sweet-toned voice with a Louisiana vibrato had the fortunate combination of southern inflections with an urbane, disarming delivery. Lonnie's blues were sometimes arch, often insinuating and occasionally straightforward and sincere. His shrewd appraisal of his audiences enabled him to offer a *double-entendre* song with panache but, when he wished, he could compose a blues of immediate relevance and social content.

> I want to go back to Helena, the high water's got me barred, (2)
> I woke up early this mornin', high water all in my backyard.
>
> They want me to work on the levee I had to leave my home, (2)
> I was so scared the levee might break, Lord and I may drown.
>
> The police run me from Cairo all through Arkansas, (2)
> Then put me in jail, behind those cold iron bars.
>
> The police they say 'work, fight or go to jail', I say 'I ain't
>   totin' no sack' (2)
> And I ain't buildin' no levee, the planks is on the ground, and I ain't
>   drivin' no nails.'

He made eight recordings on the theme of floods.

In 1927 Lonnie Johnson came to Chicago but he was soon on tour again, travelling as far as Texas and then making his way north once more to Cleveland, Ohio. In 1929 he settled in Chicago and attempted to make a living working in night clubs. The Depression interrupted his career and for five years he worked in coal mines, on the railroad and in a steel-mill, but resumed his club work as soon as he was able to secure employment. His style of singing did not change substantially and, though in his sixties he recorded little, he probably had a longer active career than any other blues singer.

A singer with a career on record almost as long as Lonnie Johnson's was Tampa Red. As a young man he was billed as 'The Guitar Wizard' and his deft use of the slide and clear, ringing tones merited the description. Tampa Red was born in Atlanta, Georgia in 1904, but his childhood was mainly spent in Tampa, Florida. His name was Hudson Woodbridge, but he took the name of his grandmother, Whittaker. Like many singers of his generation he was in Chicago by the mid-'twenties and trying to earn some money on the side from his guitar playing. His break came when he worked a short stint with Ma Rainey and made his first acquaintanceship with Georgia Tom Dorsey. Thomas A. Dorsey was born near Atlanta in 1899 and as a lanky youth learned to play piano from listening to a number of unrecorded pianists in the city, whom he remembered as Soap Stick,

Nome Burkes, Long Boy, Lark Lee and Charlie Spann. Playing for suppers and Saturday night functions, he was earning as much as $1.50 for a night's work – quite a lot for a pianist even if it hardly kept him eating. When he was about nineteen he moved to Gary, Indiana, to work in the steel mills but, weighing less than nine stone, he was scarcely able to cope with the work and instead built up a small band and played increasingly for parties. In Georgia he was 'Barrel House Tom'; now he was 'Georgia Tom' but though his music was blues he joined the Pilgrim Baptist church and took lessons in composing and arranging. After a spell in Chicago with Les Hite's Whispering Syncopators he joined Ma Rainey, organised her band for her, and with Ed Pollack on trumpet and Al Wynn on trombone, took it on tour.

One of Ma Rainey's last recording sessions, in September 1928, was made with Georgia Tom on piano and Tampa Red on guitar. Tampa Red had a little song which he wanted set to music, but it coincided with Georgia Tom's determination to devote his energies to the church and to the writing of 'gospel songs'. Eventually Tampa talked him round to writing out the tune of *Tight Like That* and they recorded it together for Vocalion. The first royalty cheque was for $2,400.19 – and Georgia Tom put off the day when he abandoned 'Race' music. It was the first of a highly successful series of issues which reflected and perhaps exploited the anxieties and optimisms of the new migrants. The homesick were to find support:

I'm a stranger here just blowed in your town (2)
Just because I'm a stranger everybody want to dog me round.

I wonder how can some people dog a poor stranger so, (2)
They should remember they goin' to reap what they sow.

I'm goin' back south if I wear out ninety-nine pair o'shoes, (2)
Then I know I'll be welcome an' I won't have the stranger's blues.

But those who had made the adjustment to urban living had their confidence bolstered by 'hokum' recordings. A minstrel show term for good-natured guying of simple folkways, 'hokum' played on the city-dweller's ambivalent mixture of condescension and nostalgia for the more innocent pleasures of rural life. Tampa Red's Hokum Jug Band or the Hokum Boys, whose personnel varied considerably but which commenced with Tampa Red and Georgia Tom singing *Beedle-Um-Bum* and *Sellin' That Stuff* were comic, ribbing 'good-time' groups who used guitars, piano, kazoo, string bass, clarinet even, in imitation of the country string bands, but with an urban sophistication. The Hokum Boys, the Hokum Trio, the Famous Hokum Boys, the Harum Scarums, the Hokum Jug Band were among the many groups of this kind. When Georgia Tom gave up the blues in 1932 and devoted his energies to the writing of gospel songs, Tampa Red continued to work and record, developing his 'Chicago Five' with Black Bob playing piano, Arnett Nelson or another musician often playing clarinet and, by the mid-'thirties, Willie B. James playing guitar.

Willie B. James, who came from Duck Hill, Mississippi, modelled himself on the Famous Hokum Boys' lead guitarist, Big Bill Broonzy, who also worked with Georgia Tom. Broonzy was born in June 1893 in Scott, Mississippi, but was taken by his family to Arkansas when he was a child. Though he played a home-made cigar-box fiddle and learned many songs from his older relatives, he did not play blues until he came to Chicago in 1920. There he claimed to have been taught guitar by Papa Charlie Jackson, the banjo-player. With the exception of one or two isolated sides in the preceeding few years, he was thirty-seven before he recorded at all extensively in 1930 and by this time he was an accomplished guitar player, capable of playing rag and dance pieces like *Saturday Night Rub* or *Guitar Rag* as well as orthodox blues. His many recordings with Frank Brasswell playing second guitar, with Georgia Tom and others, were frequently in the hokum vein and established a strain through his work which in the later 'thirties was heard in the stomps and fast 'jive' tunes of his Chicago Five. Ribald like *Good Jelly* or *Flat Foot Susie with her Flat Yes Yes* they were 'good-time music', unpretentious and confident, with rolling boogie-woogie piano from Joshua Altheimer or Black Bob and 'gaspipe' clarinet or sax played by Buster Bennett or Bill Osborn.

But there was another side of Big Bill which was expressed in a large number of slow and medium-paced blues recordings, poignant and unaffected. In his voice could be heard a quality that recalled the field holler and an authority that suggested the city-dweller. Both were present because his life was spent between his Chicago home and his Arkansas farm, and with his continued contact with both rural and urban living, Broonzy sang of each with feeling. His guitar playing made extensive use of choked notes and 'hammering-on' the strings within the framework of a rocking, swinging beat. When he sang, he seemed to cry; he had the intonation of Leroy Carr with much of the effortless instrumental technique of Scrapper Blackwell.

Look like everybody, mama got a friend but me (2)
I'm a poor boy, baby, mama good as I can be.

Baby when I'm happy, my friends are happy too (2)
So now I have fell in bad luck, mama what am I going to do?

Babe I'm motherless and I'm fatherless, sister- and brotherless too (2)
Baby today I'm so blue baby, I don't know what to do.

Big Bill was neither motherless nor sisterless, but he sang for those who were. When Leroy Carr died, he largely took his place in creating urban folk blues that yet appealed to a larger, and up to a point, unknown audience. But he had established himself as an individual artist long before, and when recording resumed after the worst days of the Depression, Big Bill and Leroy Carr were both among the first to be reinstated as artists.

The Great Depression marks a watershed in blues. Inevitably African Americans suffered worst when the stock market crash of 1929 brought the subsequent downhill tumble of the entire national economy. A quarter of the nation's total labour force was out of work by the summer of 1932 – twelve million unemployed. Of these a substantial proportion were black. They stood in rows in the breadlines, drank in silence in the soup kitchens, put newspapers inside their jackets to keep out the bitter cold of the Chicago winter. In the south, cotton prices dropped to a few cents a pound and unemployment was widespread. But the weather was warmer and the south was home; thousands streamed slowly back. Those that remained lived in unheated rooms, or in the shanty-town 'Hoovervilles' that sprang up on the outskirts of the cities. One of the very few recordings made in 1933, in the heart of the Depression told in the words of 'Joe Stone' (probably J. D. Short) the feelings of an unemployed black man.

And it's hard time here, hard time everywhere (3)

I went down to the factory where I worked years,
I went down to the factory where I worked for years ago,
And the boss man tol' me 'Man I ain't hirin' here no mo'.

And we have a little city that they call down in Hooverville (2)
Times have got so hard people, they ain't got no place to live.

In the same year, 1933, the Federal Emergency Relief Administration was established with $500,000,000 to dispose in grants-in-aid to state agencies to help them with their relief programmes, a dollar being given for every three being spent from state funds. Many States resented an alleged implication that they could not manage their own affairs, while their officials showed a reluctance to help black people with relief. One singer, Carl Martin, expressed it this way:

> Now I'm gettin' tired of sittin' around,
> I ain't makin' a dime, just wearing my shoe-soles down,
> (refrain) Now everybody's cryin' 'Let's have a New Deal'
>   Cause I've got to make a livin' if I have to rob and steal.
>
> Now you go to your workhouse, put in your complaint,
> Eight times out of ten, you know, they'll say 'I cain't . . .
>
> They don't want to give you no dough, won't hardly pay
>   your rent,
> And it ain't costin' them one dog-gone cent . . .
>
> Now I ain't made a dime since they closed down the mill,
> I'm sittin' right here waitin' on that brand New Deal.

Carl Martin, who was born in 1906, moved from Knoxville, Tennessee to Chicago in 1932; his blues was one of many which directly reflected the bitterness of the Depression and its aftermath. To President Roosevelt the greatest danger in the relief programme lay in the damage to self-respect for the unemployed in having to join the breadlines and receive handouts without being engaged in work. There were many agencies, the Red Cross among them, which undertook the work of giving aid to the hungry, but many Blacks who recalled the armed and segregated Red Cross camps during the Mississippi floods of 1927 regarded them with suspicion. Blues singer Walter Roland, equally accomplished on piano or guitar and in this case playing the latter instrument, spoke for those who found themselves obliged to accept charity handouts and 'Red Cross rice'.

> Says you know I'm gonna sing this here verse now an'
>   I soon ain't gonna sing no more
> Cause my wife an' children is hungry
>   An' speck' I'm goin' have to go
> And holler 'Oh . . .' Great Lord I'm goin' have to go,
> Says you know I just must go home and get my crocus-sack
> Go down to that Red Cross Store.

But you know one thing is certain that
  All these people see,
Red Cross don't give you everything you want,
  But they'll give you somethin' you need,
I told 'em 'No . . .'
Great Lord, says I can't go,
Says you know I cannot go to hill
I've gotta go to Red Cross Store.

In the post-Depression years, African Americans seemed to need to be given the assurance that their economic and social stresses were shared and understood, and if no one else could give it without appearing condescending, the blues singer could. The blues in this period was sometimes less rich musically than it had been hitherto, but the content of the verses, which mattered greatly to those who bought the discs, was of more immediate social relevance that at any previous time. There was also more experiment in the blues form, with verse and refrain and extended recitative blues becoming popular. There were blues on unemployment, on the Public Works Administration and the Works Projects Administration which provided employment schemes under Federal control; there were blues about high rents and low wages; blues on shootings and razor cuttings, on chain gangs and penitentiaries; there were blues about gambling and prostitution; blues about broken homes, infidelity, leaving men and forsaken women. There were blues about migration – of hoboes on the railroads and tramps on the highways. Blues about superstition and folk beliefs, blues which persisted in the cities; blues about hair straightening, about colour stratification, about beauty aids and physical features – the singers' lack of sophistication often expressed itself in those subjects which would have been anathema to the National Association for the Advancement of Colored People. There were blues, too, about sickness – tuberculosis, pneumonia, pellagra; blues about the death of wives and parents, stated sometimes with a chilling acceptance and inevitability. Disasters were often reported in similar words of fatalism – floods, hurricanes, tornadoes, conflagrations:

If your house catch on fire and there ain't no water round, (2)
Throw your gal out the window and let the shack burn down.

became commonplace.

It would seem that many blues were basically accommodative, helping both the singer and the listener to adjust to a situation over

which he had no control. Poll taxes made universal suffrage a joke –
Taxes on my Pole became an ironic sexual pun in the blues. Always
the themes, however large in conception or universal in experience,
were personalised: the singer composed his blues for the individual.
Heroes were rare – President Roosevelt or Joe Louis perhaps; other
blues singers. The death of Leroy Carr or Bessie Smith meant far more
in the blues than the activities of politicians. Blues singers spoke for
the black masses, not for N.A.A.C.P. leaders or lawyers or writers or
African American intellectuals. The blues singer did not campaign for
Civil Rights, he did not give statistics. Instead he spoke as one of the
numerals in the statisticians' tables.

As a folk song of protest, the blues was seldom outspoken, at least
on record. Sometimes a verse was addressed to 'Mister Charlie',
sometimes there was a guarded line about 'the white man' but
more direct targets were avoided or discouraged by the record
companies. Black self-assertiveness found expression instead in sexual
themes. Above all other subjects there is in blues a preponderance
of lyrics about sexual love, or merely sex. A complex language of
metaphors, often domestic or culinary, camouflaged a multitude of
sexual references. 'I want my biscuits in the daytime and my jelly
at night,' declares one singer. 'My stove's in good condition, this is
the stove to brown your bread,' his woman replies. A swaggering
list of the singer's physical attributes was common, with women no
less than with men. 'I'm a big fat woman with meat shakin' on the
bone, and every time I shake it a skinny woman leaves her home.'
Sexual virtuosity is the subject of scores of blues and the singer played
a game with the censor and hence with 'the Man' when he sang *The
Dirty Dozen* or *Shave 'Em Dry*. His words were heavily bowdlerised
but were clear enough to his listeners. Sometimes a more specific
code would be used – the number combinations of the 'policy
racket' – a kind of 'housey-housey' – in which the figures 3–6–9
would mean excreta or 4–11–44 would mean a phallus. In his sexual
prowess, real or imagined, a man could realise himself; he knew and
asserted the maturity which segregation and race legislation deprived
him of within the total society. In sexual blues the spirit of revolt
was canalised; the blues singer did not care whether he or she was
fitting popular stereotypes: 'I'm blue, black, and I'm evil; and I did
not make myself,' Alice Moore declared.

Chicago Breakdown

To what extent did the blues singers live the lives about which they sang; how much of the blues as known on record was based on personal experience? There is a reluctance expressed in some writings on blues to accept the reality of the subjects which appear in blues lyrics, a reluctance that may arise from guilt that the conditions portrayed have been permitted. Conversely there is a tendency to glamorise and to find some romantic appeal in the life depicted. The lives of blues singers were frequently hard and the conditions of crushing poverty too brutal to assume a romantic aura. 'Maybe it wasn't exactly then but I had the experience of these things. You find it's easier to tell the truth about your life so you sing about it,' Henry Townsend commented, explaining that his blues were drawn from incidents within his own life or the compass of his immediate knowledge.

In fact there was little chance for the majority of blues singers to escape the lives they described; by 1935 literally half the black families in the North were living on relief, but still the cities attracted more from the South although the disillusioned trickled back. Ghettoes burst at the seams, 'hot-bed' apartments operated on a shift basis with one family taking over from another for eight hours' use of bed and room, 'kitchenettes' offered the minimum of facilities in conditions of appalling squalor. Under such conditions crime was rife, prostitution was a commonplace, the courts filled on Friday nights and weekends with delinquents pulled almost at random off the streets. They could not take the processes of law seriously and short terms of imprisonment were shrugged off as an occupational hazard in the business of survival.

Under ghetto conditions tempers were easily frayed, arguments were settled swiftly and often viciously; underworld criminals wielded considerable power. Blacks who sought advancement or esteem but who were denied recognition and responsibility within the total society could gain them through crime or through the cult churches. Or they could become blues singers with a contract to a record company and engagement in a club. Some who played music casually found the chance of professional playing virtually thrust on them; others who sought to establish themselves as regularly employed blues singers often failed to do so. The struggle to gain work, to eat and to raise a family was sometimes too much to cope with, and many blues singers, like other jobless rootless men, took to the highways.

At the most mundane, many blues singers worked for the W.P.A., the Works Projects Administration, while scores at one time or another had been on relief. Everyday conditions in the ghetto, which constantly recur in the blues, were shared by countless singers. But even the more extreme and dramatic circumstances were to be found in the lives of some of them: Leadbelly, Son House, Robert Pete Williams, Bukka White and Muddy Waters's guitarist, Pat Hare, are among those who had served sentences for homicide; Noah Lewis, Scrapper Blackwell, Charley Jordan, Pine Top Smith, Buster Pickens and Little Walter among those who died from stabbings, shootings or 'muggings'. Blind Arvella Gray was blinded by being shot in the face, Blind Boy Fuller by lye water, Peg Leg Howell maimed by shooting. Henry Brown was a policy racketeer, Kokomo Arnold was a bootlegger, Peter Clayton and Tommy McClennan were alcoholics. Lightnin' Hopkin's ankles bore the scars of chain gang shackles; the lives of many blues singers bore the scars of indifference, suppression and segregation. But against a grim catalogue must be placed the relatively uneventful life of a Roosevelt Sykes, the quiet dignity of a Mance Lipscomb or a Mississippi John Hurt. There were some blues singers who carved out a career in another field like Black Ace, who became a photographer, or Sam Price who became a Harlem politician; some who gave up the blues and turned to the church like Skip James or Rube Lacey or Ishman Bracey. Some were temperamentally unsuited to make such an adjustment, others never had the opportunity. What was remarkable was that, however complex the circumstances or repressing the conditions of living, so many had the creative ability and the artistic stature to develop a folk music of such richness from such experience.

Blues singers, through their blues, offered an indication of the hopes and fears of black people, sometimes their anger and sometimes their apathy. There was in the blues a gauge of the frustration within the African American community, had anyone cared to listen or to consider what they heard. But blues singers sang for the 'Race' audience exclusively in the 'twenties and 'thirties and not even the black political organisations chose to listen. In the 'thirties Blacks required of the blues singer and his records the confirmation that they were not alone.

From the point of view of the record company it was preferable to have singers who were relatively stable and reliable, but they also wanted artists whose lyric inventiveness was such that they could meet the demands of the consumer market. In the uncertain years following the depth of the Depression they had a tendency to concentrate on 'star' names, building up the reputations of a limited number of singers rather than seeking out the wide range of talent to be found in the pre-Depression catalogues of the Paramount, Gennett, Okeh and Columbia companies. To a certain extent the 'star' blues singers who were drawn from the urban folk communities of Chicago and St Louis replaced the somewhat effete and stage-directed 'classic singers' of minor calibre whose work ended with the Depression. However, there were other factors at work. The classic blues singers and vaudeville entertainers were featured largely on stage or in café-cabarets like the Elites on State Street. Boogie-woogie pianists and urban folk singers played largely under cover in the speakeasies and rent-parties of the 'twenties. Such city clubs as were open were either 'dry', or they were clandestine and could not easily advertise the singers who were appearing in them.

In December 1933 all this changed. An amendment repealing Federal Prohibition was ratified and states were left to decide their own liquor legislation. This meant that in Chicago and other northern cities clubs where liquor was served could be opened freely. In the black sectors this meant work for the blues singers who provided the entertainment in them. The clubs advertised the singers who were being featured and both they and the record companies found it advantageous to employ 'name' singers. Big Bill Broonzy, Leroy Carr, Tampa Red, Lonnie Johnson, Peetie Wheatstraw, Walter Davis and many other were in wide demand. Walter Davis, like Roosevelt Sykes and St Louis Jimmy, was frequently on tour and as the 'thirties advanced, some blues singers took their own shows on the road. Some of the older blues singers were doing this too – Ida Cox, for example, who had left the legitimate stage and toured throughout the South with her travelling tent show when most of her contemporaries had retired; or Charles Cow Cow Davenport who hit the road with 'Cow Cow's Chicago Steppers'. But his 'old-style' music was less in demand; he was stranded in Florida and had to pawn his bus in 1935;

a year or two later he was in jail in Camp Kilby, Alabama, where he contracted pneumonia and lost the use of his right arm. The crowds were looking to the younger singers and the new recording blues men whose songs were more topical and technique more urbane. They liked Peetie Wheatstraw for his arrogant, insolent manner and lazy disregard for enunciation; they liked Leroy Carr for the melancholy in his voice and the poetry of his words; they liked Big Bill for the confident authority of his singing. When Leroy Carr died, there were several singers to step into his shoes. One was 'Bumble Bee Slim'.

Amos Easton – Bumble Bee Slim – was born in Georgia in 1905 and, after running away from home with a travelling show, hoboed to Indianapolis where he arrived in 1928. He had a voice not dissimilar to Leroy Carr's and was an inventive writer of blues lyrics. Though he made a few titles with Carr and Scrapper Blackwell accompanying in 1932, it was not until 1934 that he began recording steadily, making over a hundred and fifty titles in the space of three years. A large number were made for the Decca label, owned by Jack and Dave Kapp who had already several years' experience in the 'Race' record business and who retained Mayo Williams from the now defunct Paramount company as their principal talent scout. He was also contracted to Lester Melrose, one of two brothers who had also been involved in the Race record business and who was then managing for Vocalion – Bumble Bee Slim ended up making records for both companies. A poor guitarist himself, he was accompanied by Big Bill Broonzy, Charlie Segar, Memphis Minnie and Peetie Wheatstraw on some of his titles and by Bill Gaither on quite a few. Gaither himself came from Louisville where he owned a radio shop and record store. He became friendly with Leroy Carr and with his pianist Honey Hill made a large number of sides as 'Leroy's Buddy', commencing to record some months after his friend's death.

For southern listeners Bumble Bee Slim and Bill Gaither may have lacked strength in their work, though it is not without interest that such themes as Bumble Bee's *Sail On, Little Girl, Sail On* or Gaither's *Rocky Mountain Blues* fed back into the folk tradition through the distribution of their recordings. More brittle in sound was the singing of James 'Kokomo' Arnold. Born in Lovejoy's Station, Georgia, in February 1901, Kokomo Arnold learned to play guitar from an unrecorded singer named John Wiggs. He developed a technique generally associated with Shreveport and West Louisiana, playing his guitar flat across his knees and using a slide with fast finger-picking to produce a flurry of whining, singing notes. His *Milk Cow Blues* and *Old Original Kokomo Blues* were startling virtuoso pieces which immediately established him as an exceptional artist. In 1919 Arnold moved to Buffalo and later worked in the steel mills of Pittsburgh and Gary. In 1929 he moved to Chicago but the following year found him in Memphis where, as 'Gitfiddle Jim' he made a couple of recordings which did not 'take' like his later ones did. Arnold frequently worked 'gigs' with Peetie Wheatstraw, travelling to Pittsburgh with him, and though he was reticent about his life, he is known to have travelled in Mississippi and to have worked in Jackson. Perhaps it was there that he developed his use of the falsetto, but his glottal hum sung in tune with his guitar was very much his own. Often he employed traditional verses but shaped them in an original way.

> Now I'm goin' to get me a picket, right off-a my back
> fence (2)
> And I'm go'n whup my woman clean until she learn some
> sense.

> Now you know I'm your manager and you sure got to obey
> my rules (2)
> Says you ain't no schoolgirl, you sure God ain't nobody's
> fool.

> Now you sing just like Moses, walk just like the Good Lord
> above (2)
> I done had a gang o' women, but you the only one I really
> love.

It was Joe McCoy who induced Mayo Williams to record Kokomo Arnold, rather against the singer's will. Born near Jackson, Mississippi where he and his brother Charlie McCoy were active members of the group that centred on Tommy Johnson, Ishman Bracey and the Chatman family, Wilber 'Joe' McCoy was an excellent guitarist. His blues recordings under a number of colourful pseudonyms – Kansas Joe, Georgia Pine Boy, Mississippi Mudder and Hallelujah Joe among them – often popularised country themes, but McCoy's musicianship was not in doubt. The two brothers joined the Harlem Hamfats, a hokum band which was organised by the New Orleans trumpeter and brother of Lizzie Miles and Edna Hicks, Herb 'Kid' Morand. Formed in 1936 the Hamfats – with Joe McCoy now singing the ribald vocals under the name of 'Hamfoot Ham' – had a driving swing and a blues-hokum based repertoire which included such novelties as *Black Gal, You Better Use Your Head* and Tampa Red's *Let's Get Drunk and Truck*. At one stage in his career Joe McCoy had been married to

Memphis Minnie and together they produced a remarkable series of guitar duets with one or both taking vocals, which were a worthy continuation of the Dan Sane and Frank Stokes tradition.

Minnie Douglas was born in Algiers, Louisiana, across the river from New Orleans, in June 1897. At the age of seven she moved to Walls, Mississippi, some fourteen miles from Memphis and three years later her father bought her a banjo. Within a few years she had become an accomplished banjo and guitar player and at the age of fifteen was singing on the streets of Memphis under the name of 'Kid Douglas'. In 1916 she joined the Ringling Brothers Circus in Clarksdale, Mississippi and travelled all over the South with the company for several years. When she eventually returned to Memphis, she married a member of the Memphis Jug Band, 'Casey Bill' Weldon, from Pine Bluff, Arkansas, who was some nine years her junior. 'Casey Bill' – his nickname was a contraction of 'Kansas City Bill' – was a slide guitarist who played a steel guitar and was billed as 'The Hawaiian Guitar Wizard'. His own work was uneven but later he had a hokum band which he called 'The Brown Bombers of Swing' in unabashed reflected glory from Joe Louis, as well as working with Peetie Wheatstraw, Black Bob and Charlie McCoy in Chicago. His relationship with Minnie Douglas did not last long – perhaps because of the disparity in their ages – and in 1929 she married Joe McCoy. 'Memphis Minnie' was working for dimes in Beale Street barber shops, singing to the clientele when she was heard by a Columbia talent scout. As 'Kansas Joe' and 'Memphis Minnie' they worked together continuously for the next six years and recorded extensively. Memphis Minnie's voice was loud and as strong as a man's. With the features of a school mistress that belied her tough personality and with a formidable guitar technique she was an outstanding blues personality, and in the opinion of many the finest female blues singer outside the Classic idiom. The records that she made with Kansas Joe were among her best, with one guitar playing a bass line and the other playing arpeggios around it. In later years she suffered a stroke, forewarnings of which, in what she termed with irony, the 'Memphis Minnie-jitis', she may have had long before.

> I came in home one Saturday night pull off all my clothes
>   an' I lie down (2)
> And that mornin' just 'bout day the meningitis begin
>   to creep around.

My head and neck was painin' me, seem like my back
   was break in two (2)
Lord I had such a mood that mornin' I don't know
   what in the world to do.

My companion take me to the doctor, 'Doctor please tell
   me my wife's complaint' (2)
The doctor looked down on me, shook his head, said
   'I wouldn't mind tellin' you son, but I cain't.

You take her roun' to the City Hospital just as quick,
   quick as you possible can (2)
Because the condition's she's in now, you will never get her
   back home 'live again'.

After moving to Chicago in the early 'thirties, Memphis Minnie
was one of the city's best-known blues singers and her 'Blue
Monday parties' every week were celebrated, as well as providing
an opportunity for younger singers to show their paces. She married
Ernest 'Lil Son Joe' Lawlers, a competent guitarist with whom she
played and recorded many duets. Their union was lasting in spite
of Minnie's aggressive treatment of her partner. They returned to
Memphis in the 1950s, where Son Joe died in 1961 and where Minnie
died twelve years later, in poverty. There were few other women
singers to compare with Memphis Minnie in Chicago, and hardly any
who played their own accompaniment. One who did was Georgia
White from Sandersville, Georgia, west of Macon. She was singing
with Jimmy Noone's Orchestra at the Apex Club, Chicago as early as
1929. She had a strong voice and played good piano, though Richard
M. Jones often accompanied her in later years. On *You Done Lost Your
Good Thing Now* her voice had considerable range and a tough quality
appropriate to the content of her lyrics. Georgia White's blues were
extremely urban and often about prostitution, lesbianism or similar
themes stated without comment or criticism. Many were humorous
and she sang risqué songs like *I'll Keep Sittin' On It If I Can't Sell
It* and *Hot Nuts – Get 'Em From the Peanut Man*. The latter was a
favourite with Lil Johnson whose career commenced at much the
same time and who recorded often with Big Bill Broonzy's pianist
Black Bob. Her earliest recording, *Never Let Your Left Hand Know
What Your Right Hand Do* had Charles Avery playing a Yancey-like
piano accompaniment. Avery also accompanied Lucille Bogan on a
few titles including the sombre red-light song, *They Ain't Walkin' No
More*. Her earliest records, made in 1923, had otherwise unknown
pianists, Henry Callens and Alex Channey on them, and if she did

come from Alabama, as has been reported, she may have brought them with her. After 1933 Lucille Bogan was closely associated with Walter Roland and the guitarist Walter Scott, recording under her pseudonym of Bessie Jackson. Tough-voiced and uncompromising, she did not venture, as did Georgia White, into a kind of popular song form but stayed essentially a blues singer. It is probably totally inappropriate to associate her with Chicago which she may have visited only on recording trips – later records were made in New York but for both she was probably brought North; nonetheless her singing had the challenging character of the women who were working in Chicago at the time.

To a considerable extent the aggressiveness of the women singers is directly related to their position in society in the years between the wars. In the main the women were more able to get jobs than the men, and for this reason found themselves in the position of family 'head'. This probably accounts for the overall lack of women singers for they had a certain degree of security which meant that recording offered no special attraction to them. Male Blacks, a large proportion of whom were out of work or only had periods of temporary employment, were economically weak but, as the women in the lower class had little opportunity to marry into the small but growing middle class, they had a sexual advantage. 'The emotional dilemmas that arise from this awkward situation', explained the sociologists H.R. Cayton and St Clair Drake, 'have developed a pattern of defensive hardness among black lower-class women alternating with moods of lavish tenderness ... the men, insecure in their economic power, tend to exalt their sexual prowess.' Both aspects were demonstrated again and again in the blues recordings made by both men and women in the Northern cities. This applied too, of course, in other cities, most noticeably in St Louis whose singers were still recording in numbers by making the short trip to Chicago. The Chicago women had their counterparts in Mary Johnson, born in Mississippi in 1905 but a resident on Biddle Street, St Louis, for most of her life, whose suspicion of men, frequently expressed on record, earned her the name of 'Signifying' Mary Johnson; or in 'Little Alice' Moore, whose nickname was given in some cynicism and who was one of the principal St Louis women singers in the 'thirties; or yet again in Bessie 'Blue Belle' Mae Smith, who was the common-law wife of 'Po' Joe' – or 'Big Joe' – Williams, and whose blues expressed a similar point of view.

Blues fallin' down on me, just like drops of rain (2)
You give your lovin' sugar to another woman and don't
give me a grain.

I'm gonna tell you somethin' baby, want you to keep it to
yourself (2)
If you don't give me all of your sugar, you won't give it to
no one else.

Blue Belle's 'Sugar man', Big Joe Williams, was from Crawford, Mississippi, on the fringe of the Piney Woods where he was born in October 1903. One of sixteen children, he had several relatives who were musicians when time allowed, although theirs was a poor farm and the work was hard. Joe didn't care for farm work but the labour he undertook was even harder – in the levee camps, the railroad and lumber camps in and around the Knoxford Swamp. He learned to play guitar on a home-made instrument and drifted from camp to camp, eventually finding himself in Tuscaloosa, Alabama. Here he worked for the local big shot, Totsie King, playing in his joints and for country suppers. He had a spell in the Rabbit Foot Minstrels with Ethel Waters as headliner and the Birmingham Jug Band in the company. Jim Jackson was also in the troupe. Six years later, in 1935, he recorded again, when he was living with Blue Belle in St Louis. There he worked with Henry Townsend, Walter Davis and Robert Lee McCoy, an expert with the bottleneck slide and equally well-known as a harmonica player. McCoy's *Prowling Nighthawk* earned him the name of Robert Nighthawk later, but at this time he was known as 'Rambling Bob', or as 'Peetie's Boy', in recognition of his work with Peetie Wheatstraw. Big Joe and Rambling Bob made a particularly successful team, with Williams's flurries of highly distinctive guitar picking offsetting the whining slide. Big Joe had developed an unusual guitar of his own with eight or nine strings; later, in 1941, when Peetie Wheatstraw was killed as his car crashed into a train on a railroad crossing, Big Joe inherited his guitar and adapted it similarly. Big Joe's voice was rather harsh, deriving distantly from Charley Patton, and he had a tendency to accelerando which imparted an urgency to his intense and emotional singing.

On a number of Big Joe Williams's recordings the harmonica player was 'Sonny Boy' Williamson who was born in Jackson, Tennessee, in 1916. After playing as a boy in and around Memphis, where he was a strong influence on a number of musicians, Sonny Boy Williamson moved to Chicago at the age of eighteen. Though he was extremely young and working with bluesmen a great many years his senior, he was a highly respected musician. Sonny Boy played the harmonica 'crossed'; in other words, he played in a key a fourth below that in which the 'harp' was tuned. This technique developed by blues harmonica players means that the standard blues progression may be achieved by drawing the notes rather than blowing them for the majority played. Playing in the key of the harmonica means that the notes are more frequently blown than drawn for the progression. In white folk harmonica playing this is an advantage, but in the blues, which relies for its effects on the vocalisation of the sounds and the 'bending' of the notes, it is a disadvantage. Bending notes is infinitely easier when drawing – or sucking – the harp. Consequently the blues player generally uses a harmonica which is a fourth above the key played by his accompanists. This means that he plays in E on an A harmonica, or in A on a D instrument. Less frequently blues players will use other 'positions' – the third position meaning that the instrument is played two steps above the key in which it is tuned or in E on a D harmonica. For his other effects the player uses breath control, the manipulation of his tongue and the passage of air in his cheek, and the pursing of his lips. He flutters his fingers and rotates his hand, or cups his hands over the instrument, opening and closing them much as a jazz trumpet player uses a mute to produce the inflections and variations that he likes. No harmonica player was more influential in the use of this technique than was Sonny Boy Williamson.

In his early recordings, which commenced in 1937, there was still a rural sound to his music, but he arrived in Chicago when the 'hokum' bands were still popular and to some extent this affected his work. He would commence sometimes with the kind of verbal exchange and staged 'atmosphere' which the hokum bands enjoyed, but his playing was entirely blues. 'Who is that knockin' on the door? I believe that that's the collector man. Man, go tell him I ain't got a dime today, tell him I ain't made a cent all this week. Tell him I'm just as broke as I can be, honest but I'm down. Tell him that I'll have some money sometime':

Now, go open the do', here comes that collector man (2)
Well you can tell him, I say 'Come back tomorrow' because
    Sonny Boy ain't got a dog-gone thing.

Tell him that some day I'll have some money, now I want
    everybody to watch and see (2)

Well now tell him that it's hard to keep down, you know,
a real good man like me.

Tell him that I'm down and out now, but I won't be
down always (2)
Well you tell him to watch and see ole Sonny Boy'll get
him some money, Lord knows, some of these days.

Playing crossed D on a G harmonica he slurred and wailed his notes, alternating the vocal line with harp playing to produce a continuous flow of melody. Often, however, he used a percussive technique, exploiting repeat phrases, or 'riffs', which gave his work considerable drive. 'Tongue tied' with a slight speech impediment, he was inclined to extend vowels and thicken consonants, a curious vocal quality which was much imitated by other singers.

Older than Sonny Boy but not as versatile, William 'Jazz' Gillum came from Indianola, Mississippi where he was orphaned as a child. Raised by an uncle who was a church deacon, he learned to play the family harmonium, while his brothers taught him the harmonica. He was a field hand when still a boy but at the age of fourteen, in 1918, he was playing on street corners in Greenwood, Mississippi, and he migrated to Chicago five years later. Though it was eleven years before he recorded, his earliest recordings like Sarah Jane – 'my darlin' consumptive Sarah Jane' – still had a country dance swing. Gillum favoured high pitched harps and often played 'straight', limiting his technique. In contrast his voice was rich and low, so that the extended-line method of harp playing was less appropriate. From the outset he had a close working relationship with Big Bill Broonzy who was on nearly all his records, and he also used Washboard Sam to provide a gritty rhythm.

Few washboard players have the strength of voice to compete with their own playing, but Robert Brown had. With a natural timbre in his deep voice and a vibrato which seemed to have the same intervals as the corrugations of his boards he combined vocal and playing with ease. Called 'Washboard Sam' by his friends he was reportedly from Arkansas and born in 1910. He was twenty-two when he appeared in Chicago and started to record only three years later with Big Bill Broonzy, who, in the casually assumed relationship of ghetto life, claimed to be his half-brother. His blues drew from both rural and urban experience as did most of those of his friends.

I worked in a levee camp, just about a month ago (2)
Well I wind so many wagons it made my po' hands so'.

We slept just like dogs, eat beans both night and day (2)
But I never did know just when we drew our pay.

They had two shifts on day, and the same two shifts at
    night (2)
But if a man wind wagons he can't treat his baby right.

Typically, there was a second meaning in the song, for 'winding' had a sexual implication and since the 1890s 'wagon' had also meant a lover. This play on words, which made the songs both literally and metaphorically interesting, was exploited by all the group. A legion of blues singers had come to dominate the Chicago scene, including some of the more established men like Tampa Red, Lonnie Johnson and Roosevelt Sykes, but with Big Bill Broonzy and Sonny Boy Williamson as undisputed leaders. Sykes and Johnson either worked together or singly, but other pianists played frequently for most of the lead singers. Two of the older men were 'Black Bob' Hudson, who played regularly with Broonzy, and Bob Call whose *Thirty-One Blues*, made as far back as 1929, was one of the classic blues piano solos. Though he had once worked with such singers as the Louisiana-born Elzadie Robinson and James Wiggins, he had long settled on the South side.

Joshua Altheimer took over from Black Bob in 1937. He was another of Broonzy's Arkansas acquaintances, having been born in the township of Altheimer, which he claimed was founded by his grandfather, outside Pine Bluff. An exceptionally fine blues accompanist he rarely took a solo and never recorded under his own name, but he had an easy rolling style ideal for the kind of blues which was developing. When he died prematurely, at the age of thirty in 1940, he was much missed. One of the few native Chicagoans was John Davis who was some three years younger. Blinded when a child, he followed the rent-party pianists around and also picked up the music of more popularly-inclined musicians. Though Blind John Davis tended to a somewhat decorative and melodic style, he could put in a good blues background if he wished. Also a popular session man was Horace Malcolm from New Orleans, and later his fellow-pianist from the Crescent City, Simeon Henry. Malcolm was pianist with the Harlem Hamfats and sometimes worked with the McCoy brothers. It was Joe McCoy who wrote the theme *Why Don't You Do Right* for the rather sweet-voiced singer Lil Green, making a reputation for her and a bigger one for Peggy Lee. Simeon Henry and Big Bill Broonzy travelled widely with Lil Green in the early 'forties but she was far less close to the blues than was Merline Johnson. Calling herself unashamedly the Yas Yas Girl, she had a mean voice and was the best woman singer to work with Big Bill, Josh Altheimer and Blind John Davis.

One characteristic of the music of the late 'thirties in Chicago was the use of the alto sax, tenor or clarinet as a 'front-line' instrument to carry the melody, instead of a harmonica. Played by Odell Rand, clarinettist with the Harlem Hamfats, Bill Osborn or, most frequently, Buster Bennett, and augmented sometimes by Herb Morand from the Hamfats or even the old New Orleans trumpeter Punch Miller, it gave a jazz inflection to the music and anticipated later developments in the blues. But it still was blues that they played, though often of the hokum variety, or with a hard-driving, swinging dance rhythm. If the music was becoming superficial and rather stereotyped, the massive 245 pound figure of Big Maceo brought it sternly back to the tradition. Big Maceo Merriweather was born in Atlanta, Georgia in 1905 and was thirty-five years old when he turned up in Chicago, though he had been playing at Brown's Club on Hastings Street in Detroit for the past several years. He struck up a friendship with Tampa Red who had worked steadily with Black Bob and other pianists but had never really re-established the relationship he had once had with Georgia Tom. He had resorted to playing piano himself and letting Willie Bee (James) play guitar, but the appearance of Big Maceo gave him the partnership he needed. Maceo had a hoarse, rather gentle voice which was belied by the forcefulness of his piano playing. His *Worried Life Blues* became a classic of urban blues themes and his *Chicago Breakdown* one of the most dynamic recordings of boogie-woogie ever made. He seemed intent on reminding the Chicago musicians of the roots of their music 'down home'. 'What kind of jive d'ya call that?' asked Tampa Red. 'Man I call this – is the *Texas Stomp*,' Maceo replied, his left hand hammering out the figures with the propulsion of an express train. 'Come on Tampa, show me what you do in your home'. His guitar singing against the piano rhythms, Tampa Red cried, 'This is the way we do it back in my home, Macey – listen here . . . !'

But it wasn't. Tampa Red, like Big Bill or Sonny Boy, Lonnie Johnson or Jazz Gillum was playing in the brash, confident manner of Chicago which had been developing through the 'thirties. Back home, the music was very different.

Back to Mississippi

Kokomo Arnold was eighteen years old when he arrived in Buffalo at the end of the World War I. Some years later, when Sonny Boy Williamson arrived in Chicago, he too was eighteen. Georgia Tom was nineteen when he arrived North, the same age as Jazz Gillum. Bumble Bee Slim was older, twenty-three, and Tampa Red may have been a little older still. Big Bill Broonzy was twenty-seven before he arrived in Chicago, but he was the exception – many blues singers, like Big Joe Williams or Little Brother Montgomery had left home when they were little more than boys. The movement of blues singers to the North echoed the general migratory patterns as to age-groups as well as route. If a man had not migrated by the time he was twenty-five, the odds were against his doing so at all. If he waited until his thirties, the chances were that he would decide to stay in his home state and perhaps follow his children when they were old enough to send for him.

So it happened that the older bluesmen tended to remain in the rural areas and their music, like their other ways and habits of life, changed relatively little. Change, like migration, was for young men and those who moved North were more adaptable and more inclined to develop or alter their music. This meant that the older forms of the blues were preserved in the South and might have flourished steadily had it not been for the developing mass media. Not only did the sale of record players and victrolas have a follow-up service of records in the stores which brought the newer kinds of music to the townships of the South, but the general post-Depression drift to the urban areas resulted in more sophisticated forms developing in Southern cities. This was a process which took place over a number of years and in the early 'thirties the rural music, though suffering the general economic stress of the period, still survived.

In a sense the South suffered somewhat less from the Depression than did the North, though this was relative, for the South had been more depressed anyway. Most seriously affected was the cotton industry and this meant that the black farm worker was hurt more than anyone. Cotton prices had hit rock bottom, but the decision to plough under ten million acres of planted cotton so that existing stocks could be used and the prices bolstered must have seemed a desperate measure. Two hundred million dollars were paid out to the landowners and a part of the benefit was intended for the black tenants. As the landowner kept the books and the sharecropper had no legal power, he often received nothing. When the AAA – the program initiated in 1933 following the Agricultural Adjustment Act – paid the cheques directly to the tenants to redress the injustice, the plantation owners were not slow to dismiss their tenants or lower their status to labourers. The decline in Southern agriculture hit Blacks hard and there was a natural tendency to move to the towns where job opportunities for unskilled labour were more varied. It is against this background that the Southern blues in the 'thirties must be seen.

As might be expected, the older singers in the Mississippi Delta remained there, although the unrest of the times was manifest in their movements within the region. Charlie Patton seems to have been continually on the move. After his recordings began in 1929, he became more widely known and he made an adequate living from playing at country suppers, fish-fries and dances through the Delta. There are reports of his having lived in Vicksburg, Lula, Merigold and even Clarksdale, though this had been disputed. Nevertheless it is clear that he was a familiar and highly popular figure in these areas, especially with the women who bore him a number of children. In 1933 Patton settled with a young woman of sixteen, Bertha Lee, whom he had met in Lula and with whom he had a rather stormy relationship. They settled in Holly Ridge about thirty miles south of Merigold, and east of Greenville, in 1933. An extremely heavy drinker and inclined to be pugnacious when drunk, Patton must have been difficult to live with, but the dynamism of his personality came through with great power in his singing.

It was Henry C. Speir, a music store owner in Jackson who was responsible for getting Patton and nearly all the other Mississippi singers on record in the 'twenties and 'thirties. In 1933, when the Depression was still heavy on the land, Speir was optimistic enough to make test recordings of Patton, Willie Brown and his partner Son House, sending them for consideration to W.R. Callaway and Art

Satherly at the ARC – American Record Company – which had offices in New York. Callaway came to Mississippi to collect Patton and Bertha Lee and at the end of January 1934, he made his last records. Perhaps they did not flare with quite the intensity of his first sides five years before, his voice was rather hoarse and his guitar less dramatic, but they were still of remarkable depth and emotional strength. With Bertha Lee, Patton made a number of religious titles, but his last issued side was the old bawdy song, though much expurgated, *Hang it on the Wall*. He was still in his forties when he died later that year from a heart ailment which had been aggravated by fierce singing, heavy drinking and disregard for treatment.

Apparently Callaway did not consider it worth while bringing Son House to record; House had made only one session for Paramount against nearly forty issued titles of Patton on that label, and as a risk in that period of economic strain it was no doubt unwise. Eddie 'Son' House was considerably younger than Patton; he was born in March 1902 at Lyon, just outside Clarksdale, Mississippi. As a youth he had lived with his mother in Louisiana, his father and his uncle played in a small brass band. He picked moss in Algiers, across the river from New Orleans, and got a little education. On the death of his mother, he moved back to Mississippi to work as a field hand until he heard of the wages being offered up north. In 1922 he was working at the Commonwealth Steel Plant in East St Louis. It was not until he was twenty-five that, back in Mississippi, he first was attracted to playing guitar; in Matson, south of Clarksdale, he heard Willie Wilson playing a guitar with a bottleneck. Wilson lived in Leland and Eddie House heard him often, and another friend, James McCoy from Lyon, also showed him how to play. It was McCoy who taught him *My Black Mama* and *Preachin' Blues*, two of the themes which he recorded a couple of years later. The session might never have occurred, for he was playing in a juke when a man suddenly went on a rampage, shooting up the joint and hitting Son in the leg. Son shot him dead and got a fifteen year sentence at Parchman Farm.

Only a year later he was released and, moving to Lula, had the good fortune to meet Charley Patton. He became friendly with Patton who introduced him to Willie Brown, then living in Robinsonville, and in the summer of 1930 they all recorded. Son House sang *My Black Mama, Preachin' the Blues* and *Dry Spell Blues*, all of which were extended blues lasting for both sides of a record. Three years earlier the terrible disaster of the Mississippi floods had occurred; the ravages of the boll weevil were still being felt; after the inundations had come an equally devastating drought, and the full effect of the Wall Street crash was beginning to hit the South. It must have seemed that there was no end to the troubles that a Mississippi field hand had to bear. Sang Son House:

> I fold my arms Lord and I walked away (2)
> Just like God tell you, somebody got to pray.
>
> Pork chops' forty-five cents a pound, cotton is only ten (2)
> I can't keep no women, no, never nowhere I've bin.
>
> So dry, ole boll-weevil, turn up his toes and die (2)
> Now now nothin' to do – bootleg moonshine and rye.
>
> Well it have been so dry, you can make a powderhouse out' the
>   world (2)
> 'Fraid of all the money men, like a rattlesnake an' a squirrel.
>
> It's a dry ole spell, everywhere I been, (2)
> I believe to my soul this ole world is bound to end.
>
> Lord I stood in my backyard, wrung my hands and
>   screamed (2)
> And I couldn't see nothin' couldn't see nothin' green.
>
> Oh Lord, have mercy if you please (2)
> Let your rain come down and give our po' heart ease.

When he played he used a repeat phrase, rhythmic and melodic, which punctuated his words, the bass string contrasting with the bottleneck slide within the same figure. The hypnotic effect of the continual repetition offset the passionate intensity of his full, raw voice. At times his singing took on a barking tone and it was an extraordinary physical as well as emotional performance. Just a month after the session, Son House moved to Robinsonville to join Willie Brown, and together they formed a blues band playing for country balls and suppers. At different times a number of musicians joined them. One was Fiddlin' Joe Martin, who was a cousin of Jake Martin. Fiddlin' Joe played guitar, fiddle, mandolin and washboard and had played over the Delta with Charley Patton and other bluesmen from the time the left Edwards, Mississippi, at the age of fourteen in 1918 until he moved to Robinsonville in 1935. There was Leroy Williams, a harmonica player too, and all four recorded a couple of titles for the Library of Congress in 1941 when Alan Lomax came through on a field recording trip. House and Brown had a band which included both trombone and traps at one time, but the most important musician to work with them was Robert Johnson.

'He was just a little boy then. He blew a harmonica and he was pretty good with that, but he wanted to play a guitar. When we'd leave at night to go play for the balls, he'd slip off and come over to where we were. His mother and step-father didn't like him to go out to those Saturday night balls because the guys were so rough,' Son House explained to Julius Lester. Robert watched the two men, House and Brown, very closely and he attempted to copy them. Then they heard that he had run away from his home on Richard Lellman's plantation. It was six months later when they heard him again. When he came back he astounded them with his guitar playing – and alarmed them with his liking for the women, especially other men's women. Robert was not prepared to heed their warnings, and there is no doubt that he was intent on getting as much out of his life as he could. Unhappily, it wasn't a long one.

During the next few years Robert Johnson was heard and seen by innumerable blues singers – by the young Muddy Waters in Clarksdale, by the pianist Albert Luandrew, 'Sunnyland Slim', in West Helena and Memphis, in Itta Bena and other towns by David 'Honeyboy' Edwards, who grew up with him. 'Robert was tall, brown-skin, skinny, had one bad eye. He looked out of one of his eyes; one eye look like it had a cataract – in that bad eye. At that time he was playing on a Sears-Roebuck "Stella" guitar. Yeah, he was good', Edwards affirmed to Pete Welding. Perhaps Johnson's defective eye caused him to feel the need to assert himself with women, and he may have been somewhat paranoiac; whether he was or not, his blues, with the hard, angry utterances and the obsessional nature of many of his themes undoubtedly suggest it.

> Early this morning when you knocked upon my door (2)
> And I said 'Hello Satan, I believe it's time to go.'
>
> Me and the Devil was walking side by side (2)
> I'm goin' to beat my woman until I get satisfied
>
> You may bury my body down by the highway side (2)
> So my old evil spirit can catch a Greyhound bus and ride.

Some of his blues were derived from other singers, either in person or from their records, but they were transmuted through his unique expression to something essentially his own. The words of his agonised *Hellhound on My Trail* or *If I had Possession Over Judgement Day* were evidence of a tormented spirit, but his libido found release in other, more autobiographical lyrics.

If your man get personal, want you to have your fun (2)
Best come on back to Friars Point mama, barrelhouse all
  night long.

I got womens in Vickburg, clean on into Tennessee (2)
But my Friars Point rider now, hops all over me.

I ain't goin' state no color, but her front teeth crowned
  with gold, (2)
She got a mortgage on my body now, and a lien on my
  soul.

You can squeeze my lemon till the juice run down my —
  (till the juice run down my leg, you know what I'm
  talkin' about)
You can squeeze my lemon till the juice run down my
  leg, (that's what I'm talkin' about, now)
But I'm goin' to Friars Point, if I be rockin' to my end.

He was, undoubtedly, as his friends had feared, rocking to his
end. Though he worked on a Robinsonville plantation, he spent
the weekends and lay-off periods, playing, gambling and getting
entangled with women. His recordings were made in November
1936 and in June the following year, Ernie Oertle, a record salesman
for ARC, heard about him and introduced him to Don Law. Law
took him to Texas on both occasions and his recollections are of a
shy and disconsolate young man who wanted half a dollar to pay off
the woman he was with. When John Hammond tried to find him in
1938 for his 'Spirituals to Swing' Concerts at Carnegie Hall he learned
that Robert Johnson had been poisoned weeks before. According to
David Edwards he was given a poisoned bottle of whisky at a juke in
Greenwood where he was playing, and was brought home mortally
sick. Just about twenty-seven when he died, Robert Johnson, for all
his youth, was the singer who most influenced the Chicago music
of a dozen and more years later.

This was a singularly tragic period in the story of the blues in
Mississippi, for a few months after Robert Johnson made his last
recording, another era came to an end with dreadful finality. Since
the beginning of the Depression, little had been heard of the 'Classic
Blues' singers, whose careers, tied as they were to show business, were
affected by the shut-down of many of the stock shows. In spite of her
unrivalled stature Bessie Smith had been hit by this as much as any
other singer of her type. It seems likely that her habitual drinking
had also made her difficult to employ. For John Hammond in 1933,
she had made one last, glorious session, in which her rowdy *Gimme*

a Pigfoot triumphed over an inadequate accompaniment. No other dates followed. In 1934 she was on a travelling road show which hit Fort Worth, Texas, to coincide with the Fat Stock Show. It also coincided, incredibly, with Ma Rainey's appearance in the Haines Circus, singing to the guitar of the young – naturally – T-Bone Walker. She returned to Harlem, sang for the clubs and appeared at a 'Blues and Jazz Concert' at the 'Famous Door' on 52nd Street and secured a six-week engagement at Connie's Inn. The future was brightening and there was talk of a film and a new recording session; she looked forward to a retirement in 1960. It was not to be. She had a booking to join Winstead's 'Broadway Rastus Show' and was driven south to meet it. In the dim light of early morning on September 26th 1937, she was driving through Coahoma, Mississippi, just a few miles from Lula and Friar's Point when her car struck a stationary truck. Terribly mutilated and her arm nearly severed, Bessie lay in the wreckage. A passing Memphis surgeon stopped his car and tried to lift her two hundred pound body from the tangled metal when his own vehicle was struck. An ambulance took her eventually to the G. T. Thomas Hospital in Clarksdale but, though her arm was amputated, she died just after mid-day from the internal wounds she had suffered.

A score of miles to the east lay the vast, featureless spread of 16,000 acres of Parchman Farm, 'A Great Institution in a Great State', as it later proclaimed itself, having added a further 6,000 acres. A single shed marks the station on the branch line that runs right on to Parchman Farm to bring the prisoners into the largest assembly of Units in the Mississippi Penitentiary system. Only a low line of trees along the Tallahatchie River in the far distance breaks the monotony of its cotton rows, rows that were worked through the blazing noon-day sun by teams of prisoners under armed guard. When Bessie Smith died, one of its inmates was being broken into gang labour and a 'striped suit'. His name was Booker Washington White, and he'd led a tough life, tough enough to be known as 'Barrelhouse' even among the criminals on the Farm. Son of a railroad fireman, he was born in Houston, Mississippi, in November 1909, but raised by his uncle at Grenada, some fifty miles further west. His father had taught him to play a little guitar and his uncle had a piano; when he had any spare time he practised both, though he was expected to work on the farm and act as water-boy for the construction gangs. Drew and Dockery's lay another fifty miles to the west, deep in the Delta, but the fame of the musicians there was widespread and he always wanted to be a 'great man like Charley Patton.' He wasn't close enough to be under Patton's immediate influence, but he was impressed by the older man's harsh vocal strength and the rhythmic impetus of his guitar work. His own playing and singing exaggerated these elements, losing some of the subtlety but having a primitive force.

A friend from Itta Bena, Napoleon Hairiston, had got a local record store owner, Ralph Lembo, to get them a recording date in May 1930. *The Panama Limited* and *The Frisco Train* were, as their titles implied, railroad imitations whose thundering rhythms had much in common with the 'ring-shout' recorded just three years later, at Jennings, Louisiana. *Run Old Jeremiah*, recorded for the Library of Congress by Joe Washington Brown and Austin Coleman, had the same compulsive locomotive drive, urged on by cries. White sang one-line holler-blues: 'Eeeh, train time here . . . and I ain't got my fare,' and Hairiston commented 'Breeze along, boy, breeze along; going to Vicksburg in the cool of the evening . . . get your shoes boy, if we can't catch it in the bend we'll catch it at the crossin'.' With the slide ring sounding the train bell and White's guitar-wrecking flailing, it was exhilarating, and it was a form that 'Bukka' – as Booker became known – was to use many times in later years. In 1934 he teamed up with George 'Bullet' Williams, a heavy drinker like himself, who strained 'canned heat' – Sterno cooking fuel – to get alcohol, for Mississippi was technically 'dry'. They played at roadhouses in the eastern part of the state until 1937, when Bukka drew a gun in a muddled fracas and killed a man. Though he recorded a couple of titles in early September – one story says he broke bond to do so – he was in Parchman Farm within the month.

Conditions on Parchman at this time were vile and Bukka was lucky that his playing saved him from too much heavy labour. When his release was secured after two years by Lester Melrose, he could think of hardly anything else but trains, drink, prison and death, the subjects of all his blues.

> Judge give me life this mornin' down on Parchman Farm (2)
> I wouldn't hate it so bad but I left my wife in mourn.
>
> Oh listen you men, I don't mean no harm (2)
> If you wanna do good you better stay off o' Parchman Farm.
>
> We go to work in the mornin' just at dawn of day (2)
> Just at the settin' of the sun that's when the work is done.
>
> I'm down on ol' Parchman Farm but I sure wanna go
>   back home, (2)
> But I hope some day I will overcome.

While he was in Parchman Bukka White made two recordings for the Library of Congress – one of them was the traditional *Po' Boy*, sung to a tune of his own. These recordings were made 'in the field' by John A. Lomax and his son Alan Lomax, to whom must go the main credit for the extraordinary collection of black folk music in the Archive of American Folk Song in the Music Division of the Library of Congress. Their tours commenced in 1933 in a Ford car which 'carried a 350-pound recording machine – a cumbersome pile of wire and iron and steel – built into the rear of the Ford, two batteries weighing seventy-five pounds each,' a microphone, many accessories and 'scores of blank aluminium and celluloid discs,' John A. Lomax recalled. Their tour took them through Texas, Louisiana, Mississippi, Tennessee and Kentucky and later to Florida, Alabama, Georgia, the Carolinas and Virginia. Their intention was to record 'the folk songs of the Negro – songs that, in musical phrasing and poetic content, are most unlike those of the white race, the least contaminated by white influence or by modern Negro jazz.' They visited all-black communities and found that 'another source for material was the lumber camp that employed only Negro foremen and Negro laborers. However our best field was the southern penitentiaries. We went to eleven of them and presented our plan to possibly 25,000 Negro convicts.' Of the many hundreds of recordings that were made, only a minute proportion have been issued and a large number of the discs are unheard and unplayable. But this monumental achievement, which continued through 1934, 1936, 1939, 1941 and 1942, was unquestionably the greatest documentation of living folk music ever to be made.

To a large extent, however, the pre-requisite for 'uncontaminated' African American song tended to exclude blues. The greatest discovery in one man, Leadbelly, accounted for the largest number of blues which, as a songster, he included in his repertoire. But the lumber camps yielded mule-skinner's hollers but no barrel-house pianists. By the 'forties, the collectors' attitude had changed somewhat and Son House, Fiddlin' Joe Martin, Willie Brown and the then unknown Muddy Waters were recorded in the field. A built-in assumption that folk music was not to be heard in the city meant that the concentration of singers in Jackson, Mississippi, went unrecorded for the Archive and such recordings as were made of blues singers still depended on the initiative, the finances and the personal taste of H. C. Speir, Ralph Lembo and other similar record store owners and casual scouts.

And there was still much talent to be heard. Skip James, it is true, had left for Texas in 1932 but others of his contemporaries were active in Jackson and the surrounding country. Ishman Bracey was the most respected of the older generation of blues men in the city and his active life as a singer continued well into the 'forties, when, as was the case with a number of the older men, he 'got religion'. Eventually Bracey was ordained as a minister in a small church but the 'thirties saw his full maturity as a blues singer. His companion of earlier years, Tommy Johnson, was often in town but Johnson continued to live in Crystal Springs for some years. A singer by the name of Houston Stackhouse lived next to him and adopted much of his music as his own. The influence of Tommy Johnson still pervaded much of the music of the entire area. His willingness to teach others to sing and play in his style and his flair for showmanship (he played the guitar over his head, with his feet and even dancing on its rim) made him a popular entertainer. Willie Lofton, called 'Poor Boy', was one of those who was under his spell. His *Dark Road Blues* was heavily indebted to Johnson but he used words which were part tradition, part his own.

> Cryin' won't let you do me, like you did po' Shine,
>   Now don't you hear me talkin' to you pretty mama
> Won't let you do me, like you did po' Shine
> Cryin', you takin the po' boy's money, you gon' have to
>   kill me, 'fore you take mine.
>
> Cryin' I ain't gon' marry, ain't gonna settle down,
>   Now don't you hear me talkin' to you, pretty mama
> I ain't gon' marry, ain't gonna settle down . . .
> Cryin' I'm gon' stay right here, till my moustache drags
>   the ground.

Lofton tried his luck in Chicago but was unsuccessful and came back to Jackson to resume his business as a barber until his death in the 'fifties. Among other prominent singers in the area were Stack Hill, 'Peg Leg' Norwood and Lucien 'Slim' Duckett who belonged to the older generation of bluesmen. Slim Duckett's stepson, Johnny Temple, was born in Canton, near Jackson in 1906 and, because of his family interest in blues, learned to play the guitar as a boy. He worked briefly with Skip James before James left for Texas and James's *Devil Got My Woman* became his *Evil Devil Woman Blues*. A number of his early blues were derived from other singers, including his popular *Louise Louise Blues* which he seems to have learned from Big Boy Teddy Edwards who was working with Papa

Charlie Jackson in the early 'thirties. Temple made his way to New York to follow Charlie and Wilber 'Joe' McCoy, recording with them and the Harlem Hamfats. His own guitar was seldom heard on record; the changing taste of the times and of the Decca Record Company even led to Teddy Bunn partnering him. Bunn was born in New York State in 1909 and had played with the Spirits of Rhythm and the Washboard Serenaders. His immaculate, sophisticated and jazz-inflected guitar playing made an inappropriate accompaniment to the rich timbre of Temple's voice and after the New York sessions he came back to Jackson, where he died in 1966.

One of Temple's earlier recordings was a version of Little Brother Montgomery's *Vicksburg Blues*. Based on the *Forty-Four Blues* theme, it was to the piano blues of the river towns and the lumber camps what *Big Road Blues* was to the Jackson musicians. Little Brother had come back to Mississippi and Louisiana as early as 1931, forming a band in Bogalousa and later one in Jackson itself. Most of his fellow pianists continued either to work in Vicksburg, like Ernest '44' Johnson, who eventually got himself a job on the Illinois Central railroad, or in the lumber camps. In 1936 he played at a sawmill camp up in Carthage for the Pearl River Lumber Company, where he worked with K. C. Douglas, a guitarist who sometimes came into Jackson and had learned a number of Tommy Johnson's pieces there before he beat his way as a migrant worker, to California. In the same year Little Brother made an outstanding series of piano blues recordings, cutting no less than eighteen titles at a single sitting. The occasion of this session at the St Charles Hotel in New Orleans was probably without parallel for the number of blues recorded: eighteen were contributed by Montgomery, a dozen by Tommy Griffin with Ernest '44' on piano, a dozen by Lonnie and Sam Chatman, six by Eugene Powell with Willie Harris playing guitar, a couple by Walter Vincent and twelve by Bo Carter among a few others. Most of the singers for the two-day session had been collected from the Delta, although they had been associated with the Vicksburg-Jackson region at one time or another. The Chatman family had moved to the Delta region in and around Hollandale; Bo Carter lived with Mississippi Matilda Powell a few miles south in Anguilla, Willie Harris on Lake Lee at Wayside.

Of all the Chatman family, Armenter, known as 'Bo Carter' had been the most successful. Born in Bolton in 1893, he was one of the youngest of the brothers but his business head and general reliability – he was less inclined than many blues singers to get drunk on the royalty advance and the whiskey that was usually provided to loosen up the sessions – ensured him a regular retainer from the Bluebird company. Moreover he had a successful formula for *double-entendre* blues which were more amusing than profound. Even when he was singing at his most sexually exuberant, his voice had a melancholy touch, and his gently swinging guitar playing was always sensitively executed. *Flea On Me* made at that session, was typical.

> Now every time I squeeze your arm
> It makes my lovin' feelin', baby, get all wrong,
> Cause I got a flea, crawlin' on me, honey for you.
>
> Now every time I take you for a drive
> It makes my lovin' feelin' begin to rise,
> Cause I got a flea, crawlin' on me, honey for you.

Bo Carter had two more recording sessions to complete his contract with Bluebird and they indicate his movements in the last years before the War. In San Antonio, Texas in 1938, he cut eighteen titles on one day; a year and a half later he was in Atlanta, Georgia to make fourteen more. He returned to Memphis and, as the War came and the recording of blues singers was halted, slipped into penury made worse by oncoming blindness.

Bluebird, for whom most of the Chicago-based singers around Big Bill Broonzy and Sonny Boy Williamson were recording, was the last of the record companies before the War to seek artists in Mississippi. It was Broonzy who suggested to Lester Melrose that he record Tommy McClennan, and the recording manager himself went down to get him. McClennan was born in April, 1908 and worked on J. F. Sligh's farm a few miles outside Yazoo City. He was small-framed but he had a big, aggressive voice and played 'flailing', unsubtle guitar. As Broonzy commented drily, he had 'a different style of guitar. You just make the chords E, A, or B and just rack your finger across all strings and sing the blues, and change from E to A to B just when you feel like changing. Any time will do. You don't have to be in no hurry. Just close your eyes.' When McClennan sang, he roared, he slammed the guitar, he shouted with burning fury one moment and went chuckling into the run-off slot of *Black Minnie* in the next. David Edwards knew him up in Itta Bena and Greenwood where he often played with Robert Petway, a farm hand who travelled to Chicago to record wearing his blue duckins. 'Him and Robert Petway had the same style 'cause they played together all the time . . . It'd be in and out; sometimes Tommy would be by himself and then when he get something pretty large he'd go get Robert,' said Edwards. Most of his blues were about women or whiskey and they were often threatening; when he died in Chicago in the 'sixties the whiskey had got the better of him. Without his partner, Robert Petway soon slipped into obscurity.

McClennan and Petway seemed to mark the end of the blues in Mississippi, but they weren't quite the last to be brought up to record before the War.

> Babe I wouldn't a' been here, if it had not been for you (2)
> Now I'm away in Chicago you treat me like you do, you do.
>
> If I get lucky with my train-fare home, (2)
> I'm goin' back to Mississippi, Lord now where I belong.

Arthur 'Big Boy' Crudup wasn't all that lucky, but he fared better than some. He came from Forrest, Mississippi, forty miles west of Jackson where he was born in 1905, the son of a guitarist. He was thirty-six when he recorded and weighed 220 lbs, which a life as water-boy, logger, levee worker, truck-driver, sawmill-hand and farmer had not reduced. When Crudup came to Chicago from Mississippi, he lived in a wooden crate beneath the 'L' station at 39th Street and played for dimes from passers-by. For so big a man he had a high, shrill voice, but it was the shouting cry of the holler which gave his records their character; that and the slow, pacing guitar capo'd at the sixth fret to make the notes ring out. They rang out even more loudly and clearly when he came up to record the following year, 1942, for he'd fixed an amplifier to his instrument.

Travelin' Men

David Cohn, a native Mississippian, once wrote that 'the Mississippi Delta begins in the lobby of the Peabody Hotel in Memphis and ends on Catfish Row in Vicksburg.' To the Blacks who lived in the Delta the limits might be described the other way round, for Memphis was a target town for those who hoped to leave Mississippi, and for them the Delta ended, not in the sumptuous green-black upholstery of the Peabody, but the intersection of Highway 51 and Beale. When A. R. Mangus defined the *Rural Regions of the South* for the Works Progress Administration in 1940, he included in the Mississippi Delta Region the bottomland counties of Mississippi plus Arkansas, Louisiana, and Shelby County, Tennessee, to define the most densely populated rural farming region in the country. Of its one and a third million people in 1930, nearly a million were black and it is not surprising to find the greatest concentration of blues singers appears to fall within it.

From the Delta stretches eastwards a vast territory embracing most of Alabama, Georgia, and the Carolinas which Mangus defined as the Eastern Old South where four out of ten people were black and more than half of the total African American farm population lived in 1930. Most of this region lay in the great Coastal Plain, where attitudes of mind, like the patterns of agriculture, spread pretty consistently over the country it embraced. In some counties the population was predominantly black and though in others cotton had given way to truck farming, the majority of people were growing the traditional crop and following a pattern of life not greatly dissimilar from that in the Delta. To the north of the region, the plain gives way to the gently rolling slopes of the Piedmont Plateau behind which rise the Blue Ridge Mountains and the Southern Appalachians. The broken ridges and long valleys stretch across eastern Tennessee and to some extent have influenced the migratory pattern of those who circulated within the region or moved north. Two spurs of the Southern Railroad followed the south-west/north-east lie of the land on either side of the mountains to meet at Lynchburg, Virginia and to continue to Washington. In the network of railroads and highways, Atlanta, Georgia, was the hub, and its situation attracted the migrants moving from the rural districts to the city. It is also on the axis that roughly divides those who chose Chicago and Detroit as target cities for migration, and those who chose Washington and New York.

When Atlanta began to stir after the Depression, many of the older blues singers had gone. Barbecue Bob had died in 1930; Charlie Lincoln was in the penitentiary; Blind Blake was in Chicago and Peg Leg Howell had gone back to making moonshine whiskey. Howell still played with his string band in and around Atlanta with Eddie Anthony, but when Anthony died in 1934, Howell lost interest in music. His life in the late 'thirties is vague but in 1940 he managed a woodyard for a couple of years. The loss of his other leg in 1952 from sugar diabetes totally incapacitated him and when he was found by George Mitchell in 1963, he was in a sad plight. One singer, however, came through the Depression with undiminished energy. He was Blind Willie McTell.

A native of the cottonlands west of Augusta, McTell was born in 1898 and raised some fifty miles from the coast in Statesboro. He was blind from birth and his disability was also his strength, for he was determined to play music for a living. He started to play guitar as a child and as a young man he obtained the large twelve-string which provided the full and resonant sound of his numerous recordings. McTell was an intelligent, shrewd man and at the age of twenty-four he went to Macon to study at the State School for the Blind. Later he went to an independent blind school in New York and subsequently went to Michigan to read braille. Blindness did not deter him from travelling and he went, as he said himself 'from Maine to the Mobile Bay', from Florida to Arkansas, in the course of a number of years of working with medicine shows and carnivals. When he sang, it was with a nasal inflection and his oddly-turned vowels seem to reflect the broad landscape over which he had worked. Sometimes his voice had the hard quality of the white mountain singers and he displayed few of the parochialisms of the thicker-voiced bluesmen. Many of his songs were ballads and medicine show pieces, but he was a memorable singer of blues.

I got the dark night blues, I'm feeling awful bad (2)
That's the worst ol' feeling that a good man have ever had.

I followed my fair brown from the depot to the train (2)
And the blues came down like dark night showers o' rain.

I drink so much whiskey, I stagger when I'm sleep (2)
My brains are dark and cloudy, and my mind's gone to my feet.

I got the blues so bad I can feel them in the dark (2)
And one dark and dreary morning, baby when you broke my heart.

In his complete mastery over an innate disability, McTell was independent and assured. He played for coins on the streets but he was proud of being a 'professional' musician and was no beggar. Often he worked with other singers and travelled extensively with Blind Log (Randolph Byrd) a guitarist from Screven County, playing house parties, and for tobacco workers. He was married for several years to Kate Williams, who, as Kate McTell, recorded with him and also he accompanied Ruth Willis. Their keen-edged voices were ideally matched with his. McTell also worked for a number of years with Curley Weaver, who had followed Barbecue Bob and in his younger years had copied his technique, but later developed a more individual approach. The two singers often travelled to Nashville and other places in Tennessee and the Carolinas. Weaver sang a blues modelled on one of Barbecue Bob's which would have been highly appropriate as they travelled.

Went down the street I couldn't be satisfied (2)
Had the *No No Blues*, just too mean to, just too mean to cry.

I'm a stranger here, just blowed in your town (2)
If I ask for favour, don't turn me, don't turn me down.

I ain't no gambler I don't play no pool (2)
I'm just a roller, jelly-bakin', jelly-bakin' fool.

I'm a stranger here, just come on this train (2)
I long to hear some gal call my, gal call my name.

In Atlanta they played frequently at the 81 Theatre and at the Pig'n Whistle berbecue.

Both Weaver and McTell were active well into the 1950s, when they were heard together in Louisville, but McTell died of a stroke in 1959. There were a number of other singers and musicians with whom Weaver had worked who were not heard after the mid-'thirties, among them the harmonica player, Eddie Mapp, and his companion, the guitarist Fred McMullen. Like the others, McMullen could play beautifully sensitive slide guitar, as he did on his recording of *De Kalb Chain Gang*. In this, such detail as 'they beat me and they slashed me, a forty-five in my side' suggests that it was probably from personal experience. McMullen, Weaver and another guitarist named Buddy Moss played a few instrumental rag pieces of great virtuosity, including *Decatur Street 81*, which may have been a theme they had featured at the Atlanta T.O.B.A. theatre.

Of this group Buddy Moss was the most important, though he was younger than the others, having been born in Jewel in January 1914. As a boy he followed the older men in the Atlanta region and went to record in New York with Weaver and McMullen a few weeks before his nineteenth birthday. His first titles revealed him as a competent guitarist with a swinging style that made effective use of bass string rhythms and of raising a note by 'hammering on'. Vocally he sounded like a grainy-voiced version of Leroy Carr, whose tunes he often used. He obviously appealed to the ARC company, for whom he made two dozen titles in 1933 alone. The following year his voice had become richer and his guitar work, from continual playing, was exceptional. The similarity between his guitar playing and that of Blind Boy Fuller, who recorded for the first time a couple of years later, is marked. His *Dough Roller Blues* for example was probably the source of Fuller's *Rattlesnakin' Daddy* and there is a real possibility that Fuller came under Moss's influence at this time. Undoubtedly he travelled a good deal, having an address in Greenwood, South Carolina for a while and later going to Tampa, Florida, to Dalton, Georgia, and elsewhere. Moss had a reputation for having a vacillating temperament, morose and irresponsible by turns, and was reported to have spent some years in jail.

This group of North Carolina singers moved around the country quite extensively in the thirties and probably met up more than once. Fulton Allen – his name was contracted to 'Fuller' – was born at Wadesboro in Anson Country, South Carolina, in 1907, but his parents took him to Rockingham in North Carolina on the Seaboard Air Line. There he learned to play guitar and entertained at dances and suppers. The ragtime and dance character of the music remained in his work thereafter. When he was in his early twenties, the woman with whom he had been living is said to have put lye in the water with which he was washing his face, and he was blinded. Guitar playing and singing now became his livelihood and he moved into the tobacco-producing towns, in particular Winston-Salem, begging from the shift workers as they left the curing sheds and factories. The Eleventh Street 'Bottoms' and the corner of Seventh and Patterson became noted for the blues singers who begged on the streets until a city ordinance prevented them. Blind Boy Fuller played a steel-bodied National guitar with a circular diaphragm which acted as a powerful resonator. In the years before electric amplification, steel National or Dobro instruments were popular among street singers. Fuller and his companions moved on to Greensboro, Graham, Burlington and Hillsboro, which were strung out on Highway 70. Carefully dressed and small in build, his appearance belied his rhythmic steel guitar playing and gritty voice, but he was a dominant figure and attracted many other musicians. There was a strong link with Blind Blake in his playing but his singing had none of Blake's wistfulness; it was earthy and direct. His blues were bawdy at times and at other times were comments on everyday life; he used traditional themes too, like his version of *Red River Blues*.

> Whichaway, whichaway do the blood red river run?
> Run from my window to that risin' sun.
>
> Now the dumper said 'Loader, please send me six foot
>   of clay,
> Cause the blood red river risin' six foot every day.'
>
> Go down to the camp and tell my brother Bill,
> That woman he's lovin' she's sure gonna get him killed.
>
> Now reason why these here men sure don't draw no more –
> Right from that long table back to that commissary store.
>
> Now I love to hear that M & O whistle blow
> I'm in a world of trouble, God knows and I got to go.

It is probable that Fuller learned much of his technique from Blind Gary Davis who was some years his senior, born in Laurens Country, South Carolina, in 1896. At the age of five, Davis began playing harmonica; he took up the banjo the following year. By the time he was seven he was regularly playing guitar and had begun to develop the remarkable virtuosity for which he subsequently became famous in the region. It is likely that he was influenced by Willie Walker, who lived in Greenville and who was a very respected musician. When he was fourteen he organised a string band which played in many parts of South Carolina until 1915. The subsequent years are uncertain and he declined to talk about them, but during this period he was blinded and the event apparently caused him to turn to religion. He was ordained as a minister in Washington, North Carolina, in 1933 but though his earliest records, made with Blind Boy Fuller in 1935, were mainly religious he did record a couple of blues. Thereafter he insisted on playing only gospel songs, though with a blues inflection, which have been called 'holy blues'. He accompanied Fuller on a few of his earliest titles but otherwise his incredibly deft and scintillating guitar work was too little heard until the 'fifties. For many years he had been living in New York, singing in Harlem and Brooklyn and on the suburban trains or street corners, a roadside preacher and evangelist. His importance in the Carolinas is therefore mainly in the 'twenties and 'thirties, but he must have been very influential at that time.

Religious street singers may have predominated in the region; at any rate, Joshua White recalled a considerable number. He was born in February 1914 in Willie Walker's home town of Greenville, South Carolina, where Reverend Gary Davis's string band had been based. His father was the pastor of a small church in which 'Josh' sang spirituals as a small boy. He was nine years old when a blind singer named James 'Man' Arnold came to the house. Josh went with him, to act as his 'eyes' as he begged in the towns of the Piedmont Crescent. Arnold made a good enough living out of begging to own three race-horses; he was earning far more than the people from whom he begged. Josh sent home two or three dollars a week from his meagre earnings; he didn't fare much better when he acted as the eyes for other singers whom he led along the highways: Blind Columbus Williams, Blind John Henry Walker, Blind Archie Jackson and others. Many were gospel singers, some were blues singers, and over a period of eleven years Josh White led about thirty of them – the most famous were Blind Lemon Jefferson, far from his Texas home, Blind Blake and Blind Joe Taggart. At first, all he did was bang a tambourine and collect coins in it, but later he learned to play guitar from watching the singers and it was Taggart who took him, at the age of twenty, to record for Paramount with him. By this time Josh had developed a fluent guitar technique in which the blue notes were heavily emphasised. His singing voice had a curious catch in it, a half-yodel, which was singular and always attracted notice. In later years he was to exploit the twist in his voice to a point where it became a tiresome cliché, but in his early years, with the natural melancholy of a high, clear voice, it gave a tragic quality to his singing, which was stressed by the whining of his guitar strings.

Well-built and handsome, Josh travelled extensively and earned

BLUES ON RECORD

The 'Stage-Music-Movies' page of the *Chicago Defender* for September 14th 1929 carried news of minstrel troupes including the Silas Green road shows and stock companies on the T.O.B.A circuit. Advertisements were for blues records by Blind Willie Harris and 'The Masked Marvel' (a pseudonym for Charley Patton).

(*Above*) Mamie Smith, with her Jazz Hounds. Her Okeh record of *Crazy Blues* (1921) opened up a new market.

(*Left*) Georgia Tom Dorsey. Pianist and partner to Tampa Red, he later become a major Gospel song composer.

(*Top left*) Roosevelt Sykes was the first to record *44 Blues*.

(*Top right*) Leroy Carr was one of the best loved of all blues singers, and had a long partnership with guitarist Scrapper Blackwell (behind).

(*Left*) Memphis Minnie, who 'played guitar like a man'.

'The Queen', Victoria Spivey, was famous for her *Black Snake Blues*.

Walter Davis, one of the most popular singers of the 1930's, played piano with an economical style.

(*Left*) Lucille Bogan, who also recorded as Bessie Jackson, sang blues about her rough life.

Bumble Bee Slim and Memphis Minnie—

STOMP TIME

3197 NEW ORLEANS STOMP TIME and WHEN SOMEBODY LOSES (Somebody Wins)—Vocal—Guitar.
Bumble Bee Slim and Memphis Minnie 59c

(*Above*) In Chicago musicians were still nostalgic for the South.

(*Right*) Bumble Bee Slim with the singer and pianist Georgia White.

PERFECT RACE RECORDS
By THE SOUTH'S GREATEST COLORED ARTISTS

(*Above*) Perfect records sold for a quarter. Buddy Moss and Curley Weaver were among their artists.

(*Left*) Records sold on their subjects, such as *I'm Still Sloppy Drunk, Graveyard Blues, Bad Depression Blues* and *Mama Don't Allow No Easy Riders Here* on this Perfect flier.

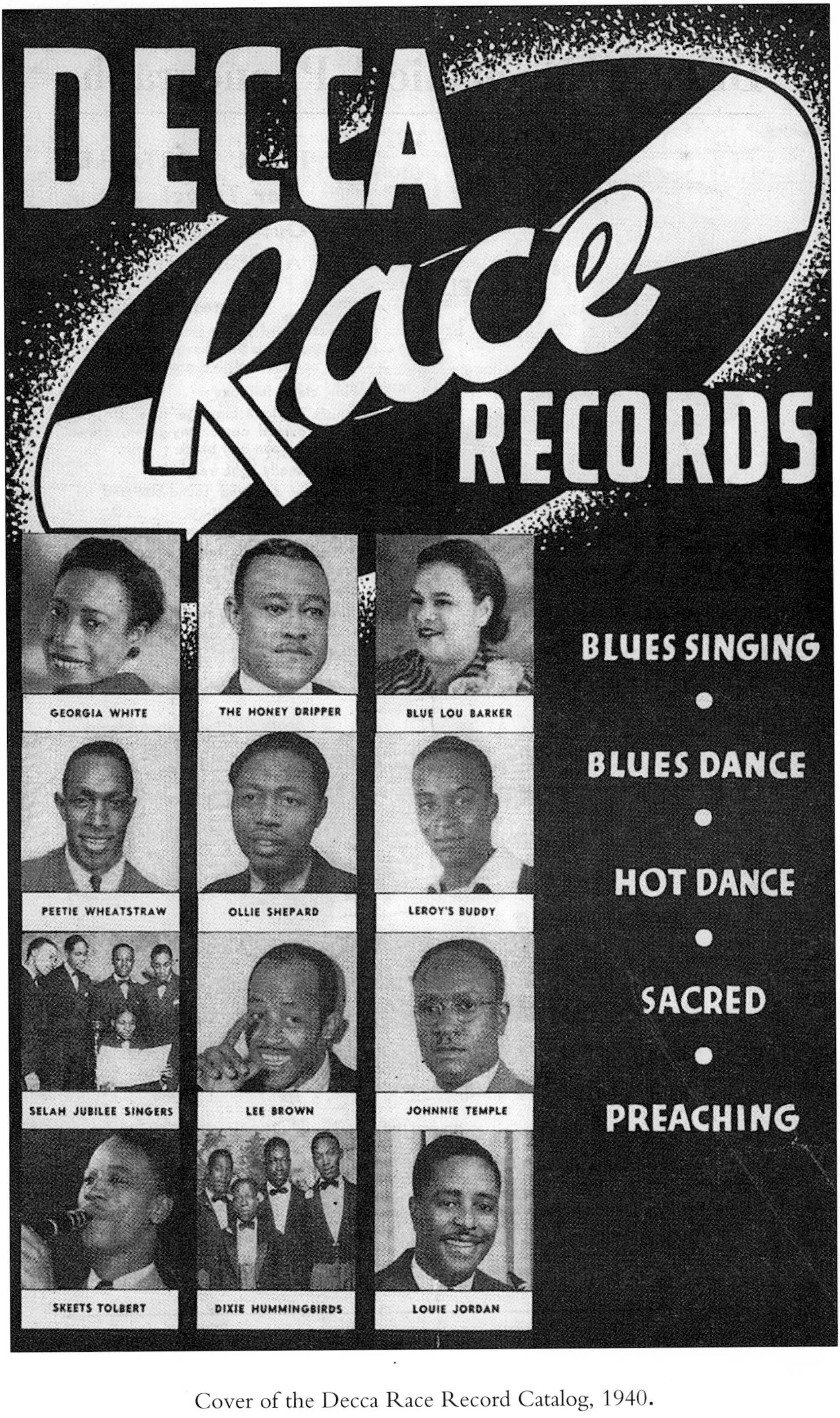

Cover of the Decca Race Record Catalog, 1940.

Pianist Little Brother Montgomery, recording manager Mayo Williams and, right, St Louis Jimmy Oden.

The decline of 'live' music is underlined by the presence in this tent juke of a piano, (right), a hand-wound phonograph (left), and a mechanical juke-box (centre).

CHICAGO BOUND

(*Above*) This Southern family
came to Chicago during
the First World War.

(*Right*) Highways 49 and 51,
the major routes of migration
north from Mississippi
to Memphis and beyond.

Chicago's South Side tenements were rapidly crowded with incoming migrants.

(*Above*) Street musicians in Chicago, c.1950, photographed by Big Bill Broonzy.

(*Right*) 'Daddy Stovepipe', who worked for many years in Chicago's Maxwell Street Market.

(*Left & Above*) Invitation cards and record advert for 'house rent' parties, or 'skittles'.

(*Right*) 'Cripple' Clarence Lofton, described as 'a three-ring circus'.

(*Above*) The celebrated pianist Hersal Thomas, who died in his teens.

(*Left*) Charlie Spand plays blues and boogie-woogie while Jimmy Yancey listens.

(*Left*) Hudson Whittaker, known as Tampa Red, played an individual style of guitar. His kazoo playing was less successful.

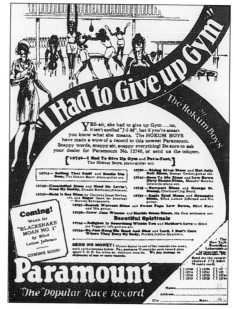

Tampa Red and Georgia Tom's *It's Tight Like That* was a major hit. It introduced the humorous, suggestive style of urban 'hokum' blues.

(*Right*) Hobos rode the freight trains to the immense Chicago railroad yards.

(*Left*) Big Bill Broonzy, was the acknowledged leader of Chicago singers of the late 'thirties. He encouraged new arrivals.

(*Left*) Tommy McClennan, the small, rough-voiced Delta singer from Yazoo City.

(*Below right*)
Boogie-Woogie pianists Albert Ammons and Meade Lux Lewis.

(*Above*) James 'Kokomo' Arnold, slide guitarist and bootlegger.

Assortment of posters for blues clubs, Chicago.

(*Above*) Memphis Slim (Peter Chatman) was influenced by Roosevelt Sykes.

(*Right*) When Big Boy Crudup came to Chicago, he lived in a wooden crate beneath the 'L' station at 39th Street.

(*Right*) John Lee 'Sonny Boy' Williamson, the influential harp player who was murdered in 1948.

(*Below*) Washboard Sam, strongest of the Chicago singers. His board had a phonograph turntable for a cymbal.

POST-WAR BLUES

(*Above left*) 'Big' Joe Turner's powerful voice matched his stature.

(*Above right*) James Rushing, known affectionately as 'Mister Five by Five', innovated a forceful style appropriate to the Kansas City blues of the Count Basie Orchestra.

(*Right*) Wynonie Harris modelled his vocal style on Joe Turner's, using witty lyrics and modern themes.

A glamorous and sophisticated image was chosen by the new Rhythm and Blues artists: *top left*, Big Maybelle who had a big voice; *top right*, blues 'shouter' Jimmy Witherspoon; *lower left*, 'the genius' Ray Charles; *lower right*, Ruth Brown, who was featured with big bands.

(*Right*) Fats Domino had an engaging blues style and toured unceasingly.

(*Below*) Bo Diddley presented the 'sharp' image of the rock 'n' roll singer.

Texas guitarist 'T-Bone' Walker was one of the first virtuosi of the electric guitar especially for the blues.

Lean and tense-voiced, Elmore James developed an electric guitar style based on Robert Johnson's technique.

Guitarist and harmonica player Jimmy Reed, off-stage.

Eddie Burns, playing in Brown's Club, Hastings Street, Detroit.

(*Left*) Willie Dixon, bass, Lafayette Leake, piano, at a recording session with J. B. Lenoir (in zebra coat).

Muddy Waters with Pat Hare broadcasting over WOPA from the Tay May Club.

Howling Wolf (Chester Burnett) playing at the
Big Squeeze Club, Chicago in 1959.

Little Milton (guitarist Milton
Campbell) played club dates
and toured widely.

Allen Bunn, whose North Carolina origin was
emphasised in his nickname of 'Tarheel Slim'.

Cornelius Green, who recorded
as 'Lonesome Sundown', remained
in Louisiana.

(*Left and above*) B. B. King brought his own band to blues clubs and appeared with R & B vocal groups at the Apollo Theater, Harlem.

(*Above*) Dee-jays or 'disc jockeys' including the veteran jazz pianist Earl Hines, reached the West Coast Market.

(*Right*) Earl Hooker, cousin of John Lee Hooker, was an outstanding guitarist.

John Lee Hooker with the record promoter Joe Von Battle in Detroit, 1959. Hooker was eventually to be the 'grand old man' of the blues.

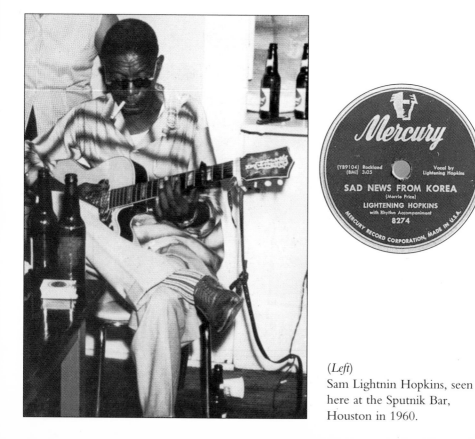

(*Left*)
Sam Lightnin Hopkins, seen here at the Sputnik Bar, Houston in 1960.

DISCOVERING THE BLUES

(*Right*) Josh White popularised black folk song among white audiences in New York.

(*Below*) Big Bill Broonzy, playing in London at the launch of his book, *Big Bill Blues*, 1955.

(*Left*) One-man band Jesse Fuller, played 12-string guitar, harmonica, cymbals and a foot-operated bass.

(*Facing page*) Texas-born one-man band Weldon 'Juke Boy' Bonner (*top left*). Champion Jack Dupree (*top right*), eventually made his home in Europe. (*Bottom left*) Big Boy Crudup in London and (*bottom right*) 'Peg Leg' Howell, at the time of his 'rediscovery'.

(*Below*) Robert Pete Williams from Louisiana sang extempore, free-form blues.

Little Walter, Sunnyland Slim, Roosevelt Sykes, Jump Jackson, author Paul Oliver and Little Brother Montgomery in Chicago.

(*Left*) Syl Johnson playing at tables in a Rush Street club, Chicago.

(*Right*) Clifton Chenier, 'King' of the zydeco blues musicians.

NOTICE!

STOP

Help Save The Youth of America
DON'T BUY NEGRO RECORDS

(If you don't want to serve negroes in your place of business, then do not have negro records on your juke box or listen to negro records on the radio.)

The screaming, idiotic words, and savage music of these records are undermining the morals of our white youth in America.

Call the advertisers of the radio stations that play this type of music and complain to them!

Don't Let Your Children Buy, or Listen To These Negro Records

For additional copies of this circular, write
CITIZENS' COUNCIL OF GREATER NEW ORLEANS, INC.
509 Delta Building   New Orleans Louisiana 70112

(*Above*) The racist Citizen's Council of New Orleans 'circular notice' opposed Rhythm and Blues.

Clarence 'Frogman' Henry was one of many musicians who remained in the South. He is seen here playing piano in a New Orleans bar.

(*Left*) Robert 'Junior' Lockwood, was influenced by his stepfather, Robert Johnson.

(*Below*) K.C. Douglas from Mississippi was one of many who migrated to the West Coast. Playing here in Oakland, California.

(*Right*) Eddie 'Son' House hollered fierce, personal blues and played a steel guitar with his brass slide. Muddy Waters learned from him.

(*Below*) Bukka (Booker) White, known as 'Barrelhouse' when he was an inmate at Parchman Farm, was a powerful performer.

Bill Williams, last of the songsters to be discovered, once worked with Blind Blake.

With the Folk Blues Festivals of the 1960's, Sonny Boy Williamson played for ecstatic audiences.

(*Left*) Buddy Guy and Junior Wells playing amongst the crowd at the Ann Arbor Blues Festival, 1971.

good money. In 1933 he recorded – as 'Joshua White, the Singing Christian' for his gospel songs, and as 'Pinewood Tom' for his blues. He accompanied Buddy Moss, Walter Roland and Leroy Carr on record and even played with the Carver Boys, a white hillbilly group. In the late 'thirties the shrewd and personable Josh White made his way to New York to try his luck in the night clubs of the city. He was a great success, as he popularised black folk song among white audiences.

New York attracted a great many singers from the Piedmont besides Blind Gary and Josh White; Sonny Terry, Brownie McGhee, Sticks McGhee and Leroy Dallas among them. Saunders Terrell was born in Greensboro, Georgia, in October 1911, but when he was three his father brought him to the Piedmont Hills above Durham, North Carolina, where he worked a farm. When he was eleven years old, 'Sonny Terry' was blinded in one eye in a children's game. A few years later a piece of iron thrown in his face caused him to lose the sight of his other eye. Withdrawn into blindness, he concentrated on playing the harmonica which he had been 'fooling with' since early childhood. He 'mocked the trains' and imitated the 'Fox Chase', making the cries of the hounds and the scream of the fox as he played the harp. His skill at combining voice and harmonica with falsetto whoops and hollers, alternating with the wails of the instrument played 'crossed' was unsurpassed in the region, even by DeFord Bailey, the diminutive player from Nashville, who came by playing his *Alcoholic Blues* and gave Sonny Terry the idea of making his living through his harmonica. He teamed up with Blind Gary Davis and the two instrumental virtuosi played on the streets of the tobacco towns together. Eventually Sonny met up with Blind Boy Fuller, with whom he became firm friends, and, after Gary Davis had left to preach on the highways they travelled as a duo. For a while they all played together and the three blind musicians must have made a commanding sight on the streets of Durham or Raleigh.

They were led by a local boy, a partial albino by the name of George Washington who lived in Durham. W.T. Blackwell's 'Genuine Durham Smoking Tobacco' with its bull trademark had given the town the name of 'Bull City', so Washington rejoiced in the name of 'Bull City Red'. He played guitar, not especially well, in imitation of Blind Boy Fuller, but he was a vigorous washboard player, accompanying them at suppers and balls. The mayor of a nearby town and owner of a department store in Durham, J. B. Long, acted as the manager for the group and got them many recording dates with the Vocalion company in the late 'thirties. Bull City Red, on a trip to Burlington, met up with another singer, Walter 'Brownie' McGhee. Son of a Tennessee farmer and 'wheeler' on the Clinch River, Brownie was born in Knoxville, Tennessee, in November 1915. His uncle, John Evans was a fiddler who played in the hill country style which was characteristic of both black and white dance functions. Evans made the boy a banjo from a marshmallow tin and on this McGhee learned his first tunes. Later he got a guitar and started to play for corn-shucking bees and similar country parties. At the age of four, just after the birth of his brother, Granville 'Sticks', he was struck by poliomyelitis, which permanently affected the growth of his right leg. Unable to do normal field work, he played guitar for vacation resorts in the Smoky Mountains until he joined a company of the Rabbit Foot Minstrels. Like many another singer he travelled with 'doctor' shows and with the Mighty Haag Carnival, played at roadhouses and jukes, 'running wild'. When he learned to use finger picks he began to play in the rocking, rhythmic-melodic style of the region which was locally called 'jukin''.

In the lean years of the 'thirties, Brownie had 'a little racket' in Knoxville. There he led a small string band with two guitars, harmonica, bass and two washboards, one played by Robert Young, who was called Washboard Slim, and the other by Leroy Dallas, who doubled on guitar. 'One board on the belly, one on the horse' was the term for the lap and saddle styles of washboard playing the band used. The harmonica player, who had a technique remarkably similar to that of his friend Sonny Terry, was a stone-mason and one-man band from Winston-Salem, Jordan Webb. It was when travelling with Webb and reaching Burlington that they met up with Bull City Red, who introduced them to J. B. Long, Blind Boy Fuller and the other musicians. Fuller was a little contemptuous at first of Brownie McGhee, but some kind of working relationship developed. Fuller's gritty voice was very different from Brownie McGhee's softer, burred intonation, but there was a similarity in their swinging styles, in the songs and blues they played and the guitar-harmonica-washboard teams they had. Brownie played a cheap Gibson guitar whereas Fuller played his steel-bodied 'National', with its hard sound and greater volume.

In June 1940, Blind Boy Fuller went to Chicago to record but he was far from well. His themes this time did not have the rowdy bawdiness of *What's That Smells Like Fish?* or *Get Your Yas Yas Out* nor the spirited instrumentals like *Jitterbug Rag, Piccolo Rag* and *Step It Up and Go* of earlier sessions, but were morbid and ominous like *When You Are Gone* and *Lost Lover Blues*. A few months later he went into hospital for a kidney operation and never came round from the anaesthetic. His fellow musicians were shocked. There had been many who had modelled themselves on him – Floyd Council, called 'Dipper Boy', who had styled himself as 'Blind Boy Fuller's Buddy' when he recorded in 1937; Ralph Willis from Alabama, who worked mainly in the Carolinas; the brothers Richard and Welly Trice – Richard Trice recording even after the war in Fuller's style as 'Little Boy Fuller'; and the obscure but able imitator, Sonny Jones. For J. B. Long the loss was a commercial one and he began to record Brownie McGhee, to the singer's irritation, as 'Blind Boy Fuller No. 2'. He was playing Fuller's 'National' and sang *The Death of Blind Boy Fuller* as a testimony to the older man, but his blues were brash and optimistic in many cases, and he sang lively dance songs.

> When I was young, in my prime,
> I could get my barbecue any ol' time,
> Now I'm old, bones is cold
> Can't get no barbecue to save my soul,
> Tell me li'l woman, who d'you give my barbecue to?
>
> I'm a poor boy, and a long, long ways from home,
> Please don't mistreat me, please don't leave me 'lone.

He had both Jordan Webb and Sonny Terry playing with him on harmonicas (even both together on *Back Home Blues*), Robert Young and Bull City Red – following Fuller's recording of Joe McCoy's song *Oh Red*, George Washington was being called 'Oh Red' now – on washboards, and Buddy Moss, who taught him to copyright his songs, playing guitar. In 1938, both Sonny Terry and Washington had gone to New York to play in the Spirituals to Swing Concert and Sonny left to try his luck in the city. He took the opportunity to meet up with Leadbelly who was now making the folk song circuit and playing in Greenwich Village clubs, and lived in the same house with him. Brownie decided to go to New York himself. New York had an audience that had an interest in blues but few blues singers and Sonny Terry had the good fortune to land a part in *Finian's Rainbow* which kept him eating and playing in the forties; later Brownie joined him and they shared a small spot for the run of Tennessee Williams's *Cat on a Hot Tin Roof*. This and a spell working for a vendor of mojo hands, love philtres and voodoo charms gave Brownie sufficient capital to open a 'Home of the Blues' school for singers and guitarists in Harlem on 125th Street – Alex Seward was one of his pupils there.

There were many other singers from the region about whom little is known at present: one such was the pure-voiced and instrumentally brilliant guitarist, Luke Jordan, who lived in Lynchburg, Virginia and who was recalled by a younger man, John Jackson, as having played in Rappahannock County, Virginia, whence William Moore also came. Julius Daniels, whose songs also spanned the blues, dance and 'songster' traditions, recorded in Atlanta in 1927 but was then living on Trade Street in Charlotte, North Carolina; he is as little known as his companions, Bubba Lee Torrence and Wilbert Andrews, the latter being on his recording of a traditional theme in the region, *Crow Jane Blues*. A favourite blues among such singers as Fuller, Moss, Willis, White and McGhee was *Red River Blues*, which was recorded in Charlotte, North Carolina, in 1938 by Virgil Childers, but his other titles include such songs as the minstrel show theme *Travelin' Man* and the white parody of the *Preacher and the Bear*. Other instances could be cited and they emphasise the existence of a blues and songster tradition which was strong in the eastern seaboard states. More considered in performance with emphasis on good execution, rhythmically free-flowing, lighter in texture and without the passionate, intense singing and fierce flailing of some of the Mississippi singers, it had a distinct flavour which mingled with that of the hill-billy and mountain singers of the white rural tradition. John Jackson, born in 1924 in Rappahannock County, or his namesake, Bill Jackson, who was born well up on the East Coast in Maryland and who learned from an otherwise unknown singer named Jim Fuller and from a stint on the B & O railroad, were late exponents of this regional tradition.

Although the Appalachians divide North Carolina from Tennessee, the mountains present no major physical barrier and there are numerous roads to break across them which the circulating blues singers used. Highway 70 was the most popular, linking the Atlantic coast by way of Raleigh, Asheville and Knoxville, with Nashville and Memphis. This was the route that Blind Boy Fuller, Sonny Terry, Sonny Jones and Bull City Red followed when the riotous car-load went to Memphis to record rather improbably, as 'Brother George and his Sanctified Singers'. In Memphis itself there was a lot of musical activity, even though some of the older musicians had died: Jim Jackson, for instance, in 1937. Some of them recorded at the same time as Fuller, like Jack Kelly, who apparently no longer had his jug band but was still accompanied by a fiddle player and another guitarist. Another was Little Buddy Doyle, a dwarf musician who was a familiar figure on Beale Street in the 'thirties, who played guitar. There were older musicians like Furry Lewis and Frank Stokes still living in Memphis, or like Joe Calicott, just outside the city, but they were not sought again by the record companies. Of the men who had recorded before the Depression in Memphis, few were heard after, but one who was again on record was Sleepy John Estes from Brownsville, Tennessee, sixty miles out on Highway 70.

> Now I were raised in Lauder' County, you know I was
>   schooled on Winfield Lane (2)
> Then what I made of myself, I declare it was a cryin' shame.
>
> Now Brownsville is my home, an' you know I ain't going
>   to throw her down (2)
> Because I'm 'quainted with them laws, and they won't let
>   me down.

sang Estes in his *Brownsville Blues*. His father was a tenant farmer not far from Ripley, when John Adam Estes was born in January 1899. When he was eleven, the family of sixteen children and their parents moved to Brownsville, where, in conditions of crushing poverty, he lived until his death in 1977. He lost the sight of one eye through being injured in a baseball game as a boy, and his vision slowly deteriorated in subsequent years. As his father played guitar, he was always trying to play the instrument but he got further instruction from an older singer, Willie Newbern, who lived in Brownsville. Newbern recorded once only, making just half a dozen sides in Atlanta in 1929 but they showed his considerable instrumental ability and the catholicity of his songs, which ranged from near-vaudeville to highly personalised blues. In his *Shelby County Workhouse Blues*, he described how he was arrested coming from Marked Tree, Arkansas, and this may have given rise to the report which could also have been true, that he was beaten to death in prison at Marvell in the 'forties.

Though Estes was not a particularly accomplished guitarist himself he shared with Newbern the ability to create songs out of his own experience. His blues were essentially personal or they were comments on the personalities in Brownsville. He told of his own rescue from drowning in *Floating Bridge* and of the burning of his friend Martha Hardin's house in *Fire Department Blues*; his blues were his autobiography and were one man's vision of his immediate world. Big Bill Broonzy described 'Sleepy John' Estes's way of singing as 'crying the blues' and it aptly fitted his broken, fragmented song which was held in tension by the contrast between the tendency to disintegration and the rhythmic impetus of his strumming. Much of the beauty of Estes's recordings lay in the mournful harmonica-playing of his unexpectedly ebullient young partner, Hammie Nixon. Though his parents objected, Hammie followed Estes to the country suppers, playing harmonica for him from 1927, when he was only twelve years old. Nixon came from Ripley where he had been under the influence of the harmonica player in the Cannon Jug Stompers, Noah Lewis, who was stabbed to death in 1937. With Nixon wailing an obligato in and out of Estes's sung phrases the two men built up a remarkable unity of sound which was given interest by their tendency to double time in the course of a song.

Mostly they played at country suppers. 'They'd take down the beds to make room, put a table 'cross the kitchen door where they'd cook catfish and sell it, sell moonshine and shoot craps in the barn. Late at night it'd get rough. They'd shoot out the lights. One night I remember Sleepy John and I had to run off; he got hung up on a barbwire fence,' Yank Rachel told Bob Koester. Rachel played mandolin and was much younger than Estes, having been born near Brownsville in March 1910. When he was eighteen, he worked on the L & N railroad as a track-hand, but in 1929 he and Estes went down to Memphis and played on Beale until they got a record session. Later, in the early 'thirties Rachel teamed up with an older man, Dan Smith; they recorded a good many titles and were paid well for it. Too well, for Smith made little secret of his newly won money. He was attacked by a burglar and left with his neck broken. That year, 1934 Hammie Nixon and a Brownsville friend with a rough voice, Son Bonds, went up to Chicago to record. Estes grabbed a freight train and followed them up to Chicago to secure for himself several recording dates. Naturally, he sang about it:

> Now special agent, special agent, put me off close to
>   some town (2)
> Now, I got to do some recordin', I ought to be recordin'
>   right now.

One day Sonny Boy Williamson 'came ridin' by on his 'bike' from Jackson, Tennessee, and he and Yank Rachel became good friends. Rachel was better able to adjust to the newer sounds of Williamson's playing and for several years he worked with Sonny Boy, going up to St Louis to be near Chicago for sessions. Son Bonds was less fortunate: a man also passed his gate when he was sitting on his front porch, but pulled a gun and shot Bonds without warning, killing him instantly. In the unlovely, neglected landscape of western Tennessee the blues singers have been stalked by tragedy, with Noah Lewis, Sonny Boy Williamson, Hambone Willie Newbern, Dan Smith and Son Bonds all meeting violent deaths. William Tucker came from Ripley and took the name of John Henry Barbee after he shot a white man in Luxora, Arkansas. He died of cancer in jail following a road accident in 1964. Though he was spared such a fate, Sleepy John Estes eventually lost his sight completely and in the years after the war was living in destitution in a cabin with neither water nor electricity. But he was still playing music occasionally in the country while, down in Memphis, the last act in the city's important part in the story of the blues was being played out.

The Number One Scab

West of the Mississippi, the effects of the Depression were not so very different from those elsewhere in the South. Farms became idle, prices dropped, the poor became poorer, especially in Texas where the lack of an effective legislation on minimum wages meant that many workers were in penury. But whereas the families who 'packed their trunks to leave' in the Delta region made for Memphis, St Louis or Chicago, and those to the east gravitated to Birmingham, Atlanta, or on to Washington and New York, in the western part of the old South, it was different. There were large cities in the region, particularly in or near Texas, to which displaced workers migrated and Shreveport, Dallas and Houston witnessed considerable growth rates. This internal migration meant that the contact with the North was less. It also meant there is less known data and less recorded material on the blues. It is almost twice as far from Chicago to Dallas as it is from Chicago to Memphis and the distance made talent scouting or bringing singers to the North uneconomic. One or two trips were made, in fact, but Texas blues in the 'thirties was recorded internally, and much of it – including whole sessions by Willie Reed, Funny Paper Smith, Black Ace, Black Boy Shine and Bernice Edwards – remained unissued or had a token coupling issued only.

These singers represent a fair cross-section of the considerable army of guitarists and pianists who were active in the westward-expanding cotton frontier, the logging camps and the cities as the recuperation from the worst of the Depression gathered strength. One, Babe Kyro Turner, was born in Hughes Springs, not far from the Louisiana border, in December, 1907 on a farm, where he worked until he was in his late twenties. Typically, too, his first instrument was a home-made one and he was a young man before he was able to buy a guitar. When the farm could no longer support the family,

Babe Turner made for Shreveport, and there met Buddy Woods, a man some fifteen years his senior, who had a small string band. Oscar 'Buddy' Woods played the guitar flat across his knees Hawaiian style, and used a slide; it was not a technique that Turner was accustomed to, but he copied it and soon became proficient, using as a slide a small medicine bottle. The two men worked at the joints and at house parties and made relatively good money until Turner broke away on his own. In 1936 he was broadcasting over Station KFJZ, singing in his burred, warm tones his theme blues:

> I am the Black Ace I'm the boss card in your hand (2) –
> And I'll play for you mama if you'll please let me be
>   your man.
>
> Sometimes the Black Ace never comes in sight (2)
> But I'll play for you mama if you please will treat me
>   right.

By now he was known as 'The Black Ace' and was doing well until 1943 when he went into the Army, eventually to play for service functions as 'Buck' Turner. But when he came out, he had no employment, and it was not until he was given a job helping at a photographic studio in 1955 that he had regular work. By then the guitar and the blues were left behind, but for him they were being actively played by one of his followers, Andrew Hogg.

In the 'thirties Andrew Hogg used to 'run around' with Black Ace, playing second guitar to him. Hogg was eleven years younger and had also been raised on a farm, near Cushing, Texas. He learned a little guitar from listening to his father play and in his early twenties he was playing for country suppers with Turner. He modelled himself on the records of Peetie Wheatstraw just as Ace had been influenced to some extent by the records of Kokomo Arnold, at least to 'cover' Arnold's *Milk Cow Blues* with his own *Lowing Heifer*. Later, Hogg began to establish his own identity, though he always retained a buzz-tone in his vocals that related to the singing of both Ace and Wheatstraw. Then in 1936 he, Andrew Hogg, Black Ace and Alex Moore, still rolling out the blues in Dallas, travelled to Chicago for one session for Decca. Hogg made just two sides and did not record again for eleven years. When he did it was with the indistinct enunciation that gave him the name of 'Smokey' Hogg. Many of his post-war records were made with a small group including drums and piano or a similar combination. Sometimes Alex Moore played on these too. The veteran Dallas pianist was now fifty years old, still carting junk 'from North Dallas to the East Side', and playing piano at nights. He too, had a blurred, rather hoarse voice but his piano playing was as vigorous as ever and his blues had the same quirkish lyrics that had distinguished them in the past.

> When you neglect your woman she'll compare you with
>   someone else (2)
> I don't blame that woman – I'd feel the same way myself.
>
> I believe each and every woman should have a chance
>   at the Tree of Life (2)
> Just treat her nice and kind, be patient; that's the way
>   to control a man's wife.

Alex Moore represented the older generation of blues singers in Texas and was one of the few to record after the War. But he was by no means alone among those who were still singing, and though Blind Lemon Jefferson had died years before, Texas Alexander was still to be heard in Dallas or in the country between Dallas and Houston, or out in West Texas, following the migrant cotton-workers who were now being driven out in trucks to the labourer's camps that served the newly opened-up fields. As Alexander did not play a guitar, he still used an accompanist, and in the late 'thirties Funny Paper Smith was travelling with him. There were few Texas blues guitarists of note who did not claim to have played for Texas Alexander at one time or another, and one who often worked with him was Sam Hopkins. A complex of family associations suggests a vague relationship between the Hopkins family and Alexander. The Hopkins' were born on a farm at Centerville, Texas; the oldest, John Henry, in 1901. He left home at an early age and led a tempestuous life, but his brother Joel Hopkins, who was born in 1904, started playing guitar when he was nine and after working as a medicine show buck-and-wing dancer met up with Blind Lemon Jefferson in 1922. By this time Sam Hopkins was ten years old, but as a child he, too, followed Lemon around when he was working in the country and, compared with the hard strumming and strident singing of his brother Joel, learned more from Jefferson. Sam developed still further the arpeggio technique of answering phrases for which Lemon was famous and moulded this into a very personal one of his own.

For some years, Sam Hopkins wandered with Texas Alexander, off and on, playing while the older man sang. But he also travelled a good deal by himself, playing for suppers, in the streets, wherever he could.

He had a remarkable gift for improvising blues both instrumentally and lyrically, following Lemon's leadership in the invention of new verses out of fragments of everyday experience. His blues became, like those of Sleepy John Estes, an extended essay in autobiography.

> You know the doctor says 'I got somethin' to tell you I
>   been had on my min' for a long time
> You better stop drinkin' whiskey Sam and turn over,
>   and drink some wine.'
> You know I cain't drink no whiskey boys, like everybody
>   else,
> For the reason you know I got to quit drinkin' whiskey
>   boys,
> You know it's bound to ruin my health.

These were some of the important blues singers whose formative years were between the wars, but who were virtually unknown until the late 'forties. Before any further discussion of the complex pattern of post-War developments, it is necessary to take a look at the south Texas piano tradition, the development of the local record industry and the popularisation of electric instruments. In the lumber camps of the Piney Woods in the belt running from East Texas deep into Louisiana and the southern part of Mississippi, the piano traditions continued unabated from the 'twenties. Timber was still being felled, the camps on the shacks mounted on railroad car chassis, moved deeper into the woods as the forest was reduced to stump lands. The barrelhouse moved with them. In these unapproachable regions, piano blues of a kind almost unrecorded was the fundamental music. Many of the pianists moved further west or drifted to the towns, in particular the wide-open towns of Richmond, west of Houston, and the seaport of Galveston. Here were to be heard the hard-hitting boogie and blues pianists like Conish Burks and Son Becky, Rob Cooper and Black Boy Shine, Andy Boy, Robert 'Fud' Shaw and Edwin 'Buster' Pickens, and the singers Joe Pullem and Walter 'Cowboy' Washington.

Detailed discussion of these powerful and dynamic groups of piano players is not practicable here; together they formed a group sometimes known as 'The Santa Fe' who travelled on the branches of this line from the lumber camps to the oil fields to the open towns. In the latter centres they were to be heard in the red light district of Galveston's Post Office Street or Church Street, on Houston's

West Dallas Street or in Richmond's Mud Alley. Though they formed a 'school', they had individual characteristics, with Andy Boy and Rob Cooper displaying strong ragtime influences, Burks and Son Becky playing a driving blues with walking bass figures and Buster Pickens favouring slow and contemplative blues. Their voices tended to be pitched fairly high and they sang in the relaxed, slightly blurred manner favoured by many Texas singers. An exception to this generalisation was Joe Pullem whose diction was exceptionally clear and who sang in a shrill, unstrained falsetto which contrasted with the barrelhouse piano that Andy Boy and Rob Cooper played for him. He gave an effective impression of the country-to-urban population movement in the combination of elements in his records as well as in the choice of words he sang.

> See that train comin' mama, up the railroad track (2)
> I want you to catch it baby, and don't ever come back.
>
> See me standin' here with my dirty, dirty duckins on (2)
> That means my baby's in trouble, hustlin's going on.

A contrast in the careers of these singers is effectively emphasised by Shaw and Pickens, neither of whom recorded at the few isolated sessions which put most of the others on wax. Many bluesmen worked joints in the townships and camps served by the railroad. Robert Shaw was one: 'When you listen to what I'm playing, you got to see in your mind all them gals out there swinging their butts and getting the mens excited. Otherwise you ain't got the music rightly understood.' Shaw was born in Stafford, Texas, a cattle town near Richmond and, as a teenager, joined the group of pianists working the Santa Fe triangle of towns. He played with the red-light pianists, followed the labour gangs to the cotton-picks and beat his way up to Kilgore during the oil boom years. His path took him as far north as Kansas City and when, after a spell playing on a radio station in Oklahoma City, he made his way back to South Texas and settled in Austin, he began to be a runner for a policy wheel. It was the attitude of the police to his later activities that made him give up, in 1932, a career of barrelhouse piano playing for the more sedentary one of barbecueing spare-ribs. Edwin 'Buster' Pickens was younger, born in Hempstead in 1916, but he was barely more than a boy when he began to follow the older blues pianists into the lumber camp barrelhouses. He played piano with Doctor Sugar's Medicine Show and worked with the Sugar Foot Green Minstrels, but his main work was, like that of the others, in the lumber and oil camp barrelhouses and the joints of Richmond and Houston's Fourth Ward.

Work in these joints was, in his own word, 'rugged', but he tried to take care of himself and to avoid an early death from 'exposure' by coming out of an overheated shack into cold night air too often, the fate of most of the piano-players he had known. But life could still be rugged in the city joints and in November 1964 he was shot to death in a dispute over a few coins. A dozen or so years before he had made his only commercial recording, and such was the interweaving of traditions, that it was as pianist in Leon Benton's Busy Bees, accompanying the ageing Texas Alexander on his only post-War record. Soon after, Texas Alexander died, while the curfew imposed on the rural barrelhouses by the police had killed the main employment Buster Pickens had ever had. In the years before he died, Pickens was generally to be found playing piano in Lightnin' Hopkins's club dates. Small, serious, unable to adjust to changing circumstances, Buster Pickens was the antithesis of the ebullient, resourceful and ultimately successful Robert Shaw, who made for himself a profitable business in Austin. They represent the polarities of personality within the blues, but both shared a music in a strong localised tradition which met the needs of the black populace while social conditions permitted.

But the social conditions were changing, and the blues had to change with them. The movement from rural to urban centres within the state was creating job competition which the work opportunities could not meet. On the west coast, the defence factories were offering employment on a scale which made migration attractive to African Americans in the south-west region. Between 1920 and 1930 Los Angeles's African American population increased by one-and-a-half times and the rate continued through the 'thirties. In California as a whole, there were only just over 80,000 Blacks in 1930 and during the next decade, the number increased by a half – the increase in Los Angeles and San Francisco was indicative of the concentration of migrants in the cities. But between 1940 and 1950 this number increased by well over 300,000 to a total in California of 462,000 and the inflow continued to grow. The massive migrations from the Mississippi Delta to the North were paralleled by no less vast movements to the West. And of these, by far the largest proportion came from Texas, with others coming from Louisiana or Oklahoma – or migrating from those States into Texas itself.

With the exodus of African Americans went many blues singers, some to go and remain in the new domain, others to migrate for a period of time, to play music in the opening bars and joints of Oakland and Watts before drifting back to Texas and the central states. So it happened that Smokey Hogg was recorded extensively in Los Angeles as well as in Dallas and Houston, and so, too, was Sam Hopkins. He travelled to the West Coast with his pianist, Thunder Smith, who played in the manner of the Santa Fe men. With them was a younger man, Amos Milburn, who had been born in Houston in 1926 but who had spent the war years, under age, in the Marines. Texas Alexander wanted to go too, but Mrs Cullum, who was Milburn's manager and had arranged for the session in Los Angeles, was frightened by the old, rough man who had only recently come out of jail. In Los Angeles, Sam Hopkins and Wilson 'Thunder' Smith made a number of exciting sides which led one of the engineers to call them 'Thunder and Lightnin' – which latter name stuck with Hopkins. Milburn, on the other hand, played a smoother, more sophisticated style of piano which made Thunder Smith's appear rugged and anachronistic. Thunder Smith and Lightnin' Hopkins played on the West Coast for a while to the newly settled migrants from Texas, but soon they found themselves back in Houston to stay.

Two streams of blues were beginning to emerge in the immediate post-War years; the 'Down-Home Blues' of the older singers and the first phase of 'Rhythm and Blues'. Of these the former had a clearer pattern and the deeper roots but eventually both currents were to meet and intermingle through the increasing importance of mass media of communication. In the 'twenties and 'thirties, phonograph records had been distributed to the 'Race' mainly through the music and furniture shops and by means of travelling salesmen who followed up their sales of hand-wound phonographs with supplies of new discs. They ensured that the blues of the North was widely disseminated in the South, but distribution methods were coloured by the kind of market which had been ascertained for a particular singer. This was often of local interest only, but whether local or not, its effect was damaging to music-making.

A hand-wound phonograph could now provide music for dancing more cheaply, and often with greater variety than could a single singer, a duo or even a string band. In the late 'thirties the inroads made in group entertainment by the record industry were bolstered by the introduction of the mechanical players, which could handle as many as fifty records at a time. They were set up in the country districts at every crossing cafe, and in every joint and juke. The latter gave them their name – juke-boxes began to replace live musicians everywhere; florid, chromium plated and enamelled in genuine 'pop' art fashion, they were installed at roadside booths, even on breakfast counters. Their cheap sophistication offered an urban image to rural joints: by 1940 the juke-box industry had a sixty-five million dollar turnover.

Radio similarly had made great strides in the exploitation of the African American market; the potential of large untapped commodity sales overcame lingering prejudice about beaming blues records to black audiences. Disc-jockeys with fanciful names and a swift, jivey line of patter introduced the records; advertised goods sold, and the blues began to boom. If there was an adverse effect in the steady wearing away of live music in some districts, there was a bonus in the opportunities that the demand for discs gave to singers to record. Before the War the record industry had been in the hands of a few major concerns whose Decca, Bluebird, Okeh, Vocalion and Victor issues, together with those appearing simultaneously on a batch of labels owned by the American Record Company and issued through chainstores and mail-order catalogues, decided what would be heard of the blues. In 1942 the growth of the juke-box industry had reached such proportions that James C. Petrillo, President of the American Federation of Musicians, declared that the record was 'the Number One Scab'. Record companies were 'musical monsters that were killing employment' for musicians, he ranted, and banned his members from recording for the industry. This and the strict rationing of shellac effectively stopped the recording of blues, although such singers as Bing Crosby, Perry Como and Frank Sinatra, along with the big swing bands, were still bringing in plenty of money for the industry.

When it seemed that the big companies were unlikely to show any interest in blues again, a mushroom growth of small labels appeared all over the country. They were particularly prominent on the West Coast where the appropriately named Juke-Box label started as early as 1943. Some time after, Gilt-Edge appeared and Bob Geddins started his Down Town, Big Town and Rhythm labels. In Texas, Bill Quinn's Gold Star label, Don Robey's Peacock and his later acquistion, the Memphis-based Duke and a host of minor companies including Blue Bonnet, Freedom, and Star Talent sprang up. Though such labels appeared only intermittently in the late 'forties, by 1952 most of them had come on the market. Some, like Peacock or the west coast Jaxyson, were black owned and gave further indication of the demand for the blues, both Down-Home and Rhythm and Blues. Lightnin' Hopkins was firmly in the first category. His blues were sometimes harsh, sometimes introverted, sometimes outgoing dance tunes. His flair for lyric invention seldom failed him and he commented on his fear of airplanes, on the war in Korea, on tornadoes and on private disputes with equal freedom and personalisation.

> You know this world is in a tangle, baby, yeah I feel, they're
> gonna start war again (2)
> Yes there's gonna be many mothers and fathers worryin',
> yes there's gonna be as many girls that lose a frien'.
>
> I got the news this mornin', right now they need a million
> men (2)
> You know I been overseas, woman, po' Lightnin' don't
> want to go there again.

He answered every phrase with a flourish on the guitar, and his slow blues often had extended improvisations in which single chords and whining blue notes were set against flashing arpeggios. Hopkins made a remarkable series of records for Gold Star, and though some did not survive Bill Quinn's unorthodox bathroom methods of producing discs, there were many masterpieces among them. Another of Gold Star's singers was Melvin 'Lil Son' Jackson who had been persuaded by his friends to send a demonstration record, made in an amusement arcade booth, to Quinn. His guitar work had a rolling rhythm and his taut and plaintive voice a distinctive quality. Jackson was born in Tyler, half-way between Dallas and Shreveport, in August 1916 and liked a small group to accompany him. He toured for some years in Oklahoma and Texas and made many records for Imperial until a car crash led him to give up playing blues. A sincere and nervous man, 'Lil Son' Jackson retired to work in an auto wrecking firm.

Along Highway 90, on the route from Houston to New Orleans, is situated the small town of Crowley where J. D. Miller, a local record man, gathered together some of the talent in West Louisiana and recorded them for the Nashville-based Excello company. Of these, the guitarist Otis Hicks, who was born in St Louis in 1915 but brought by his parents to Baton Rouge, was the most interesting. He shared much in common with Lightnin' Hopkins, including a nickname, recording under the name of Lightnin' Slim. Though he used the same arpeggio-based guitar technique, Lightnin' Slim was a simpler man and a rougher singer with the 'real sound of the swamp', as *Billboard* commented. Around him were loosely gathered a number of musicians who played on his records or on dates. Few had the humour of his *Hoo-Doo Blues* or the weight of *Bad Luck and Trouble*, but Lonesome Sundown's *My Home is a Prison* was a moving blues by one of the younger singers. The name concealed the identity of Cornelius Green, who was born in Opelousas, Louisiana in 1928. He played an effective and melodic guitar. Almost the same age, James Moore from West Baton Rouge, who recorded as Slim Harpo, played harmonica and sang, making a hit record with his *Rainin' in My Heart* and *I'm a King Bee*. Like Lazy Lester who was also from Baton Rouge, Slim Harpo played amplified harmonica. All these blues singers played electric instruments in spite of their 'down-home' character; in the southern jukes, a band or singer could only be heard live by playing with the volume, and even the distorted amplification, that the juke-boxes produced. Taking electric guitars in their car trunks, they worked dances and 'battles' from Baton Rouge to Houston.

One singer who emphasised the cross-fertilisation of blues styles was Lowell Fulson, who was born in Tulsa, Oklahoma, in 1921 into a family with musical talent. His father was part-Indian but Fulson's music was essentially blues. He played with the Wright Brothers' String Band in Texas as a youth and when he was seventeen met up with Texas Alexander, whom he accompanied for some three years. Such is the continuity of the Texas singers that he replaced Funny Paper Smith in this role, and continued until the War. While in the Navy he played with United Services shows and was often accompanied by the boogie piano, drums and guitar groups which were popular in the Swing era. On his discharge he went to Oakland on the West Coast and began playing in the clubs. The high pay in the shipbuilding industry had led to the opening of many of these clubs and so to a further influx of blues singers from Texas, Oklahoma, and Kansas City. At first, Lowell Fulson sang and played with his brother, Martin Fulson, accompanying him, but after the death of his brother, he began to use a small group, with a positive change of sound from the Down Home character of the early work to a more modern flavour. The pianist was frequently Lloyd Glenn, a Texas pianist of long standing who had much experience in the 'thirties working with the San Antonio and Dallas jazz bands of Terrence Holder and Boots Douglas. At other times he was accompanied by Jay McShann on piano, and a contingent of West Coast or Kansas City musicians.

This transition from Southern blues to the modern idiom of the West Coast represented in the work of Lowell Fulson the change that was taking place in the blues in California. Lloyd Glenn's contemporaries, Charles Brown, the pianist, and the brothers Oscar and Johnny Moore, had popularised a bland, fluent technique.

Though lacking in strength or conviction, they were capable of adapting themselves to popular ballads or boogie-blues with equal confidence. Similar in character and also coming from Texas, Floyd Dixon played a delicately melodic blues piano and sang in a plummy, sophisticated voice. They had all followed Ivory Joe Hunter out to the West Coast and together formed a style of blues which was peculiar to the region. Hunter had been born in Wiergate, Texas, in 1914 and had gone out to California in the 'thirties. Though he made frequent trips back to Texas, he was extremely popular in Oakland and Los Angeles and always returned there. In 1945 he formed his own record company, Ivory, and had 'The Three Blazers' – Charles Brown and the Moore brothers – to accompany him. Oscar Moore had played for a considerable time with the popular ballad singer Nat 'King' Cole and his influence coloured their work. Hunter also played piano for Lowell Fulson at one time, and, though Fulson's high, strained voice and instrumental technique were more firmly rooted in the Texas blues of his youth, the blend was apparently successful.

For many tastes the work of this group was too effete, but for others it was agreeably sophisticated in sound. A formula which had been arrived at by the pianist Cecil Gant was to couple a rolling boogie-woogie or 'jump' item with a more sentimental blues-ballad on one record. Gant was born in Nashville, Tennessee, in 1915 and had been influenced by Leroy Carr, whom he resembled on blues numbers. He moved to the West Coast and served in the Army during the War. When he was discharged he began to record for the Gilt Edge Company on North Western Avenue, Los Angeles, who billed him as 'Pvt. Cecil Gant, the G.I. Sing-Sation'. It was a clever device for it played on his lowly Army role. His first record, *I Wonder*, was an outstanding hit and played a part as important as Mamie Smith's *Crazy Blues* in 1920, in opening up the new blues market.

There were parallels between the blues of the East Coast 'Classic' singers of Harlem and Atlantic City in the 'twenties and the West coast singers of this school in the late 'forties: they softened the market and prepared the way for a more vigorous music to follow. The harder strain of 'Rhythm and Blues' came quickly and was driven home by three veterans of earlier days, who came from the mid-west. In December 1938, the pianist and vocalist team of Pete Johnson and Joe Turner made the coupling, *Roll 'Em Pete* and *Goin' Away Blues*, which largely anticipated the 'R & B' post-war music. The record was a tremendous success and the two men decided to stay in New York on the strength of it. They had come from Kansas City where

Pete Johnson was born in 1904. There he learned to play piano from Udell Wilson, Nero Edgar, Stacey La Guardia, Good Booty Johnson, Slamfoot Brown and his uncle, Charles Johnson – pianists who worked at the Entertainer Club and the Independence Club and who taught him to play walking basses. In the mid-'thirties he began working at the Sunset Crystal Palace on 12th and Woodlawn and built up a small band in the Kansas City tradition: hard-hitting, blues-based, riffing. The Sunset was owned by the local 'boss', Piney Brown, who had installed a tall and massively-built young bartender, Joe Turner. Turner, born in 1911, struck up a friendship with Johnson and the two made a sensational team with Johnson's rolling piano and Turner's immense, shouting voice. After an abortive attempt to break into New York engagements in 1936, they were invited back by John Hammond, to play the Carnegie Hall, and to work at Café Society Uptown with Albert Ammons and Meade Lux Lewis. These pianists had been located by John Hammond, and the 'Boogie-Woogie Trio' rode in on the swing craze.

In the late 'forties Pete Johnson and Joe Turner, after a period of separation, came together again in California, working at the Memo Cocktail Lounge in San Francisco, and later in spots in Los Angeles and Long Beach. They were on the coast from 1947 for three years and their driving bands, with Art Farmer on trumpet or Maxwell Davis on tenor sax, were a timely reminder of the impact of Kansas City shouting and boogie piano. It was a form which was followed with gusto by Saunders King and Crown Prince Waterford, and Pete Johnson even played piano for Waterford on some of his records.

Out on the coast at the same time was Aaron 'T-Bone' Walker. Actually, he had been a resident there since 1934, and with the exception of a couple of years touring with the Les Hite Orchestra in the 'forties, had been playing there for twenty-odd years. T-Bone Walker was another migrant from Texas, where he was born in Linden, in 1910. At the age of sixteen he had recorded a couple of titles under the name of 'Oak-Cliff T-Bone', but it was to be a long time before he recorded again. He played with the Coley Jones String Band, accompanied Ma Rainey and Ida Cox, and was an exceptionally fine guitarist when he reached the West Coast. His technique was dazzling with its runs and flamboyant arpeggios and ideally suited to an electric instrument. The Basie guitarist, Eddie Durham (born 1906 in San Marcos, Texas) had pioneered the use of the electric guitar, and his lead had been followed with brilliant effect by Charlie Christian, Dallas-born but raised in Oklahoma City, who was thirteen years his junior. T-Bone Walker was one of the first, if not *the* first, blues guitarists to use an electric instrument and his influence on Oscar and Johnny Moore and, eventually, innumerable other guitarists, was immense. His clowing often distracted attention from his highly skilled musicianship.

Out of the complex currents of Kansas City jazz bands, blues 'shouting', boogie-woogie and Texas piano, electric guitars and small group improvisation, one strain of Post-War Rhythm and Blues got under way in both California and Texas. Singers like Sonny Parker, Eddie 'Mister Cleanhead' Vinson, 'Bull Moose' Jackson, Clarence 'Gatemouth' Brown, Dwight 'Gatemouth' Moore, 'H-Bomb' Ferguson and many others took some or all of these elements and moulded them into their own blues. Record labels like Swing-Time, Peacock, Imperial and Modern recorded them in considerable numbers and the trading of metal masters, the sub-leasing of issue rights, the disc-jockey radio programmes and the ubiquitous juke-boxes spread their music, and sometimes killed it.

There were other singers, like Percy Mayfield, whose blend was palatable to the more sensitive tastes, and they moved further away from blues and into commercial popular music with blues colouration. And some trod a delicate path between the two, like Jimmy McCracklin, a native of St Louis where he was born in 1931. While in the Navy, he took up boxing – as a number of other blues singers, including 'Champion' Jack Dupree, Willie Dixon and Eddie Kirkland had done. On his discharge, he turned professional and had twenty-three victorious bouts in succession before he was injured in a road accident. He recuperated in hospital in Los Angeles and there began to play the piano. When he started to record, it was initially with piano and guitar and sometimes fuller rhythm, but by the early 'fifties he was using a three-brass and full rhythm section band, later employing the vocal choruses and 'rock' beat which were inclined to detract from the originality of his lyrics. Though McCracklin later moved into the popular-ballad area and virtually gave up the blues, his best records were notable for the presence of such guitarists as Lafayette Thomas and even B. B. King.

A studied exploitation of blues idioms was to be found in the music of Ray Charles, whose records have taken in every kind of idiom from the blues of Big Maceo to 'country and western' ballads. Born in Albany, Georgia, in 1930, he was raised in Florida and there, at the age of six, contracted the disease which left him blind. At blind school, he studied braille and eventually, music, and by 1947 could play piano, trumpet and saxophone. McCracklin acknowledged Percy Mayfield, Joe Turner and Billy Eckstine as his influences; Ray Charles was openly indebted to Charles Brown and Nat 'King' Cole. Of his accomplishment and technical ability, his talent as a composer and as a singer there is no doubt; nor is there any question of his eclecticism and his methodical use of 'gospel' techniques, blues enunciation, rock-and-roll off-beats and sentimental balladry in his work. He did not have the genius that was claimed for his versatility, but he could undoubtedly put in as convincing a version of *Let The Good Times Roll* as he could *Carry Me Back to Old Virginny*.

Simpler, far closer to the blues, as well as to jazz was Antoine 'Fats' Domino, who was born in New Orleans in February 1928. His piano-work was an effortless boogie-blues, rolling below his engaging, winsome voice and backed by a swaying blues band, more Kansas City than New Orleans. His slightly melancholy, reedy singing of blues like *Going to the River* and *Please Don't Leave Me* gave an impression of smiling through tears and the amiable Fats Domino was in tremendous demand in the 'fifties, travelling over thirty thousand miles in one year of one-night stands. He took two hundred pairs of shoes and thirty suits with him on the road, living luxuriously and working hard, as his counterparts, the Classic Blues singers like Mamie Smith were able to do. *Poor Me* and *Bo Weevil* were the titles of two of his recordings but they owed nothing whatever to Charley Patton. Yet curiously, at much the same time, there were other singers at their peak who undoubtedly did.

King Biscuit Time

Dogface, Lord Faunteleroy, Jet Pilot of Jive, Fatman Smith, Bonnie Prince Charlie Geter, Sweet Chariot Martin or Rockin' Lucky – 'Sensational, Saturant, Satisfying' – the names of the disc-jockeys on the black radio stations were as deliberately colourful as those of the blues singers whose records they played: Howlin' Wolf, Muddy Waters, Bo Diddley. Beaming to a black market of over a hundred thousand from Jackson, Mississippi, on WOKJ, to as many from WXOX in Baton Rouge, to half a million over WAOK Atlanta and WRMA in Montgomery, these radio stations had vast audiences which meant 'sales power'. 'Man, he moves merchandise!' bragged San Francisco's KSAN of one of its most successful disc-jockeys, Willie Mays. The disc-jockey was at the centre of black radio and the insatiable demand for records meant an ever-increasing importance of the industry to the blues singer. Some radio stations went over to total black 'interest' in the early 'forties, like WJLD in Birmingham, Alabama, in 1942, or WHAT in Philadelphia in 1944. Others beamed up to half their time to a black market and then turned over to a total programme in the late 'forties and especially in the early 'fifties.

WDIA, Memphis, 'America's only 50,000 watt Negro radio Station', with a potential market of one and a quarter millions became fully directed to the black audience in 1948, though it had commenced a couple of years before. Its powerful beam and continuous programmes of blues and gospel music, mainly on record but sometimes live, for twenty hours a day, seven days a week was one of the contributing factors to the concentration of blues activity in Memphis in the early 'fifties. There were others. It was still a 'target' city for migrants and a halt for others who had joined the mass exodus from Mississippi after the war. It had, anyway, a long and lively tradition and the record men began to come again to seek out talent. A young pianist, Ike Turner from Clarksdale, who was born in 1931, was always on the lookout for singers for the RPM and Modern labels which were operated by the West Coast brothers Saul and Jules Bihari. But they had to make the long trip to Memphis and hire an empty garage when they wanted to record. To Sam Phillips, an Alabama-born white disc-jockey there was good reason to start his own label. Sun began issues in 1950 and Phillips leased masters of recordings to Chess, the developing Chicago independent label which was cornering the blues market there. When bluesmen did migrate, they had a record company to go to in Chicago, though not without legal risk. Later the Biharis started their Meteor and Flair labels, while down in Jackson, Mississippi, Mrs Lillian McMurray had her Trumpet label in operation. Between them they recorded, if not quite all, nearly all the major influential blues singers of the post-war period: Howlin' Wolf, Elmore James, Sonny Boy Williamson, B. B. King, as well as many of their successors and popularisers, Junior Parker, Johnny Ace, Bobby 'Blue' Bland – and Elvis Presley.

For the new media at any rate, Sonny Boy Williamson was the most important of the first group. He was not the Sonny Boy – John Lee Williamson – who had gone north from Tennessee in the 'thirties to shape the pre-war Chicago blues, but an older man. John Lee Williamson had been murdered in 1948, stabbed with an ice-pick on his way home from the Plantation Club where he had been working. There is some doubt as to which Sonny Boy Williamson was the 'first', but no denying which was the senior man. His friends said his name was Willie or Alec 'Rice' Miller and that he came from Glendora, Mississippi. Stooped, buzzard-like in posture, he had a reputation in his younger years for being 'mean and ornery'. But he was unquestionably one of the finest and most influential blues harmonica players. He had an uncanny sense of timing, marked by short sung phrases, finger-snaps and tongue-clicks which crackled against the rhythmic-melodic phrases of his harp. In 1938 he was invited to play regularly on 'Sonny Boy's Corn Meal and King Biscuits Show' which promoted the Interstate Grocer Co.'s 'Sonny Boy Cream Extremely Fancy White Corn Meal' and the Buhler Mill & Elevator Co.'s 'King Biscuit Enriched Phosphated Bleaching Flour'. With him were Joe Willie Wilkins, guitar, Dud Low, piano, and James Peck Curtis, drums. Over thirty years later, Sonny Boy and Curtis still played the 'King Biscuit Time'. It went out daily at 12.45 pm on Station KFFA from Helena, Arkansas. The show gave employment to Willie Love, the guitarist Joe Willie Wilkins and many other bluesmen but the principal artist was Rice

Miller, 'Sonny Boy Williamson No. 2' – the 'original Sonny Boy' as he always claimed. His sensitive, nervous harp and his warm, broken words made beautiful and poignant blues out of simple themes.

> Been so long till I just can't sleep at night, (2)
> I couldn't eat my breakfast in the mornin' and my teeth
>   and tongue begin to fight.
>
> Yes it been so long the carpet have faded on the floor, (2)
> If she ever come back to me I'm not goin' to let her
>   leave no more.

Such themes as *Eyesight to the Blind* or *She brought life back* were uniquely his own, but his harmonica playing was as important as was that of John Lee Williamson. Yet it was the latter who left his mark on the work of most of the younger harp players, even in the region, and Forrest City Joe Pugh from Arkansas made his *Memory of Sonny Boy* as a tribute to him, one of a long line of such memorial records to blues singers made by their friends. Pugh was himself killed when still quite young, dying in a road accident, as before him had a number of blues singers who travelled long distances when tired after all-night playing. Rice Miller travelled extensively but it was not until 1954 that he took a band with Willie Love up to Detroit. Love died three years later but by this time Sonny Boy had moved up North to stay, settling in Milwaukee, East St Louis and Chicago for brief periods.

It seems likely that for commercial reasons, or merely for reflected glory, Miller exploited the 'Sonny Boy' tag; but this is unimportant. What *is* important is the fact that intermittently he was playing over KFFA for so many years. After a period of success in the North, and even, to the total disbelief of his accompanying musicians, in Europe, he returned to Helena and was still playing on the show when he died in 1965. This meant that live blues was being continually beamed to an audience of tens, even hundreds of thousands for a quarter of a century, in the Arkansas and Mississippi Delta region. Instead of being a guitarist or guitar-and-harmonica team, it was a blues band, southern in feeling but with the instrumentation of a Chicago group, and this contributed to the tendency to the larger combination that was marked in the 'forties and 'fifties.

With Sonny Boy was the pianist Willie Love, who came from Duncan, Mississippi, in the Delta, in what is normally considered to be 'guitar country'. Though the emphasis may have been on guitars, this can be misleading. Just south of Duncan on Highway 49 West is Vance, where Albert Luandrew, Sunnyland Slim, was born in September 1907; he was a pianist and got his first job in Vance before travelling with the alcoholic and highly popular blues singer Peter 'Doctor' Clayton who claimed to have been born in Africa. In Clarksdale itself Eddie Boyd first learned to play – he was born there in 1913. Down on Highway 49 in Belzoni, where Charley Patton was once in jail, the veteran pianist Friday Ford taught Otis Spann to play blues piano. There is much evidence, from the reminiscences of these men, from Roosevelt Sykes and Little Brother Montgomery among others, that a pattern of piano blues existed as an underlay to the more striking guitar blues in the Mississippi Delta. Willie Love, who was born in 1906, was a part of this. He lived for some years in Greenville, where Freddie Coates was once the principal pianist, and his premature death at the age of forty-six was much regretted in the Delta.

One of his friends was a guitarist named Elmore James. He played a sizzling electric guitar, vibrating a bottleneck on the high E and alternating it with a walking bass that derived from Robert Johnson (Music Example 10). There are stories of his having worked with Johnson at jukes in the Delta, and it might be so, for he was only a few years younger, having been born in Richland north of Jackson in January 1918. Though he was a religious man and played largely in church, he developed his technique and sang blues adapted from Johnson, like *Dust My Broom*, in a tense, agonised voice against a lurching rhythm. He played often with Sonny Boy and made forays to the North, but got a job as a disc-jockey on WOKJ in Jackson and preferred to stay at home or work in his radio shop. However, his records caught on, tours were arranged for him and he was recorded by the Bihari brothers in places as far apart as Los Angeles and New Orleans. Eventually he settled in Chicago, reluctantly. The cold and the dusty atmosphere didn't suit his asthma, but when he died in 1963, he left a generation of disciples to carry on his work.

Back in 1941 Alan Lomax and John Work came to Mississippi to look for Robert Johnson; they didn't find him because he was already dead, and they didn't find Elmore James either. But they did get directed to a well-built, good-looking sharecropper with a slight oriental cast in his features who played in a manner remarkably like Robert Johnson and had apparently learned off the latter's records. His name was McKinley Morganfield but everyone called him by his childhood nickname of Muddy Waters. He only recorded a couple of blues for them then, but they were back the following year and with trembling guitar slide he sang of work on Howard Stovall's plantations.

Man I tol' the man, baby, 'Way up in Dundee' (2)
Well you go on to Mister Howard Stovall's place, he got all
the burr clover you need.'

Well now the reason that I love that ol' Stovall's farm so
well, (2)
Well-a you know we have plenty money and we never be
raisin' Hell.

Well we raise plenty cotton and we are booked out with the
corn (2)
Well you know we have to carry the place on, now the main
boss been here and gone.

Though he'd been born down in Rolling Fork in April, 1915,
Muddy Waters was raised in Clarksdale and learned to play guitar on
the usual home-made instrument. He played with a string band and
also played harmonica, and after Lomax had left, he joined a company
of Silas Green from New Orleans, playing harp on the tour. When he
came back, he was restless; his Uncle Joe Brant was already in Chicago
and Muddy went up north to join him, getting a job in a paper mill
and later driving a truck. Sunnyland Slim had come north too, and
they often played together in the clubs and joints on West Lake and
on the South Side. Because he had left Mississippi as early as he did
and did not get to Memphis, Muddy Waters was one of the major
singers from the region who was not recorded commercially at the
time. But when his first records were made for Aristocrat in 1947/48
they were relayed on every local radio station in the south. Baby Face
Turner had got the phrases off exactly when he accompanied 'Drifting
Slim' – Elmon Mickle – on *Good Morning Baby* in Little Rock, a year
or two later. Mickle had himself played over the local KDRK and
KGHI stations in Arkansas in the 'forties and had worked often with
Sonny Boy Williamson, even getting him a spot on KGHI.

With Muddy Waters on some of his Library of Congress recordings
had been a ragged country band called the Son Sims Four, which
included Charley Patton's fiddle player, Henry Sims. Patton, of
course, was long dead, but they did record Son House on location
at Lake Cormorant. At the time Charley Patton's pupil, Willie Brown
– if it was he, though the guitar technique seems to have changed a lot
– was recorded with Son House and Fiddlin' Joe Martin, but his other
major pupil, Chester Burnett had been drafted in the Army. Burnett
had learned a little guitar from Patton but mostly he learned his songs
and he sang in a manner which, though not similar, had the same
aggressive fierceness. He couldn't manage the falsettos popular with

many Delta singers and gave a call instead; though he has given other, conflicting reasons, it may be why he was nicknamed – by the white singer Jimmie Rodgers, he once claimed – 'Howlin' Wolf'. Working on a plantation near Ruleville in Sunflower county 120 miles west of Aberdeen, where he was born in June 1910, Howlin' Wolf was able to learn from the older singers. His voice was less vibrant and sounded strained and constricted when he sang, but the physical impact of his blues, and the angrily burning eyes in the massive head made him unforgettable. After Patton's death, he went to farm on a plantation near West Memphis and after his discharge from the Army returned to continue working there. He formed a band in the late 'forties, which included a small and difficult tempered guitarist in his twenties, named Pat Hare, a thirteen-year-old harmonica player from Tunica, Mississippi named James Cotton, another harmonica player who was born in West Memphis, Little Junior Parker, and guitarist Willie Johnson, also from Tunica. It was a powerful country-styled band and with Wolf's harsh vocals rapidly drew attention. He was offered a job as disc-jockey on KWEM from West Memphis and, not surprisingly, prominently featured blues.

Ike Turner got Wolf on record for Bihari's RPM label and the raw and vital *Moaning at Midnight* and *Crying at Daybreak* with Turner himself on piano, Willie Johnson and Pat Hare playing guitars and Wolf singing and blowing his harmonica in searing lines of sound, captured the group's compelling primitivism. Jimmy Cotton was probably not up to playing on Howlin' Wolf's records at this time, but within a couple of years, in 1953, he made his *Cotton Crop Blues* with Pat Hare on guitar. He'd played dates with Sonny Boy Williamson and Willie Love, sitting in on guitar, drums or harmonica, and played for Willie Nix, 'The Memphis Blues Boy', a thirty-year-old guitarist and drummer with a vocal and guitar technique that showed he had been listening to the records of T-Bone Walker. Several of the Memphis blues singers of the period could play two or three instruments – even at the same time. Joe Hill Louis played guitar, harmonica and traps and was the most esteemed 'one-man band' in Memphis. There had been one-man bands before of course: Sam Jones, known as Stovepipe No 1 in Cincinnati, 'Daddy Stovepipe' – Johnny Watson – who played harmonica, guitar and drums from Mobile, Alabama, and the veteran Jesse Fuller from Jonesboro, Georgia, who had been out in Oakland since 1929 and who played harmonica, kazoo, twelve string guitar and his own invention, a foot-operated bass he called the 'fotdella'. But these were songsters who included occasional blues in their repertoires and were part of the medicine show tradition; Joe Hill Louis was a blues man. He died of tetanus in 1957 but by this time, 'Doctor' Isaiah Ross who was another Tunica musician, born there in 1925, had made a one-man band of himself. He recorded for Sam Phillips a roaring *Chicago Breakdown* in Memphis, which in spite of its name was an exhilarating piece of country dance music with guitar, washboard and broom, no less, accompanying his harmonica.

Doctor Ross and Jimmy Cotton both left Memphis in the same year; Ross to go to Flint, Michigan, Cotton to join Muddy Waters in Chicago. This was in 1954 and by that time most of the Memphis singers had gone or were contemplating leaving. In general they went north but one or two, who had been cultivated by the record and radio industries, chose to go south to Houston, Texas. Radio continued to be a major influence in Memphis itself, even though the musical scene was active. In fact, it may have contributed to the decline of Memphis music in showing the pickings that were to be had through recording for large companies in the North – largely an illusion, but this would not have been evident on the d-j programmes. When Sonny Boy Williamson was out of town his drummer, James Curtis, would take over the King Biscuit show on KFFA, sometimes with one of the older Jackson musicians, Houston Stackhouse, playing guitar. Stackhouse was an influence on Robert Lee McCoy – 'Robert Nighthawk', born in Helena in 1909, who was always commuting from Chicago or St Louis to Memphis and took bands on the road as far as Mexico or Florida. Back in Memphis he would play over Clarksdale's station WROX with a blues pianist Ernest Lane. In Memphis a group of younger singers were getting more attention.

They were all born within a few years of each other – Herman 'Junior' Parker, who played harmonica, was local to West Memphis and born in 1927; Robert Calvin Bland came from Rosemark, Tennessee, played guitar and was three years younger; John Marshall Alexander was born in Memphis itself, played piano and was a year older than Bland; the youngest was Roscoe Gordon who played piano and was born in Memphis in 1933. To these must be added a young man from out of town, Riley King, who came from Indianola, Mississippi. Such is the fabric of the blues that this innovator of a new blues form was a cousin of Bukka White, whose companion in 1927 when Riley was only four years of age was Napoleon Hairiston. His background was in the church and he began as a boy to sing with the gospel quartets which were now becoming popular, and playing his guitar in a manner influenced more by the records of T-Bone

Walker than by the sounds of Mississippi. He started singing on occasional dates in Indianola before moving the twenty-six miles to Greenville where he got a job as a disc-jockey on station WGUM, which beamed about a third of its time to the black audience. Don Kern, the head of WDIA in Memphis heard him and invited him to join the station as disc-jockey, billing him as 'Blues Boy' King. The 'Blues Boy' soon became just B. B. King.

In 1948 the younger Memphis singers, Roscoe Gordon, Johnny Ace (Johnny Alexander), Bobby Bland and a drummer, Earl Forrest, formed themselves into a group they called the 'Beale Streeters', based on the trio which Roscoe Gordon, though the youngest, had been leading. With his position as disc-jockey, B. B. King soon recorded and the others swiftly followed. James Mattis, a disc-jockey on WDIA, decided to form his own record company, which he called Duke, and while B. B. King was recording for Bihari, he signed up Johnny Ace and, soon, Junior Parker. The sound of these young singers was frankly modern and though Parker had worked with Sonny Boy Williamson and Howlin' Wolf, and Bland had worked with Billy 'Red' Love, they tended to become progressively more inclined to commercial ballads in the ensuing years. Their initial records, which included Junior Parker's *Mystery Train* (with Pat Hare on guitar) for Sun, Johnny Ace's *Ace's Wild*, Bobby 'Blue' Bland's *Army Blues* and Roscoe Gordon's hit *Booted* on RPM, were closer to the blues tradition, but it was clear that they were geared to stage presentation. When Duke was bought out by Don Robey's Peacock label in Houston, Bland, Parker and Johnny Ace went with the company. Parker and Johnny Ace, in particular, were extremely successful and were toured with Big Mama Thornton. She had been touring since the age of fourteen with the Hot Harlem Review, a road show from Atlanta which she had joined in her home state of Alabama. She stayed with the show until 1948, travelling down the Gulf Coast as far as Corpus Christi before deciding to settle in Houston. She had a big, powerful voice and was heavily-built; her singing and presence recalled the Classic singers of the 'twenties, but she played drums as well and learned to play harmonica from Junior Parker. Later she joined the Johnny Otis show and it was while travelling with the company that she made her song, *Hound Dog*. It was only a minor hit but it later made a fortune for Elvis Presley who built his rock n' roll singing and guitar successes on Junior Parker's *Mystery Train* and other blues by Arthur 'Big Boy' Crudup and Nashville's Arthur Gunter.

For Big Mama Thornton the subsequent years brought some good records but little attention; for Bobby 'Blue' Bland and Junior Parker, they brought increasing commercialisation of their work, and for Johnny Ace they brought oblivion. On Christmas Eve, 1954, in the intermission of a concert at the City Auditorium in Houston he drew a revolver loaded with one slug, jokingly spun the chamber and played Russian Roulette by placing the muzzle to his temple and squeezing the trigger. The hammer fell on the bullet and Johnny Ace was dead.

Though several of these young singers had gone south to Houston, the predominating trend was to follow the general migratory movement to the North, in particular to Chicago and Detroit. In the 'forties the African American population of the northern states increased phenomenally; in 1940 there were 387,000 black people in Illinois and within ten years this had increased to 645,000 while in Michigan the increase had been from 208,000 to 442,000. Most of the gains were caused by the mass emigration from the South which continued unabated in the 'fifties. One and a half million Blacks left the South within the decade, a quarter of them going to California and most of the rest going north. This massive infiltration caused great social pressures which flared up in 1942 and 1943 with serious racial riots in Detroit, but the migrants were not deterred. With them came many blues singers, who worked in the automobile plants during the day and played in the clubs at night. The immense scale of unemployment that characterised Detroit in 1960, when as many as four out of ten Blacks were out of work in one district, had yet to hit the city. There was money around and the clubs on Hastings Street accommodated them. One blues pianist, Bob White who called himself Detroit Count, recited a *Hastings Street Opera* which described some of the saloons and joints: 'Sally Wilson's, the longest bar in town . . . cross the street, Jake's Bar . . . Garfield and Hastings: Mary's Bar . . . Hung One Ranch – that's the onliest place you can fight all you wanna fight and nobody run out . . .' He continued with 'Dixie bar – one way out, never go in that joint . . . Leland and Hastings – Leland Bar, where the bartenders carry pistols . . . cross the street, Joe's Record Shop – he got everybody in there but a T-bone steak . . . Blue Star Bar – call the fire department to put the band on the bandstand . . . Skid Row Club better known as Brown's Bar . . .'

Several of the places he mentioned were famous for their blues singers. Brown's Bar was Big Maceo's principal spot. Joe's Record Shop was run by an Alabaman named Joe Von Battle who had started his career junking old records in a barrow and re-selling them; later, on Hastings, he opened a shop and off-beat recording studio which

pulled in such unlikely musicians as One-String Sam, a street singer
with a monochord instrument who sang in a broken voice:

> Y'know I talked with mother this mornin',
> Mother talk with the judge,
> I couldn't help but eavesdroppin' –
> Y'know – understood the words.
> She said 'I need a hundred dollars,
> You know I need a hundred dollars
> You know I need a hundred dollars
> Just to go my, my baby's bond.'

Many of Detroit's active musicians were obscure. One of the oldest
was Washboard Willie who played a variety of instruments including
harmonica and washboard, and was often to be heard playing behind
the Detroit singers, though he seldom recorded. In 1948, when he
was thirty-eight he came from Columbus, Georgia, to Detroit.
About the same time, Baby Boy Warren arrived in Detroit from
Memphis, though he was born in Lake Providence in 1919. He
had a forceful voice and highly rhythmic technique on electric
guitar and had played with Sonny Boy Williamson No. 2 when
he was on his visit to Detroit. Of his generation was Bobo Jenkins
from Arkansas, the son of a sharecropper, who came to Chicago in
the 'thirties and arrived in Detroit at the same time as Warren. He
had witnessed the Depression in Chicago and the economic stresses
that were already becoming apparent in Detroit in the 'fifties; the
widespread alarm at the Republican victory was tellingly illustrated
in his *Democrat Blues*:

> Well do you remember baby, '19 and '31,
> That's when the Depression baby, just begun
> > Yes I know, yes you know what I'm talkin' about
> > Well the Democrats put you on your feet baby
> > You had the nerve to vote 'em out.
>
> You didn't have to plant no more cotton baby
> You didn't have to plough no more corn
> If a mule was runnin' away with the world baby
> You tell him to go 'Head on', Yes I know . . . etc.
>
> Well do you remember baby when the steel mills shut down
> You had to go to the country
> Cause you couldn't live in town, yes I know . . .

Jenkins was accompanied by Robert Richard, a young Georgia

harmonica player who used the warbling tone that had become popular with the increased use of the amplified instrument in the 'fifties. Like 'Little Sonny' Willis, who came up from Alabama and played harmonica with Eddie Burns from Belzoni, Mississippi, or Little Eddie Kirkland who could play harmonica, organ and guitar and came from Louisiana, these men were born in the mid- and late 'twenties. Most of them 'scuffled' – played at the Club Carribe or the Apex Show Bar or similar places for their fellow factory workers but were not, in the full sense, professional musicians. For this reason they were essentially blues singers, unflustered by the pressures of the record industry to build them, though always hopeful that they might make a 'hit' recording. John Lee Hooker, a decade older – he was born in Clarksdale, Mississippi in 1917 – was the biggest name in Detroit blues and the one singer who broke out of the confines of its ghetto. He had a guitar technique which made extensive use of 'hammering on' the strings and his heavily accented foot-beat as he played was integral to his performance. A slight speech impediment in his deep and rich voice gave it an oddly expressive urgency. He would use Boogie Woogie Red on piano and Eddie Kirkland as his second guitarist and his passionate, deeply-involved blues were contrasted with the hypnotic, infectious rhythm of *Boogie Chillen*. For years Hooker played in such places as the Monte Carlo Club, Apex Club, Club Basin or the Muddy Color Bar, joining touring shows for short periods and returning to Detroit to play the Club Carribe or the Harlem Inn. He recorded heavy, slow blues with his unique guitar style, contrasted with lively boogie instrumentals.

Whereas Detroit was dominated in the 'fifties by one singer, Chicago had several major artists. The typical Detroit group used two guitars, harmonica and sometimes piano and drums; the Chicago group was similar, but infinitely louder and more aggressive. The use of the electric 'Fender' bass gave a dark, underlying rhythm pattern while the drummers who followed Judge Riley and Jump Jackson's 'sock rhythm' of heavy beats in the 'forties now used the fractionally delayed 'back beat' developed by Freddy Below. Through the 'fifties the emphasis was on ever-increasing volume, with amplifiers turned to their maximum and almost every instrument electric – Sunnyland Slim even played electric piano. Blues harmonica players still preferred their cheap Hohner models which might only last for an evening's blowing but they cupped their hands round a microphone to amplify the instrument. Dominating the Chicago blues scene of the mid-'fifties were the bands of Muddy Waters, Howlin' Wolf and later, Little Walter, and Elmore James.

When he left Memphis, Muddy Waters was still playing an acoustic guitar but in Chicago his uncle bought him an electric instrument which he played with a bottleneck. His early records were virtually solo, with Leroy Foster playing second guitar, but in 1951 he was joined regularly by Little Walter Jacobs playing harmonica. Much younger, Little Walter had been playing 'harp' for a living since the age of eight when he begged on streets in Monroe and Alexandria, Louisiana. In 1947, at the age of seventeen, he came to Chicago and began to play on Maxwell Street Market. This desolate wasteland off Halstead, Peoria and Sangamon Streets on the South Side was not only a street market but a centre for scuffling musicians, who rented power lines from the adjacent houses to amplify their guitars. On Maxwell could be heard Robert Nighthawk, Blind James Brewer, Blind Arvella Gray, Daddy Stovepipe and younger musicians like King David and Maxwell Street Jimmy Davis, Little Walter, Shakey Horton and many others. Here Big Bill Broonzy heard Little Walter and encouraged him as he had done Muddy Waters; they were soon working together.

Though Jazz Gillum, Washboard Sam and others had largely retired following the murder of Sonny Boy Williamson, the brash, extrovert sound of their music was carried on by their successors, with Big Bill acting as a continuity link. Muddy Waters and Little Walter, new from the South, added the stark Down-Home quality that urbanisation had gradually destroyed in the playing of the older men. In 1951 Muddy Waters moved in to Smitty's Corner, a large club on the corner site of 35th and Indiana Avenue. His band, indisputably the finest of its kind in blues, included on its best days Muddy Waters singing and playing slide electric guitar, Jimmie Rogers or Pat Hare playing second guitar, Little Walter on harmonica – sometimes joined by the youthful Junior Wells or Jimmy Cotton – Muddy's half-cousin, Otis Spann playing piano, Big Crawford and, later, Willie Dixon on bass, and Freddy Bellow or Francey Clay on drums. The personnel varied as musicians joined other groups or temporarily left, but the overall sound, wailing, strident, harmonica warbling over a ground bass of piano-drums-bass rhythm and slashed by electric slide guitar, with Muddy Water's violent, physical vocals as he roared out *Forty Days and Forty Nights, Hoochie Coochie Man* or *Manish Boy*, was unforgettable.

Over on West Lake at Sylvio's in the expanding West Side, or down at the Big Squeeze Club on the South Side, Howlin' Wolf led his band, the sweat pouring off his vast and rugged head as he shouted in harsh tones his strained and impassioned *Evil is Going On,*

Smoke Stack Lightning or *Forty Four*. He generally played harmonica, rough but adequate, and was supported by the deft, unerring guitar of Hubert Sumlin, with Jody Williams supporting on bass guitar and piano and drums. Howlin' Wolf's aggressive music was less subtle than Muddy Waters' but it was a matter of degree. For a brief period in the late 'fifties it was possible to hear Elmore James, too, playing with his bass guitarist, Homesick James Williamson, Sunnyland Slim or Johnny Jones on piano, Odie Payne's drums and J. T. Brown playing tenor sax. Lean and haggard Elmore James sang in an agonised, tense voice, his guitar singing its triplets and walking its basses in throbbing rhythm to *Rollin' and Tumblin'* or the inevitable, if ever-satisfying *Dust My Broom*. Through the heavy amplification, the smoke, the urban haze, could be discerned still a line of descent which was sired in the music of Charley Patton, Son House and Robert Johnson. It was a thrilling, dramatic culmination of a remarkable tradition exemplified in numerous lesser bands led by Snooky Pryor or J. B. Hutto, Walter Horton or J. B. Lenoir all over the South and West Sides. But it was not to last much longer.

Blues and Trouble

For every blues singer who became well known through records, a dozen were unknown and unsuspected. In the 'fifties, the extremes became even more marked as record companies sprang up everywhere and cultivated those singers whose sales encouraged further investment. Blues singers, once on record, have always been vulnerable to commercial interests, as the work of those singers of the 'thirties who tried to adapt themselves to the demands of the record companies clearly shows. In the highly competitive post-war recording scene, the distinction between those artists who became successful and those who failed to do so became even more marked. A surprisingly large number of minor singers did, in fact, record, because their music was intrinsically good and worth the risk to issue, but did not sell in sufficient quantity to secure many more recording dates.

Naturally, the reasons for this are various; in part they reflect the policies of the record companies themselves, and in Chicago particularly, those of Leonard and Phil Chess's label, Chess. 'A singer can't perform effectively without records; a company soon grows broke if no one hears their products. Hence the pop status of most recording artists; hence the recurrent payola scandals,' wrote Charles Keil, observing that although the 'artists have to bow and scrape to record company moguls, they can take some satisfaction from the fact that these companies are usually in a similar position vis-à-vis the radio stations.' Chess solved this problem by purchasing radio station WHFC in 1963 and, under its new name of WVON, beaming their own records to an audience of over a million.

Muddy Waters, Howlin' Wolf and Little Walter were contracted to Chess and sold exceptionally well; their esteem as performing bands ensured large sales, but others were not so lucky. Often they recorded, if at all, for tiny backroom labels: J.O.B., States, Chance,

Bea and Baby, Keyhole, Colt, Abco, Club 51 and so on. Some major singers got their start this way: even Little Walter's first record was on a Maxwell Street label, Ora-Nelle, which issued just two records. But for many singers these were the only chances that they had to break in on the market. The fine singer-guitarist Johnny Shines, for instance, who came to Chicago from his Memphis home in 1941 at the age of twenty-six, was one. His tests for Columbia were never issued: his few records for J.O.B. were ended when he displeased the powerful Al Benson and could get no recording contract. Again, Arthur 'Big Boy' Spires, a blues singer three years his senior, who was born in Yazoo, Mississippi and who played in South Side clubs when he came to Chicago in 1943, had two sessions for Chess. One record was issued on the Checker subsidiary; the other was withheld.

Some singers appear to have suffered from a personality problem, like Walter 'Shakey' Horton, a superb harmonica player who largely pioneered the Chicago warbling style. He was born in Memphis in 1918 and played with the Memphis Jug Band and Buddy Doyle. A shy and rather nervous man, his introverted playing reflected his sensitive nature. His personality was little suited to the kind of musical showmanship that the clubs and the record company organised tours demanded. Many singers felt the cold wind of Chicago blow on them. As John Brim sang:

> I had a good job workin' many long hours a week,
> They had a big lay-off, and they got poor me,
> I'm broke and disgusted, in misery
> Can't find a part-time job, nothin' in my house to eat,
>> Tough times, tough times is here once more,
>> If you don't have no money you can't live happy no more.

Probably, however, the main failing of many singers was that they were no longer suited to the times. In their thirties and forties by 1955, they were unable to adjust to the demands of the youthful audiences. By 1954 the nation's African American population had a median age of 25.1 and in the northern cities more than half the black masses were under this age; they did not wish to hear the blues of the South that their parents still liked – the South meant nothing to them. Muddy Waters, Howlin' Wolf and Elmore James were already seeming 'old' but their dynamism, their fierce shouting and the collective power of their bands expressed the swelling anger of the younger Blacks. They didn't really want to hear John Brim singing about *Tough Times*; they knew times were tough and what they wanted was a brash, confident music which suggested that change might be fought for. When Muddy Waters sang *Manish Boy*, declaring that he was a MAN in no uncertain terms, and spelling it out, he was singing a blues composed by a younger artist, Ellas McDaniel.

Called by his childhood nickname, Bo Diddley, Ellas Bates, or McDaniel, had come up from McComb, Mississippi as a boy and had been raised in Chicago where he played violin on the street in a trio. He had an urban wit and when, in 1955, he began recording at the age of twenty-seven, his lyric inventiveness was very evident. Though he would use the blues musical structure, his words and verse forms were quite different. They played on the current fads, fears and fantasies of the young blacks and his first record *I'm a Man* and *Bo Diddley*, which was a major hit, was followed by such titles as *Cops and Robbers, Diddy Wah Diddy* and *Bo Meets the Monster* which displayed an attractive disrespect for old themes. Often he played on the records of his contemporary, Chuck Berry, and it was no accident that they both recorded for Chess.

It is an indication of the importance of mass media in the 'fifties that *Maybellene*, Chuck Berry's first title, should have been given the Billboard Triple Award as the Biggest Rhythm and Blues record, the Biggest R & B Record on the radio stations, and the Most-Played R & B Record on the juke-boxes. Direct sales, radio and juke-box provided a measure by which the purse of the record companies could evaluate their artists. By this token Chuck Berry was a gold-mine. He'd been born in 1931 in St Louis and was only twenty-four, having had a group of his own for some three years. When he came to Chicago, Muddy Waters encouraged him and caught the ear of the Chess Brothers. Chuck did the rest, following up with *Roll Over Beethoven, Rock and Roll Music, Memphis, Tennessee* and many others. Often he smuggled in the rapid stream of words some ironic lines, unusual even in blues:

> I met an English girl in Germany, she went to school,
>   in France,
> We danced in Mississippi at an Alpha Kappa Dance.

'Uh-uh, boys, it wasn't me', he commented, having hinted in the couplet at national, racial and class prejudice with a cynicism that would not have escaped his hearers. Maybe not his white ones either.

For now there was a growing white teen-age audience to buy the records of the 'Rhythm and Blues' singers, or 'R & B' as they were called for convenience. The old term 'Race' had been dropped long before, but now a new one was in currency: Rock n' Roll. Invented by a disc-jockey, Alan Freed, it was an old blues term which was now applied to the Rhythm and Blues/Country and Western amalgam which was being popularised by Elvis Presley, Bill Haley and his Comets, Ray Charles – even Pat Boone. Chuck Berry and Bo Diddley had a foot in both camps, but anyhow the frontiers were undefined.

Rhythm and Blues itself covered a variety of forms, as had Race in the past, embracing the bands of Bill Doggett, Earl Bostic, Louis Jordan and Fats Domino. Some of the bands featured powerful 'blues shouters' who combined blues with ballads and novelty songs. In the forefront of these was the witty, licentious and promiscuous Wynonie Harris, born in Omaha, Nebraska in 1915. He admired Joe Turner and adopted the shouting style of Turner and Jimmie Rushing, backed by orchestras, notably Lucky Millinder's. He worked in Los Angeles and New York and recorded extensively, with *Good Rockin' Tonight* being a major hit in 1947.

One of the singers influenced by Wynonie Harris was Roy Brown, born in New Orleans in 1925. Once a gospel singer he was active on the West Coast and also toured extensively in the 1950s. Less raucous and more expressive than Harris he has been regarded as among the first of the 'Soul' singers. Women now figured more prominently than at any time since the Classic Blues decade; Big Maybelle (Mabel Smith), a contemporary of Brown, was one of several strong performers of the 'fifties and early 'sixties, working with orchestras in New York, Chicago and eventually Cleveland, where she died in 1972, three years after Wynonie Harris.

These singers featured blues in their acts but Rhythm and Blues embraced popular song, and the sleek performances of the vocal quartets and quintets, which were not really blues in character at all. They had their origins in the vocal groups like the pre-War Ink Spots and Mills Brothers on the one hand, and the gospel groups who sang in the store-front churches on the other. Their acts were highly sophisticated, superbly timed and often athletic on stage. Calling themselves the Platters, the Drifters, the Charms, the Meadowlarks, the Five Keys, the Five Royales, they dressed uniformly in loud check suits or even in turbans and lamé suits. From the gospel 'quartets' like the Five Blind Boys of Mississippi or the Spirit of Memphis they acquired frenetic, screaming vocal techniques which were alternated with harmonised crooning. Secular themes were draped in a religious cloak and they were the direct forerunners of the 'Soul' groups. Solo singers used the same devices, like the diminutive, mop-haired, wild-acting Little Richard Penniman, or the bizarre Screaming Jay Hawkins whose act commenced as he leapt out of a coffin on-stage.

Out of the Rhythm and Blues-cum-Rock n' Roll scene emerged a few singers whose roots were still deep in the blues itself but who had distinctive, individual features of their own which appealed to the young audiences. Jimmy Reed was one of these. He began recording in December 1953 and his first issues came out the following year, when *Boogie in the Dark* was a major hit on disc-jockey programmes from coast to coast. This was an instrumental; others, like *Big Boss Man* and *Meet Me* were vocal items. In all his recordings a four-beat walking bass was the characteristic ground and the vocals were sung lazily, negligently, sloppily. Reed followed a style once recorded, a decade before, by 'Mushmouth' Robinson – the words almost slobbered from the side of the mouth. In 1950, when he was twenty-four, Jimmy Reed had decided to quit his work at a Gary, Indiana, iron foundry and try his luck in Chicago as a professional musician. He met up with a childhood friend from their home in Leland, Mississippi, Eddie Taylor, who had a band at the Jamboree Club with Walter Shakey Horton. Jimmy joined the band, and, having been playing harmonica as well as guitar for a few years, soon took over. They toured extensively, made a few records on the west coast, and got a break when Jimmy heard that a Gary disc-jockey, Vivian Carter, was starting her Vee-Jay label. He stayed with Vee-Jay and helped make its fortune. A heavy drinker, his alcoholism exaggerating his slurred enunciation, Reed was relaxed to the point of collapse where singers like Howlin' Wolf or Elmore James had developed a hard, taut style. When they shouted, he smiled an amiable, lop-sided grin; for him at least, his odd formula worked, but he slowly deteriorated in subsequent years. He died from epilepsy in 1976.

Among the younger blues singers unquestionably the most influential was B. B. King. Unlike the other Beale Streeters he went west instead of south after his successful period as a disc-jockey on WDIA, for which he did a daily two-hour programme. Having signed up with the Bihari brothers he moved to California where he formed his bands. These were modelled on the Kansas City form with riffing brass and blues-playing saxes. Though the personnel varied, with Floyd Jones playing trumpet and Bill Harvey tenor at one time, and later with Lloyd Glenn, the Texas pianist, on piano, the structure of his bands remained similar. Influenced by T-Bone Walker, Charlie Christian, and well aware of Django Reinhardt,

B. B. King developed a fluent, sometimes flashy electric guitar technique of great proficiency. His themes were nearly always 'woman trouble', with *Sweet Little Angel, 3 o'Clock Blues* and *Ten Long Years* sung in impassioned, if somewhat uninvolved and mannered phrases. His singing was greatly influenced by Joe Turner and Walter Brown, many of whose blues, such as *Cherry Red* and *Confessin' the Blues*, he sang. The very first notes of a performance brought screams of delight from his audiences and his sung phrases triggered off immediate responses from his ecstatic young listeners.

In the playing of Otis Rush, Albert King, Freddie King, Magic Sam Maghett and Buddy Guy could be heard the reverberating echoes of B. B. King and through him, the guitar of T-Bone Walker and Guitar Slim. These younger guitarists, born in the mid-'thirties, elaborated on the technique that he had popularised, contrasting long and whining notes with rapid runs falling in a cascade of clear sounds, making explosions and flurries, scintillating embellishments and repeated riffs with the vibrato amplified in pulsating sound and the volume turned to maximum. Buddy Guy, perhaps the best and most flamboyant of these guitarists, was born near Baton Rouge in 1936, and was therefore contemporary to most of them. Though he learned from listening to the Baton Rouge musicians like Lightnin' Slim and Lazy Lester, it was the concerts of B. B. King and Bobby Bland which most impressed him. He came to Chicago in 1957 and, after some unsuccessful 'gigs', won a blues contest in which both Otis Rush and Magic Sam were competing; they helped him get on record and eventually he was signed up by Chess. Guy's *First Time I Met the Blues* was typical of the technique favoured by the younger men, with falsetto singing, repetitions of short word phrases and stuttering, gospel-inflected emotional outbursts emphasised by guitar patterns in identical vein.

Buddy Guy became extremely popular in Chicago, much more so than his friend Otis Rush, who came to Chicago in 1956 at the age of twenty-one from his Philadelphia, Mississippi, home. Less of a spectacle on stage, Otis Rush was an excellent musician, and his trembling vocal on *So Many Roads, So Many Trains* was one of the finest blues of 1960. It is evident, however, that Guy's antics, his deliberate and entertaining showmanship, while adding nothing to his music, made him extremely popular while Rush's more reserved personality did not suit the demand for spectacle. Showmanship also counted to some extent in the relative success of Junior Wells, who played harmonica with Buddy Guy on recordings and dates. Born in Memphis in 1934, he was twelve when he came to Chicago and only fourteen when he began to play harmonica with Tampa Red and Big Maceo. Though Little Walter was somewhat contemptuous of his age – forgetting perhaps, his own extreme youth when his career began – he was a strong influence on Wells, who developed the amplified harmonica technique in a style of his own. Whereas Little Walter relied on instrumental rhythmic-melodic dynamics and a compelling command of tonal variety, Junior Wells applied the flourishes of the young guitarists to the harmonica.

That the Soul trend – the blend of gospel techniques of exaggerated mannerisms and screaming, passionate entreaties with blues instrumental techniques and commercial 'pop' words – was immensely popular with young Blacks and Whites alike is undeniable. It meant vastly increased sales for the record companies and, combined, with the sleek and successful Detroit Tamla-Motown 'sound', dominated the record catalogues which were directed to a black market, and so in turn, the juke-box and disc-jockey promotional devices. This was damaging to the blues as a form in its own right and blues singers who had been unwilling or unable to adapt their music to the demands of 'soul' found themselves without engagements. The more geared to the record and radio industries music became, the greater was the pressure on blues singers to accede to popular taste. As Buddy Guy explained to Peter Guralnick, 'you got to keep up with the latest songs. You got to have it down, man, what James Brown or Wilson Pickett may put out. You forget your own . . . Unless you make a hit.'

Soul, it seems, replaced the blues as the music that spoke for the younger generation of Blacks, while it drew from blues for part of its expression. Like the blues which was also, in its early stages, a form which drew off many traditions, Soul established its own identity and had lasting value. Once the blues had determined its own specific character it did not lend itself to hybridisation, but change was internal, the result of natural growth modified by a cultural ecology. The exception is probably 'Zydeco', or 'La-La music', a blues off-shoot of marked folk character, sung and played by the French-speaking Blacks of Louisiana and east Texas. Drawing off the 'Cajun' music of the French settlers of Acadian descent, it combined with the blues to produce an unusual, localised form. Apparently adapted from the phrase 'Les Haricots sont pas selés' – meaning 'snap-beans are unsalted' – Zydeco is a rhythmic dance music played on accordion, violin and guitar. Probably the first player was Amadé Ardoin, who recorded in the late 'twenties, and there were many other exponents, unheard on record, in subsequent years. With the migration of the French-speaking Blacks to Houston – perhaps the last southern city with an active blues life – it became very popular, with Clifton Chenier, who was born in Opelousas, Louisiana, in 1925, being the best-known musician. His uncle, Morris 'Big' Chenier, Clarence Garlow and Boozoo Chavis were among the fiddle, guitar and accordion players who made of Zydeco a strong, regional music.

With the exception of Howlin' Wolf, Muddy Waters, B. B. King and Jimmy Reed, few of the northern blues singers of Chicago and Detroit were working regularly in the mid 1960s unless they were playing in the white clubs and on the college circuit, and even the first two named appeared ever more frequently in such contexts. This had been one of the most marked developments of the 'sixties, and in a sense is less of the story of the blues than of the white recognition of it.

In the 'forties it seemed that the surviving exponents of guitar blues were Leadbelly and Josh White; of the blues shouters, Jimmy Rushing and Joe Turner, and of the pianists Meade Lux Lewis and Pete Johnson. Of these only Leadbelly appeared to present an unadulterated and authentic blues idiom. After a violent life Leadbelly became an idol of Greenwich village clubs and sang for audiences of all kinds. He died in 1949 after a brief visit to France; a visit too short to make much impact but one which did sow the seeds of an interest in blues which took root in Europe.

Three years later Big Bill Broonzy was invited to France and in subsequent years he toured Europe regularly, gaining huge followings in England and Belgium as well as France. 'It could readily be said that the story of the traditional blues as a living, creative force had come to its end,' wrote Bill Grauer and Orrin Keepnews on the death of Leadbelly; now Broonzy was saying, as he wrote in his autobiography a few years later, that 'even the young people in the South are learning to play fast time and jump, the young people like to jitterbug and if I was to stop playing the real old slow blues I don't know what would become of it.'

In Europe Big Bill Broonzy epitomised the blues singer. His first concert in London in 1951 marked the beginning of the blues 'boom'. While he prophesied the impending demise of the blues in his conversation, he mentioned enough singers to indicate that at the time, many blues singers were still actively working. In Great Britain in particular, his large following began to create their own music in imitation of the rent-party and country dance musicians. Noisy, unsubtle, depending heavily on the repertoire of Leadbelly and Broonzy, 'skiffle' was a rough out-crop from the New Orleans jazz revival of the early 'fifties.

It took its name from the recordings of Dan Burley's 'Skiffle Boys' made in 1946 with Brownie and Globe-Trotter McGhee in New York for Rudi Blesh's Circle label. Following the pre-war researches into boogie-woogie by William Russell and Dan Qualey's recording of the pianists on his Solo Art label, Blesh had discovered the whereabouts of the pianist Montana Taylor, had likewise found Hociel Thomas and had recorded Taylor, Thomas, Chippie Hill, Jimmy Yancey, the pianist 'Mr Freddie' Shayne and Dan Burley, a reporter with the *Amsterdam News* and a pianist. Rudi Blesh's book *Shining Trumpets*, published a few years later, had considerable influence on the New Orleans jazz 'Revival' in the United States, Australia and Great Britain. In 1950 Harold Courlander, on grants from the Wenner-Gren Foundation for Anthropological Research, did field work in Alabama and Mississippi, recording old black songs, hollers and religious music. The following year, one of the co-editors of the pioneering work *Jazzmen*, Frederic Ramsey Jr, began a series of five probing field trips in Alabama, Mississippi and Louisiana, and, assisted by the John Simon Guggenheim Memorial Foundation Fellowships for 1953 and 1955, further extended knowledge and recordings of surviving but fast-fading rural traditions.

With Big Bill Broonzy on one of his last visits to Europe was Brother John Sellers, a young singer born in 1924 in Clarksdale, who had worked with rhythm and blues bands in Chicago before devoting himself to the Church. Through his help to Jacques Demetre and the author valuable insights on contemporary blues were gained. Broonzy died in 1958 and the following year Jacques Demetre left France for an intensive tour with Marcel Chauvard, documenting New York, Chicago and Detroit blues. The same year, 1959, saw Samuel B. Charters in the South doing research on country blues and interviewing surviving members of the Memphis Jug Band and Gus Cannon, and Alan Lomax doing exhaustive field work which resulted in the last recordings of Forrest City Joe Pugh and the first by Fred McDowell, who was born in Rossville, Tennessee, in 1905 and who, after a dozen years in Memphis, moved to Como, Mississippi, in 1940. In 1960 the author, on a State Department research grant made an extensive tour in the northern cities aided by Bob Koester and Charles O'Brien in Chicago and St Louis; and joined by Chris Strachwitz in Memphis and Mack McCormick in Texas made field recordings, and many interviews for the British Brodcasting Corporation. Strachwitz's Arhoolie label was one of the

first of many to make location recordings, and a couple of years
later Pete Whelan's Origin label began to reissue an unparalleled
documentation of the earliest blues records.

Within the next few years the 'rediscovery' of blues singers began
to snowball. A younger generation of blues collectors, critics and
white guitarists made forays to the south following clues from
records and the careful interviewing of blues singers to support
the work being done by Harry Oster in Louisiana and Pete Welding
and Robert Koester in Chicago. John Fahey, Nicholas Perls, Henry
Vestine, Dick Waterman, Dick Spottswood, Pete Lowry, George
Mitchell, Gayle Wardlow and David Evans in the United States
and Georges Adins, Neil Patterson, Mike Leadbitter, Mike Rowe,
John Broven and Bruce Bastin, enthusiasts from Europe, researched
on field trips. Interestingly, the American researchers largely concentrated on the veteran singers; the European ones on the modern
Chicago, Houston and West Coast blues men. As a result of these
latter-day researches most of the present knowledge of the story of
the blues has been gained. From Mance Lipsomb and Mississippi
John Hurt to Robert Wilkins and Furry Lewis, Will Shade and Gus
Cannon, Son House and Skip James, Black Ace and Sleepy John
Estes, Bukka White and Big Joe Williams, Whistling Alex Moore
and Speckled Red, Henry Brown and Sonny Boy Williamson
No. 2. Sippie Wallace and Victoria Spivey and in a sense, Little
Brother Montgomery, Roosevelt Sykes, Sunnyland Slim, Lightnin'
Hopkins, Lil Son Jackson, even Muddy Waters, John Lee Hooker
and Howlin' Wolf – had been 'discovered'. Of the discoveries, few
were young men. Snooks Eaglin, who was born in 1936 and left
blind from a brain tumour when less than two years old, played
guitar in the streets of his home city of New Orleans. He learned
from records a wide variety of songs and was attracted to the blues of
older men as well as a Spanish *Malaguena* or Jimmie Rodgers' hill-billy
songs. Less sophisticated, the sturdy Mississippi singer Wesley 'Short
Stuff' Macon was only three years older and his hollered, modal
vocals indicated the persistence of the oldest blues forms. But in
general the discoveries were of older, veteran blues men. In some
of these cases there was genuine discovery, in others withdrawal
from retirement, in others merely awareness of the music that they
had been playing; 'discovery' and 'rediscovery', though widely used
terms meant recognition by the white community, or a part of it at
least, in the United States and Europe.

The growth of blues interest in Europe and Great Britain is
indicative of a wider phenomenon. When Big Bill Broonzy died,

Brownie McGhee and Sonny Terry took his place, and his pianist after the death of Joshua Altheimer, Memphis Slim – Peter Chatman – who was born in Memphis in 1915 became exceedingly popular in France. A close associate of Memphis Slim was the massive Willie Dixon, a powerful bass player and prolific composer of blues for Muddy Waters and other Chicago singers. Dixon was on the records of Muddy Waters, Howlin' Wolf, even Buddy Guy and Otis Rush and, as principal talent scout for Chess, was highly influential in Chicago. Apart from singers like Speckled Red, Little Brother Montgomery, Champion Jack Dupree and Roosevelt Sykes, who had been brought over independently to work on tour with Chris Barber's Jazz Band, singers from the Chess stable were booked, largely through the contacts of Memphis Slim and Willie Dixon. When Muddy Waters first played in Leeds, he used an electric guitar and his audience was unprepared for it; his pianist, Otis Spann, nearly stole the show. When next he came tastes had quickly become adjusted to the Chicago sound, and the mushrooming beat and blues clubs in Great Britain were soon booking prolonged tours for Little Walter, Howlin' Wolf, Bo Diddley, and many other blues singers including the much-loved Sonny Boy Williamson.

Williamson's enigmatic personality never quite revealed why he felt so at ease with English teen-age groups; he wanted to make Europe his home as Champion Jack Dupree had done, and as had Curtis Jones – a Texas-born blues pianist long resident in Chicago, or Eddie Boyd. Several of these singers had toured in Germany, France, Sweden, Denmark, Holland, Belgium and Great Britain – even, in some cases, Spain and Morocco, coming over with the German-initiated American Folk Blues Festival and staying on to tour with a small group. The Folk Blues Festival, an annual event since 1962, had brought singers like Skip James and Son House, Victoria Spivey and Sippie Wallace, Buddy Guy and Otis Rush; by the mid-'sixties, incredibly, European blues enthusiasts had heard more blues singers in person than most of their American counterparts had ever done.

The singers were lionised perhaps, and returned wonderingly saying 'man, they treated us like we were artists'. In the rhythm and blues clubs, many of the young dancers hardly knew who they were dancing to; they liked the music, and a generation in revolt found that the music of a segregated minority was the symbol of gulf between themselves and the values and attitudes of their parents. As American electric blues groups sprang up through the States, the college clubs and concerts and the Newport Folk Festival, featured able white imitators of the blues who could often play the music they admired in the older generations of blues singers with more skill than the survivors could themselves. Once Leadbelly could assert 'Never has a white man had the blues, 'cause nothin' to worry about' and the implication was that he couldn't play or sing them either. There had been white blues singers – Jimmie Rodgers, Frank Hutchison, the Allen Brothers – but they were a tiny minority and no threat to the music or to blacks' independence. Now, suddenly, the blues was being played by white bands everywhere – country blues guitar and harmonica, city blues with searing slides on electric guitars. White singers could play the blues too well and, up to a point, could sing them, but they hadn't got the magical quality of 'soul'. The blues bands of Howlin' Wolf and Muddy Waters played the jazz and folk festivals and the college shows while the lesser blues singers of Chicago, unknown and forgotten, 'scuffled' in obscure South and West Side dives, or more frequently laid up their guitars and went back to driving trucks, working at the mill, acting as porters. 'His guitar was in hock', 'he hadn't got a piano in his home', 'he hadn't touched an instrument for years' became almost as much the clichés of blues reportage as did 'he was born in the Mississippi Delta and went to Chicago when he was twenty-five'; the facts were so often repeated as to become a commonplace.

In the words of his biographer Charles Sawyer, the 'arrival' of B. B. King took place in 1968 at the Fillmore West in San Francisco before 'an adoring crowd of white youths'. Sawyer numbered the bench-marks of B. B. King's 'climb' as touring with the Rolling Stones and concerts in Europe and Australia, a world tour in 1972 and one in Africa sponsored by the State Department, summit billing with Frank Sinatra and, the ultimate accolade, appearance on the Ed Sullivan Show. Arrival was equated with recognition by the white Middle America, and by an international middle-class audience.

Black bluesmen who escaped the 'chittlin' circuit' to perform for the college and concert circuits may have been better paid than before, but none made the fortunes that some of their admirers who extended the blues into the rock and pop world acquired. By the 1980s blues was being heard in Russia and Siberia, and soon after, blues were being sung in a dozen languages in countries literally thousands of miles from their place of origin. Blues were providing the soundtrack for T.V. commercials for beer and autombobiles, and were used to symbolise poverty or alienation in television feature films just about anywhere.

Not surprisingly, young Blacks abandoned the blues; 'it was

"depressing", "backward" or "accommodating white values,"' as Nelson George noted. He dismissed their view, arguing that blues was 'suffering the same fate that was soon to come to its successor, soul.' 'The most fanatical students of blues history have all been white,' he added. 'Blacks create and then move on. Whites document and then recycle.' Well, that may be, though the 'fanatical students' who document the music are not necessarily those that recycle it.

In the processes of arriving and receiving recognition blues was subtly separated from its creative context: histories focussed on the artists and their art, diminishing the sources of their inspiration and motivation. 'Nothing but the Blues' was not an idle phrase.

This revision and recycling of *The Story of the Blues* is made without apologies, for it endeavours to place the making of this great African American music and song form in its socio-historic context. Since it was first published, in 1969, much has happened as blues became part of an international musical vocabulary. But that, quite simply, is *another* story.

Music Examples

Transcriptions by Donald Kincaid.

1. Thomas Marshall *Cornfield Holler* (*Arhoolie*)
The notes marked 'X' are sung with a catch in the voice like a descending yodel. In the whole call there is a falling pattern from tonic (D) to A and from dominant (A) to tonic.

2. Garfield Akers *Cottonfield Blues*
The flattened seventh (Bb) and the flattened third (Eb) are particularly marked with the Eb itself emphasised on the descending vocal phrases, the line at 'X' denoting a glissando from F to G through F#.

Akers played a half-barré on the first three strings of his guitar in the rhythmic accompaniment.
Commencing at the third fret and sliding up to the fifth, the little finger extended to add the C and slid back to the Bb.
A right-hand strum placed a stress on the crotchet beats, with a downward stroke.

3a. Charley Patton *Down the Dirt Road Blues* (vocal)

The major third in the rising voice is indicated by an 'X'.

3b. Charley Patton *Down the Dirt Road Blues*
Part of the persistent rhythm in the accompaniment to this blues

is punctuated by slapping on the guitar, and by figure *i* or *ii* with the characteristic G to C. Each verse ends with the guitar phrase *iii* which includes semi-quavers.

4. Bass figures as played in versions of *Big Road Blues*
In this version the 6th string is tuned down to D and the 'walking' bass is played by forming a barré *over the top* of the fingerboard across to the fourth string and picking on the 4th and 6th.

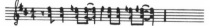

The syncopated phrase is obtained by changing the D chord at the 2nd fret to G7 on the first three strings and making a crotcher beat on the low-tuned bass E string.

5. Blind Lemon Jefferson *Black Snake Moan*
i. Answering guitar phrase

ii. Vocal line. Blind Lemon's employed range was wider than the usual octave and he used, typically, the flattened 7th, and both the major 3rd and flattened 3rd.

6. Jimmy Yancey *Eternal Blues*

The movement of the bass figure by slight variations and shifts to give a richness to the left hand while retaining the essential quality of the pattern, is evident here. The bass figure is not constant but has the following appearing at the end of a chorus:

Another variant employed by Yancey in the same performance.

Shown below are examples of his use of the flattened 3rd being played with the major 3rd (A♭ (G♯) in F and C♯ (D♭) in B♭) to give a pungent discord in triplets.

7. Henry Brown
i. Example of bass figure

ii. Extension of bass figure
This figure is of the kind used by Hersal Thomas. The top line rises to a 7th – F♮ in the key of G and, though the dotted shape is maintained, the bass descends in ragtime fashion in order to modulate to C.

8. Albert Ammons bass figures
Typical of an Ammons bass pattern this example contains the open 5th followed by a minor and then major 3rd (E♭ – E♮) and includes other familiar aspects in the 6th (A) and the dotted rhythm. In the right hand he played a repetitive syncopation adding this same 6th (A) in C which becomes the 3rd of the chord of F. A change of colour is brought about by E of this syncopated group becoming E♭ in F.

Other bass figures used by Ammons and his contemporaries, and deriving from Pine Top Smith in particular, have a running quality. Here the bass ascends from C to A and omits E♭; the rhythm is still dotted and there is no 5th (C – G).

9. Charles Avery *Dearborn Street Breakdown*
In this bass figure the pattern changes with the emphasis thrown on new notes – the dotted quaver on the second beat, marked 'X' in bar 1 comes on the fourth beat in bars 2 and 3, though apart from the quaver pulses the rhythm was not dotted.

10. Robert Johnson *Rambling on My Mind*
i. Bass figure

The bass figure, fragmentary at first, grows gradually. High triplets in quavers appear in the treble, and the dotted bass gives lift.

ii. Variation: Elmore James *Dust my Broom*

Elmore James used the Robert Johnson figure, but more regularly placed with almost continuous triplets. The bass guitar would play a heavily stressed second and fourth beat.

References

BIBLIOGRAPHY

ALBERTSON, Chris, *Bessie* (New York: Stein and Day, 1972).

BASTIN, Bruce, *Crying for the Carolines* (London: Studio Vista, 1971).

—*Red River Blues: the blues tradition in the Southeast* (Urbana: University of Illinois Press, 1986).

BLESH, Rudi: *Shining Trumpets*, Cassell, London 1949.

BLESH, Rudi and JANIS, Harriet: *They All Played Ragtime* (1950); Revised edition, Oak Publications 1966.

BOTKIN, B. A. (ed.): *Lay My Burden Down, A Folk History of Slavery*, University of Chicago Press 1961.

BRADFORD, Perry: *Born with the Blues* – his own story. Oak Publications 1965.

BROONZY, Big Bill, and BRUYNOGHE, Yannick: *Big Bill Blues* (1955), Oak Reprint 1964.

BROVEN, John, *South to Louisiana: the music of the Cajun bayous* (Gretna, LA: Pelican, 1988).

— *Walking to New Orleans: the story of New Orleans rhythm and blues* (Bexhill-on-Sea: Blues Unlimited, 1965).

CABLE, George: 'The Dance in Place Congo'; reprinted in *Creoles and Cajuns* (Arlin Turner, Ed.), Doubleday Anchor 1959.

CALT, Stephen, *I'd Rather Be The Devil: the blues of Skip James* (New York: Da Capo, 1994).

CALT, Stephen, and Wardlow, Gayle, *King of the Delta Blues: the life and music of Charlie Patton* (New Jersey: Rock Chapel Press, 1988).

CHARTERS, Samuel B.: *The Country Blues*, Rinehart 1959.

—*The Bluesmen*, Oak Publications 1967.

COHN, David: *Where I was Born and Raised*, University of Notre Dame Press 1967.

COHN, Lawrence (ed.). *Nothing But the Blues: the music and musicians* (New York and London: Abbeville Press, 1993).

COLLINS, Tony, *Rock Mr Blues: the life and music of Wynonie Harris* (Milford, NH, 1995).

COURLANDER, Harold: *Negro Folk Music, U.S.A.*, Columbia University Press 1963.

DANCE, Helen Oakley, *Stormy Monday: the T-Bone Walker story* (Baton

Rouge: Louisiana State University Press, 1987).

DEMETRE, Jacques, and Marcel Chauvard, *Voyage au Pays du Blues / Land of the Blues*) (Paris: CLARB, 25 rue Trezel, 92300 Levallois-Perrett, 1994).

DIXON, R.M.W., Godrich, John and Rye, Howard, *Blues and Gospel Records* 1890–1943 (Oxford: Oxford University Press, 1996).

DIXON, Willie, *I Am the Blues* (London: Quartet, 1989).

EPSTEIN, Dena J., *Sinful Tunes and Spirituals: black folk music to the civil war* (Urbana: University of Illinois Press, 1977).

EVANS, David, *Big Road Blues: tradition and creativity in the folk blues* (Berkeley: University of California Press, 1982).

FISHER, Miles Mark: *Negro Slave Songs in the United States*, Cornell University Press 1953.

FORTEN, Charlotte: *A Free Negro in the Slave Era* – The Journal of Charlotte L. Forten (R. A. Billington, Ed.), Collier 1961.

FRAZIER, E. Franklin: *The Negro in the United States*, Macmillan 1949.

—*The Negro Family in the United States*, Dryden 1951.

GARON, Paul, *The Devil's Son-in-Law: the story of Peetie Wheatstraw and his songs* (London: Studio Vista, 1971).

GARON, Paul, and Garon, Beth, *Woman with Guitar: Memphis Minnie's blues* (New York: Da Capo, 1992).

GEORGE, Nelson, *The Death of Rhythm and Blues* (New York: Pantheon, 1988).

GROOM, Bob, *The Blues Revival* (London: Studio Vista, 1971).

GURALNICK, Peter, *Searching for Robert Johnson* (New York: E.P. Dutton, 1989).

HANDY, W.C.: *Father of the Blues*, Sidgwick and Jackson 1957.

HARALAMBOS, Michael, *Right On: from blues to soul in black America* (Ormskirk: Causeway Press, 1994).

HARRIS, Sheldon, *Blues Who's Who* (New Rochelle, NY: Arlington House, 1979).

HARRISON, Daphne Duval, *Black Pearls: blues queens of the 1920s* (New Brunswick: Rutgers University Press, 1988).

HEARN, Lafcadio: 'Levee Life', *Cincinnati Commercial*, March 17, 1876; reprinted in *The Selected Writings of Lafcadio Hearn* (Henry Goodman, Ed.), Citadel Press 1949.

HERSKOVITS, Melville J.: *The New World Negro* – Selected Papers in Afroamerican Studies, Indiana University Press 1966.

—*The Myth of the Negro Past*, Harper 1941.

HIGGINSON, Thomas Wentworth: *Army Life in a Black Regiment*, Collier 1962.

JACKSON, Bruce, *Wake Up Dead Man: Afro-American worksongs from Texas prisons* (Cambridge, Mass.: Harvard University Press, 1972).

JOHNSON, Charles S.: *Shadow of the Plantation*, University of Chicago (1934) 1966.

—*Patterns of Negro Segregation*, Gollancz 1944.

JONES, A.M.: *African Music in Northern Rhodesia and Some Other Places*, Livingstone Museum Occasional Paper No. 4,

KEIL, Charles: *Urban Blues*, University of Chicago 1966.

KEMBLE, Fanny: *Journal of a Residence on a Georgia Plantation* (1835);

reprinted Alfred A Knopf 1961.

LEADBITTER, Mike, and Slaven, Neil, *Blues Records, 1944–1970 Vol. One, A-K.*

LEADBITTER, Mike, Fancourt, Les, and Pelletier, Paul, *Blues Records 1943–1970 Vol. 2, L-Z.* (London, Record Information Services, 1987 1995)

LEVINE, Lawrence, *Black Culture and Black Consciousness* (New York: Oxford University Press, 1977)

LIEB, Sandra, *Mother of the Blues: a study of Ma Rainey* (Amherst: University of Massachusetts, 1981).

LIPSCOMB, Mance, *I Say Me For a Parable: the oral autobiography of Mance Lipscomb, Texas bluesman*, ed. Glen Alyn (New York and London: W.W. Norton, 1993).

LOMAX, Alan, *The Land Where the Blues Began* (London: Methuen, 1993).

—*Mister Jelly Roll* (London: Cassell 1952).

LOMAX, John A.: *Negro Folk Songs as Sung by Leadbelly* (Macmillan 1937).

—*Adventures of a Ballad Hunter* (New York: Macmillan 1947).

MACLEOD, R.R., *Yazoo 1-20; Yazoo 21-83; Document Blues vols 1-3;* (Edinburgh: PAT Publications, 1988–1996) [Series]

MANGUS, A. R.: *Rural Regions of the South*, Works Progress Administration 1940.

METFESSEL, Milton: *Phonophotography in Folk Music* (University of North Carolina Press 1928).

NATHAN, Hans, *Dan Emmett and the Rise of Early Negro Minstrelsy* (Norman: University of Oklahoma Press, 1962).

NILES, John Jacob: *Singing Soldiers* (Scribners, 1927).

NKETIA, Kwabena: *African Music in Ghana* (London: Longmans 1961).

OAKLEY, Giles, *The Devil's Music: a history of the blues* (London: British Boradcasting Corporation, 1976).

ODUM, Howard, and JOHNSON, Guy B.: *Negro Workaday Songs*, University of North Carolina Press 1926.

—*The Negro and His Songs* (1925), Folklore Associates 1964.

ODUM, Howard W.: 'Folk-Song and Folk-Poetry as Found in the Secular Songs of the Southern Negroes', in *Journal of American Folk-Lore*, Vol. 24, July-September 1911.

OLIVER, Paul: *Bessie Smith*, Cassell 1959.

—*Blues Fell This Morning: Meaning in the Blues*, Cassell 1960. (revised edition, Cambridge: University Press, 1990).

—*Conversation with the Blues*, Cassell 1965 (revised edition Cambridge: University Press, 1997).

—*Screening the Blues: aspects of the blues tradition* (London: Cassell and Company, 1968; New York: Da Capo, 1988).

—*Blues and black folk music entries in Jazz on Record*, (Albert McCarthy, ed.), Hanover Books 1968.

—*Savannah Syncopators: African retentions in the blues* (London: Studio Vista, 1970).

—*Songsters and Saints: vocal traditions on race records* (Cambridge, UK: Cambridge University Press, 1984).

OLMSTEAD, Frederick Law: *A Journey in the Seaboard Slave States*, New York 1856.

OLSSON, Bengt, *Memphis Blues and Jug Bands* (London: Studio Vista, 1970).

OSTER, Harry, *Living Country Blues* (Detroit: Folklore Associates, 1969).

PALMER, Robert, *Deep Blues* (New York: Viking, 1981).

PARRISH, Lydia: *Slave Songs of the Georgia Sea Islands* (1942); (New York: Folklore Associates reprint, 1965).

RAMSEY, Frederic, Jr.: *Been Here and Gone*, Rutgers 1960.

—and SMITH, Charles Edward (eds.), *Jazzmen* (1939); (reprinted Sidgwick and Jackson 1957).

ROSE, Arnold: *The Negro in America*, Harper Brothers 1948.

ROWE, Mike, *Chicago Breakdown* (London: Eddison Press, 1973; as *Chicago Blues: the city and the music*, New York: Da Capo, 1981).

RUSSELL, Tony, *Blacks, Whites and Blues* (London: Studio Vista, 1972).

SACRE, Robert (ed.), *The Voice of the Delta* (Liège: Presses Universitaires de Liège, 1987).

SAWYER, Charles, *The Arrival of B.B. King* (New York: Doubleday, 1980).

SCHLESINGER, Arthur M., Jr.: *The Coming of the New Deal* (The Age of Roosevelt. Volume 2). Heinemann 1959.

SHAW, Arnold, *Honkers and Shouters: the golden years of rhythm and blues* (New York: Macmillan, 1978).

SPEAR, Allan H.: *Black Chicago* (University of Chicago Press, 1967).

TILLING, Robert (ed.), *'Oh What A Beautiful City': a tribute to Rev. Gary Davis 1896–1972* (Jersey, CI: Paul Mill Press, 1992).

TITON, Jeff Todd, *Early Downhome Blues: a musical and cultural analysis* (Urbana: University of Illinois Press, 1977); (reprinted, University of North Carolina Press, 1994).

TODES, Charlotte: *Labor and Lumber*, (Labor Research Association 1934).

U.S. BUREAU OF THE CENSUS, *Statistical Abstract of the United States* for years as cited.

VAN RIJN, Guido, *Roosevelt's Blues: African-American blues and gospel artists on President Franklin D. Roosevelt* (Oxford: University of Mississippi Press, 1997).

WATERS, Ethel, with SAMUELS, Charles: *His Eye is on The Sparrow* (W. H. Allen 1951).

WEBBER, Malcolm: *Medicine Show* (Caxton Printers 1941).

WHITE, Newman I.: *American Negro Folk Songs* (1928); (Folklore Associates reprint 1965).

WITTKE, Carl, Ph.D.: *Tambo and Bones* (Duke University Press 1930).

WOLFE, Charles, and Lornell, Kip, *The Life and Legend of Leadbelly* (New York: Harper Collins, 1992).

BLUES PERIODICALS

News, biographies and record reviews are published in many journals. Among those published in Britain and the USA are the following:

Blues Access: Editor Gary Wolfson
    Dept BRQ, 1514 North Street, Boulder, CO 80304–3514, USA

Blues and Rhythm: Editor Tony Burke
    82 Quenby Way, Bromham, Bedfordshire, MK43 8QP, England

Blues Revue: Editor Bob Vorel
    Rt 2, Box 118, West Union, WV 26456, USA

Juke Blues: Editor Cilla Huggins
    PO Box 148, London W9 1DY, England [Quarterly].

Living Blues: Editor Peter Lee
    Center for the Study of Southern Culture, University, MS 38677, USA

78 *Quarterly*: Editor/Publisher, Pete
Whelan P.O. Box 283, Key West,
FL 33041, USA

RECORDINGS
In excess of 3000 Compact Disc issues and reissues of blues records are
in the catalogues at any one time.
All known blues and gospel titles
listed in Dixon, Godrich and Rye's
Blues and Gospel Records 1892–1943 (see
Bibliography) have been reissued, the
majority on Document and related
labels. For details write to Document
Records, Eipeldauerstr. 23/43/5 A-
1220 Vienna, Austria.

No such complete reissue programme exists for Post World War
II records, but a high proportion
has been reissued on Ace. Details
may be obtained from Ace Records
Ltd. 42–50 Steele Road, London
NW10 7AS.

Many post-war reissues and field
recordings from the 1960s have been
issued by Arhoolie Records. Details
from Arhoolie Records 10341 San
Pablo Avenue, El Cerrito, California
94530, USA.

As recording and musical quality
is variable and duplications occur,
this author with John Cowley has
edited a number of articles by acknowledged experts on all types and
periods of blues recordings on CD.
Some 560 CD issues are discussed,
and placed in the historical context
of the music. John Cowley and Paul
Oliver (eds), *The New Blackwell Guide
to Recorded Blues*, Blackwell Publishers
Ltd, Oxford UK, 1966.

Index

The following abbreviations are used:

acc	accordion
bjo	banjo
coll	collector
comp	composer
clt	clarinet
dms	percussion
ent	entertainer
group	small band/group
gtr	guitar
hca	harmonica
jug	jug/stovepipe
mand	mandolin
pno	piano
prom	promotion
sax	saxophone
tmb	trombone
tpt	trumpet
vln	violin, fiddle
vo	vocal
wbd	washboard

other instruments are entered in full.

The entry 'group' includes vocal and instrumental groups and bands. The entry 'prom' (promotion) includes managers, owners of clubs and record companies, recording promoters, etc. The entry 'comp' refers to composers of written blues music.

The entry 'ent' (entertainer) includes performers in road shows, minstrel, medicine and stock companies.

The entry 'coll' (collector) includes collectors of material in the field irrespective of other occupations; and other researchers.